Schools Council
Research Studies

Gifted Children in Primary Schools

Eric Ogilvie
B.Sc., M.Ed., Ph.D.

The report of the Schools Council enquiry into
the teaching of gifted children of primary age 1970–71

Macmillan

© Schools Council Publications 1973

First published 1973

SBN 333 149408

Published by
MACMILLAN EDUCATION LTD
Basingstoke and London

The Macmillan Company of Australia Pty Ltd
Melbourne

The Macmillan Company of Canada Ltd
Toronto

St Martin's Press Inc
New York

Companies and representatives
throughout the world

Printed in Great Britain by
Hazell Watson & Viney Ltd, Aylesbury, Bucks

Contents

Part III: The future

Appendices

Figures and Tables

Figures

Tables

Note : item numbers refer to the questionnaire in Appendix 3

Abbreviations

AVT	Audio-visual technology
BBC	British Broadcasting Corporation
EPA	Educational priority area
FA	Football Association
HMI	Her Majesty's Inspector (of Schools)
IAPS	Incorporated Association of Preparatory Schools
ILEA	Inner London Education Authority
IQ	Intelligence quotient
ITA	Independent Television Authority
i.t.a.	initial teaching alphabet
LEA	Local education authority
NAGC	National Association for Gifted Children
NFER	National Foundation for Educational Research
PE	Physical education
PSR	Post of special responsibility
PTA	Parent-teacher association
RE	Religious education
SES	Socio-economic status
SRA	Science Research Associates
VRQ	Verbal reasoning quotient
WISC	Wechsler Intelligence Scales for Children

Preface

In the spring of 1969, the Schools Council set up a working party to study the teaching of gifted children in primary schools. The working party found that our knowledge of what is actually being done for gifted children by Local Education Authorities and schools was very limited and inconsistent, and felt that it was essential to have a lot more information about current practice gathered together for publication. The Council's Programme Committee approved an initial grant of £3,500, and an enquiry began in September 1970. The following paper describes very briefly the conduct of the enquiry, and reports the findings resulting from it.

The enquiry was considerably disrupted by the prolonged postal strike at a crucial stage when study groups were in the process of formation. We wish therefore particularly to record our thanks to the LEAs involved, and to the members of the study groups themselves, for pursuing so ably and conscientiously the work they set themselves to do on our behalf. Despite the breakdown in communications, a good proportion of those who expressed an initial interest in the project contrived to provide accounts of their deliberations by June 1971. In the end, therefore, the impact of the strike was negligible.

Thanks are due also to a large number of teachers, tutors and advisers, including some four hundred who completed the questionnaire; and to LEAs who offered schools for study and supplied information to us about their provisions for gifted children; and to the staffs of schools which were visited during the year. The willingness with which teachers described how they worked with and felt about provisions for gifted children and the hospitality so readily extended to the director of the project, have been constant sources of gratitude. This high level of co-operation may well have been predictable but we feel it nonetheless worthy of mention on that account.

We are glad to take this opportunity of expressing our appreciation of the valuable assistance received from the National Association for Gifted Children; the Incorporated Association of Preparatory Schools; the various Subject Committees of the Schools Council; and Mr Yehudi Menuhin.

In addition we would like to record our gratitude to Her Majesty's Inspectorate. The invaluable help which we have received from its members has greatly facilitated the work and expanded the scope of the enquiry.

Introduction

One major premise has been quite fundamental to all the working party's discussions on 'giftedness'. This was that we were concerned with those conditions, results and evaluations of learning which were of particular relevance to teachers, and which were related specifically to problems arising directly or indirectly from the presence of outstanding or potentially outstanding pupils within a school. Although on the whole neither the working party itself, nor the teachers' study groups which were subsequently established, felt the need for precise definitions as an essential preliminary to useful discussion, some justification of the definition of 'giftedness' which the working party ultimately adopted is probably necessary. For convenience of exposition this will be attempted in Chapter 1, and we shall concern ourselves here merely with a brief review of the programme of work which forms the main basis for the remainder of the report.

A STUDY OF THE TEACHING OF GIFTED CHILDREN:
GUIDELINES

Guidelines for the study proposed by the working party and approved by Steering Committee A of the Schools Council:

   1   A survey to be made of all LEAs to discover what help and support they provide for the teaching of gifted children between the ages of 5 and 11. These children may be of high general intelligence or with gifts in one specific area—e.g. music, ballet, drama. For the most part this LEA help is likely to fall into one of three categories:
   (*a*) help provided more or less directly in the form of home visiting teachers of music, Saturday morning art classes, sports facilities, etc.
   (*b*) help provided in the form of scholarships or exhibitions to outside specialist institutions—e.g. the Royal Ballet School and the Colleges of Music.
   (*c*) support for the organization of 'enrichment' groups during school hours in schools or among groups of schools.
   The survey should seek to discover who detects these gifted children, and by what means, and who arranges provision for them. The experience of the LEAs such as Essex, Oxfordshire and West Sussex, known to have concerned them-

selves more than most with the problems posed by gifted children, to be studied with particular care.

2 A brief questionnaire to schools (including independent schools) regarded by HMIs, LEA advisers etc., as schools which make good provision for gifted children in some or all aspects of the curriculum. A selected number of the schools to be visited and their experience written up in a series of case studies. These to include a description of organizational arrangements, of materials and equipment thought to provide opportunities for gifted children to develop their strengths and of the cues or pointers which indicate to experienced teachers that children of particular ages are gifted in this or that direction. Schools for the detailed study to be chosen as far as possible to show variety of methods and background circumstances.

3 A small-scale study to be made of teachers' views on the identification and selection of gifted children.

4 Some gifted children to be asked to talk or write about themselves and their work.

5 The study to seek information and views from the Directors of Schools Council and Nuffield Primary and Middle Years Projects and to establish close contact with the work being done under the direction of Professor Tempest and Dr Bridges.

Steering Committee A also expressed a wish that the Schools Council's Subject Committees should provide their own views on the problems of giftedness, in the following terms:

[The Committee] appreciates of course that fundamental questions as to the aims of primary education are involved. Nevertheless it hopes that within the context of any general views which they may wish to express Subject Committees will comment specifically on:

(a) The extent to which it is desirable for gifted children to be selected for special activities;

(b) the form which such activities might take;

(c) the cues or pointers which indicate to experienced teachers that children of particular ages are gifted in this or that direction. It may be that Committees would like to describe gifted children's behaviour (in its widest sense) at, say, age 9-10.

In response to item 1 of the guidelines, all LEAs were sent a letter requesting answers to a series of questions concerning their provisions for gifted children. Those LEAs from whom replies were not received were again approached during June 1971. The text of these letters are included as Appendix 1.

In accordance with item 2, a questionnaire was formulated which enabled teachers to express views on a number of problems related to giftedness, and the questionnaire was distributed to both those schools which were visited by the director and to the teachers' study groups. Altogether some thirty schools were visited across the country; and eighteen study groups were established, the locations of which are given in Appendix 2. The numbers given to the study groups in the text do not correspond with this list, which is arranged alphabetically. A copy of the questionnaire, together with the notes for study groups, are added as appendix 3. The notes specifically requested the groups to consider problems of identification and selection, as required in item 3 of the guidelines; but preliminary findings related to item 4 were not very encouraging and it receives attention of a more incidental kind.

It did not prove possible to carry out fully the intentions expressed in item 5; the director was however able to visit Professor Tempest's group at Southport, and one of the schools involved currently in the Brentwood experiment. Brief exchanges occurred with the Middle Schools and Science Projects but the correspondence could not be pursued, nor could other project directors be consulted.

The purpose of this report is not to present definitive findings or recommend particular lines of action. The project has been exploratory and fact-finding in nature, so that any comments and suggestions made must be regarded as more or less tentative. Any conclusions drawn are to be interpreted as pointers towards further study rather than as authoritative statements, and this will be made clear by the character of the evidence, particularly that deriving from the work of the study groups. Study group reports have been extensively quoted at the risk of appearing to be no more than anecdotal in character; the reason is that these reports form not a collection of anecdotes but a compendium of statements made by groups of highly responsible teachers following on considerable discussion and careful study of the problems to which they refer. It is for this reason that we have preferred to quote relevant extracts from these deliberations as often as possible rather than attempt a count of apparent generalities put forward by some given number of study groups. To present such findings in some sort of table would not be difficult: it would however disguise the situation rather than illuminate it. The method adopted here has the merit of enabling statements to be seen in something of their general contexts, and the essential correctness or otherwise of judgements put forward can be evaluated more exactly.

Somewhat similar considerations apply with regard to evidence from case studies. The actual size of a problem can never be judged from single instances but this trite platitude should not be permitted to disguise the value of selected individual experiences as demonstrating that a very real problem exists. Demonstration of a problem's existence is an essential preliminary to any consideration of the degree of its general impact,

Part I

The recognition of gifted children

1 Definitions and dimensions

It can be argued with some cogency that problems of recognition are always spurious: that what we fail to recognize or realize is *ipso facto* incapable of generating sufficient stress for there to be anything of more than minor or peripheral importance involved. Basically the position becomes one based upon a presumption that where objects or events do not thrust themselves upon the attention then they cannot warrant it, and that to imagine such objects or events as problems of recognition must be to attribute to them an importance which, in the general scheme of things, they do not deserve or justify.

It may thus be argued that so-called problems of recognition are created or engineered for motives beyond themselves. Proponents of such a view may not see these motives as necessarily evil or calculated to advance selfish causes; on the contrary the motives may even command respect and so much is readily demonstrated by quoting a statement from one of the study groups:

There is not, so far as we know, any evidence that specific talent exists independently of general intelligence. We suggest that the belief that it does rests on either our ignorance about the complex interaction of factors which makes anyone the person he is, or the difficulty of predicting an individual's response . . . and finally on the wish of many people of undoubtedly high ability to find a tangible equality of worth in others less obviously able than themselves.

It is interesting to observe that in this instance the motives underlying this attitude to recognition are considered to be wholly laudable. But they then become even less convincing than if they had been mischievous and not simply misguided.

The viewpoint suggested above needs no debate at this stage. It merely serves to draw attention to a need to demonstrate, however briefly, the wide range of views amongst educationists, not as to whether there are problems of recognition, since these must always be secondary, but whether there are any problems at all which might usefully be collected under the heading 'giftedness'. Opinions relevant to this matter have been variously expressed in our correspondence:

1　As a small authority we very rarely seem to be faced with the problem of educating the gifted primary school child and indeed I do not recall any problem which has arisen in this way for the past twenty years.

2　The best possible arrangements are made for all children according to their abilities, aptitudes and needs . . . 'gifted children' are not particularly identified . . . it is not the practice here to identify groups of individuals more than is necessary.

3　In this area teachers' study groups are not likely to be welcome in order to study gifted children . . . teachers would feel that they had other more pressing problems.

4　It is contrary to our educational philosophy for us to seek to define a category or categories of gifted children. Our primary schools are so organized that we try to provide for the needs of individual children whatever their gifts.

5　I am not aware of any [schools] which feel the need to make special provision for outstandingly gifted children, or indeed which have encountered any such children.

6　I am personally extremely doubtful about the wisdom of special provisions for gifted children except . . . where some particular skill is involved.

7　By and large we do not believe that gifted children need special attention over and above what a good school reckons to provide for them—except where the specialism required is not available in that school.

8　I have some doubt as to the responsibility of a local education authority towards the so-called gifted child as opposed to his normal peers . . . on what exceptional talents should public monies be spent? To produce a concert artist? An Olympic champion? An international football player? Where do we draw the line?

9　The education of gifted children seems to be an area where opinions are often subjective and on balance we feel there is little to be said for discriminating in their favour . . . [there is] a large proportion of socially deprived children . . . and the devising of appropriate educational stimuli for this large group is a much more pressing problem for us.

10　This authority has always had a particular interest in the identification and the needs of the 'gifted' child but this concern has always been in the context of making the best possible provision for all primary age children, the fostering of excellence at all levels and in all activities and in giving all children individual care and encouragement . . . [our] general policy . . . rests upon a recognition of the dangers of 'elitism' at the primary age.

11　We are very interested in this much neglected issue.

12　A very clear definition of 'giftedness' seems to be needed before any kind of special educational provision can be discussed . . . Giftedness, at least at 'prodigy' level, must I imagine be a serious burden and embarrassment . . . and a possible source of great unhappiness at least up to later teens.

13　It is recognized that gifted children may present problems . . . highlighting gifted pupils in the school situation can lead to undesirable consequences just as highlighting subnormal pupils causes concern to the pupils themselves and their parents.

14   Any attempt on the part of schools to single out groups or individuals of high ability academically for special consideration is open to misinterpretation by the main body of parents.

15   It is generally true that over the past twenty years attention has been concentrated on the less able, and it is time that more attention was devoted to the problem of gifted pupils . . . there would appear to be about ten to fourteen pupils with an IQ of 140+ in the whole county.

16   [In my] generally integrated happy school [we have] lots of hard work for all of my gifted children . . . the whole concept has an unpleasant flavour of *Brave New World* about it.

17   I believe that this is the greatest problem in education but is comparatively ignored because it is less obvious than the problem of backwardness.

18   . . . the process of destreaming and mixing abilities seems to have highlighted the problem of the exceptionally able child . . . it would seem neither appropriate nor sensible therefore to be seeking ways of separating exceptionally able children from the rest. The difficulty is always that one never knows how many or what proportion to select or separate.

19   Though special attention is given to the backward, and rightly, I am not sure that the converse ought to be true.

It is clear even from this small sample of general comments that no simple dichotomy of views exists. To attempt to divide educationists into those who are, as it were, 'for' the gifted child and those who are 'against', would be grossly to oversimplify the position as it reveals itself in the correspondence. The comments more usefully draw attention to the following points:

(*a*) It is probably expecting too much to ask people who are daily confronted with the immense educational difficulties presented by massive illiteracy and deprivation to consider the term 'giftedness' as indicative of more than a peripheral set of problems confined almost wholly to 'middle class' areas. At the same time, the fact that the actual numbers involved may be small does not invariably entail that the problems created by them are seen to be wholly unworthy of attention.

(*b*) Problems of giftedness, in so far as they are seen to exist, are more likely to receive consideration in the context of the educational needs of individuals, *qua* individuals, than if they are related to hypothetical groups.

(*c*) The notion of special provision will need at some stage to be distinguished from what will more usefully be termed 'proper' provision. It may turn out that where there is a considerable consensus on the need to educate according to 'age, aptitude and ability', this agreement weakens immediately the concept of special provision is proposed.

(*d*) There is amongst some educationists an intuitive scepticism with regard to the apparently very reasonable notion that if children at the low end of a scale of ability require special treatment, then children similarly located at the upper end must require special treatment also.

(*e*) Educationists tend to use the term 'gifted' generically to indicate not only those who seem to possess high general academic ability, but also those who display more specific talents.

(*f*) It is possible that the degree of precision required of the description 'gifted' has to do with a person's attitude to special provision, and in particular to segregation, rather than to any real misunderstanding about the difficulties of educational measurement.

Each of these points will be raised again in the appropriate context. They are sufficient justification for assuming that educationists are agreed on the probability that giftedness, however defined, is a very real problem, even though the degree of importance attached to it depends upon a number of factors and particular circumstances which will require our attention.

A definition of giftedness

The definition of giftedness adopted here is available as a frontispiece to the questionnaire included in Appendix 3, but is reprinted for convenience below:

The term 'gifted' is used to indicate any child who is outstanding in either a general or specific ability, in a relatively broad or narrow field of endeavour. . . . Where generally recognized tests exist as (say) in the case of 'intelligence', then 'giftedness' would be defined by test scores. Where no recognized tests exist it can be assumed that the subjective opinions of 'experts' in the various fields on the creative qualities of originality and imagination displayed would be the criteria we have in mind.

The intention was that this definition should be considered in the general context of the questionnaire itself and, taken thus, it appears to have several advantages:

(*a*) There is no pretence at a spurious precision.

(*b*) The use of the term 'outstanding' focuses attention on the wish of the working party to consider problems of teaching and not problems of definition. It is significant in the present context that Miles (1957) found himself 'struggling with the awful fact that the word "definition" itself has twelve definitions' (quoted by McNemar, 1964), and there is thus a grave danger that discussions which are intended to result in action can readily get bogged down in some philosophical argument which has no practical outcome beyond that of diverting attention away from the real purposes of the discussions. This the working party was determined to avoid if at all possible.

(*c*) The problems to be considered are not confined only to those concerning intellectually gifted children. A broader field is envisaged.

(*d*) We are not faced with preliminary problems regarding disagreements about 'mental structure'. For example, the extent to which a belief in 'general cognitive ability' is in fact justified becomes a secondary issue, if indeed it appears at all.

(*e*) Similarly an unfruitful engagement in a nature–nurture controversy is avoided since we are concerned not so much with the reasons as to how and why any child becomes outstanding, but rather with the simple fact that he is. This does not mean that we cannot concern ourselves with problems of potential as well as performance. The first will always somehow have to be inferred from some element in the second.

(*f*) Finally, and perhaps most vitally, the term 'outstanding' enjoys a greater degree of freedom from emotive overtones than 'gifted', and is more obviously relative to given contexts. It manifestly invites certain questions, amongst which are the following:

(i) Outstanding in relation to what kind of group?

(ii) Outstanding in what particular activity?

(iii) Outstanding as evidenced by location in what upper proportion of the designated group?

Each of these last three questions requires separate consideration.

OUTSTANDING IN WHAT KIND OF GROUP?

The answer proposed here rests on the hypothesis that the presence of outstanding pupils in any teaching group poses problems for the teacher. Two kinds of 'outstandingness' are important. In the first place there are those teaching difficulties which are associated simply with the presence of an able pupil within what is otherwise a fairly average group; the 125 IQ pupil, perhaps, in a small village school. In the second, there are those further problems which arise when a pupil is not only outstripping his peers, but also outstrips his teacher. The latter possibility is most obviously demonstrated perhaps in the learning of instrumental music, but it is unlikely to be confined to this area of activity alone.

It is pertinent to note that the degree of truth which attaches to our premise is closely related to the presence of artificial constraints in the curriculum. Where these exist, individual differences will be minimized; and the teaching problems associated with them can arise only in a much attenuated form. Where the individualization of learning has been carried forward to a massive degree, a perhaps paradoxical situation arises wherein the progressive solution of an important set of teaching problems actually operates to make them more acute, and thus to increase our awareness of them.

A degree of vagueness is thus deliberately injected into the preliminary deliberations as promised, and it is necessary to note that the study groups, which were not in any way constrained with regard to definitions, found themselves in more than broad agreement with the working party's own conclusions regarding a need for tolerance of ambiguity. This statement is not intended to hide or minimize the difficulties involved in definition which everyone who wishes to consider problems of giftedness must face. Typical experience in this regard is best described by the following direct quotation from a representative study group report:

Considerable difficulty was experienced in trying to find an acceptable definition of giftedness which could be used by the discussion groups. It was felt that giftedness was not just high IQ but that a child could be gifted in a particular area. A problem also considered was whether 'talented' children should be included in the definition of 'gifted' children. It was suggested that gifted children could be defined as children 'outstanding in any area'.

A further problem however was whether a definition of giftedness should also include those children whose gifts were only outstanding in relation to those of the rest of his class or school. It was decided that for the purpose of this discussion these children should be included but it was important that the two types of giftedness were not confused.

It was therefore decided that a gifted child is:

(a) a child who is gifted in absolute terms, i.e. his ability or his achievement in any area (or several areas) is outstanding with regard to all children of his age group, not just those in his own school. Such a definition includes children with a high IQ, or a talent in a particular area.

(b) a child who is gifted compared with the rest of his class or school, i.e. his ability is not outstanding in relation to all children of his age but the teacher may have problems in ensuring that he is given adequate opportunities to realize his potential.

Although this definition was accepted it was found impossible in the discussions to ensure that a distinction was always drawn between which type of gifted child was being referred to. However in several sections the discussion did not apply only to gifted children but to the importance of ensuring that all children realize their potential. In this context the importance of distinguishing the two types of gifted children diminished.

But the following note from another study group also deserves attention:

We find it almost impossible to answer the Schools Council's questions constructively, primarily because we do not know what *they* mean by a 'gifted' child.

Faced with this comment, it is perhaps fortunate that we found far more agreement between our views on definitions of giftedness and those of this team than they themselves appear to have anticipated.

OUTSTANDING IN WHAT PARTICULAR ACTIVITY?

It is apparent that our definition of giftedness implies a particular view of the school curriculum; this is most economically presented in the diagrammatic model[1] shown in figure 1.

Any school curriculum may be said to comprise a number of more or less distinguishable activities, or 'dimensions', represented by the arrows on the diagram. (For the purposes of this discussion, the relative angles of the arrows are unimportant; nor is it necessary to assign specific subject areas to particular arrows.) Each dimension is characterized to a greater or lesser extent by developmental sequences, and on each the individual achieves a certain position. Here the feathered end of the arrow represents high achievement, the pointed end a very elementary or low level. The goal of both

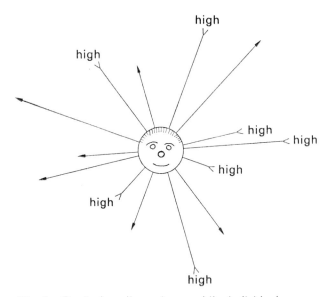

Fig. 1   Curriculum dimensions and the individual

teacher and learner is to change the pupil's location on some or all of the dimensions in a forward direction (i.e. so that he proceeds towards the 'high' position in each case) at optimum speed.

It would be easy now to become involved in fundamental questions regarding the aims of primary education but this is not our function. It must suffice only to consider the most important points relating general aims to the curriculum model. These are most conveniently stated separately below:

1   'Individuality' arises from the location of a person at the focus of a number of dimensions, each one of which is 'thrust through' to a different extent probably. This does not however imply that there is nothing more to personality development than this; the sum may well be greater than the parts in any event. It will later become apparent that teachers do not visualize the curriculum as comprising only those dimensions which have traditionally been vehicles of talent but such views are readily compatible with the model.[2]

2   The number and character of the dimensions envisaged is to some

extent arbitrary and can best be determined empirically. As with any other conception of human abilities and activities there are possibilities of infinite subdivision. It does not follow that teachers need to pursue such possibilities endlessly, but it will be made clear in what follows that the utility of the model does not depend upon prior agreement as to the precise nature and number of dimensions.

3   The 'thrusting through' process of development, alluded to above, whereby any individual moves along any particular dimension or dimensions has no implications for teaching method. Movement will occur through direct didacticism or 'discovery' method; as a consequence of both internal and external motivation; and indeed as the result of any number of approaches.

LOCATION IN WHAT UPPER PROPORTION?

Terman (1954) of course chose 140+ IQ as his cut-off point for giftedness and Hoyle (1969) believes there is some consensus about this. De Haan and Havighurst (1961), however, suggested pupils among the top ten per cent; Gallagher (1964) states (p. 12) 'the group labelled "gifted" usually refers to about the top two per cent of the population', and, as is well known, the National Association for Gifted Children interests itself in the highest two or three per cent. Gold (1965) contents himself by arguing that 'the cut-off point is significant because it may defeat its own purpose if set too high or too low. If set too high it may eliminate youngsters of high ability who for one reason or another do not test well. If set too low it may include so wide a range that highly advanced, challenging or difficult programs become impossible because they would result in frustration for a proportion of the selected group'.

Proctor (1966) provides the best tentative answer to this question by noticing the possibility that 'from a teaching point of view the implications of these different concepts of giftedness will be much the same', and perhaps many teachers intuitively agree with this since it has been our experience that they are frequently very reluctant to state given percentages of gifted children either with regard to their own schools or to some random group. When teachers are pressed into giving estimates, these vary markedly, as may be seen in the following table. These findings are intended as illustrative only. Nineteen headteachers and college of education primary tutors with one administrator were asked the question, 'What proportion of children gifted in a general intellectual sense would you expect to find in a random group of children?'

Additional evidence will be reported later which suggests that the readiness with which teachers are prepared to recognize children as gifted varies considerably, and one reason is probably embodied in this same table. Our experience further suggests that many teachers are unaware of the precise relationship between an intelligence quotient and a cut-off percentage, so

Table 1.1 Teachers' estimates of numbers of intellectually gifted children in a random group

Percentage intellectually gifted	<1%	1–2%	3–5%	6–10%	11–20%	21–30%	31%+
Equivalent IQ ($\sigma = 15$)	135+	130+	125+	119+	113+	105+	104–
Number giving response	1	2	6	4	3	3	Nil

that had the question been framed in terms of IQ scores, there would have been an apparently greater degree of agreement than the information in the foregoing table would justify. Most teachers who have been consulted suggest that 130 IQ probably indicates a useful cut-off point for intellectual giftedness and it seems that general opinion focuses on a 2–6 per cent band as marking off children who are likely, in most situations, to be sufficiently outstanding to warrant consideration on that account. A few of the study groups made comments broadly indicative of the proportions of intellectually gifted children they had in mind, thus:

Group 19 The names of 14 children had been submitted from 1500 . . . fewer than one per cent are rated as outstanding by their schools.

17 We would accept the definition of giftedness in that sense [verbal reasoning] for those scoring in the top two per cent of intelligence tests.

16 It has been suggested that an academically gifted child will have an IQ over 130 and this group forms a very small percentage of the population.

14 There was general agreement . . . that giftedness should be understood as being concerned with the top 5–6 per cent of the ability range.

5 Intellectually gifted children probably lie in the top $3\frac{1}{2}$–4 per cent of the population.

But the majority took the view expressed most succinctly as follows:

2 We cannot recommend that any particular proportion of children be designated as talented . . . this form of categorization . . . would introduce a rigidity antagonistic to our intentions for the children.

The recognition of general and specific giftedness

Most discussions of giftedness have been confined to problems concerning only the intellectually able pupils and have moreover generally assumed the existence of a 'g' factor (general intelligence) as being overwhelmingly important. Consideration of the relationships between the number of dimensions along which individual differences are recognizable and the total number of pupils likely to appear as gifted seems thus to have been neglected. It is necessary here, however, to examine this question in some detail since the definition of giftedness proposed does not necessarily involve recognition of a 'g' factor, and certainly specifies that several dimensions of giftedness will in all probability be recognizable.

Two rather different cases require attention. The first arises by stating that the only type of giftedness worthy of note is a kind of polymathic capacity which enables a pupil to be outstanding at practically everything. The theoretical expectations as to the actual numbers of such pupils likely to be found are calculated in table 1.2. Thanks are due to Gilbert Peaker for the information in this and the following table.

Table 1.2   The incidence of polymathic giftedness

	Coefficient of correlation (r)	Number of dimensions of giftedness							
		1	2	3	4	5	6	7	8
5·5% gifted	0·00	5.5	0·3	0	0	0	0	0	0
	0·25	5·5	0·7	0·2	0	0	0	0	0
	0·50	5·5	1·4	0·6	0·3	0·2	0·2	0·1	0·1
1·8% gifted	0·00	1·8	0	0	0	0	0	0	0
	0·25	1·8	0·1	0	0	0	0	0	0
	0·50	1·8	0·3	0·1	0	0	0	0	0

The upper half of the table shows the numbers of pupils who would remain gifted if they were first selected from the top 5·5 per cent in one dimension and then assessed again for two dimensions, and so on to a total of eight. Clearly the level of intercorrelation among the dimensions is crucial and three levels are taken to illustrate the effect. Contrary to what common sense might suggest, 0·3 per cent remain across two dimensions even though the correlation is zero. The main point however is that with intercorrelations approaching those found among intelligence test items, the original 5·5 per cent becomes a mere 0·3 per cent with four dimensions, and with seven dimensions only one child would remain from the original fifty-five per thousand.

The second half of the table illustrates the situation when only the top 1·8 per cent are chosen initially, and it is clear that the numbers of polymathically gifted children within this order of selection reduces dramatically to near zero with as few as three dimensions. Indeed with a curriculum comprising only four dimensions it will be something of a waste of time to attempt recognition unless the activities concerned are correlated very highly indeed.

There can be seen in these results some basis perhaps for the contention that the truly gifted are 'rare birds' who emerge of their own accord since they are so few.

It is the second case to be examined however which is more in the spirit of the definition of giftedness adopted here. This occurs in response to the question, 'If a given proportion of children is taken along each curriculum dimension separately and we designate them all as gifted regardless of their levels of performance in other fields, how does the total number recognized as being specifically gifted vary with the number of dimensions involved?' The necessary information is given in table 1.3.

Table 1.3 The incidence of specific giftedness

| | | Number of dimensions of giftedness | | | | | | | |
	r	1	2	3	4	5	6	7	8
5·5%	0·00	5·5	10·7	15·6	20·2	24·6	28·7	32·6	36·3
gifted	0·25	5·5	10·2	14·4	18·2	21·6	24·6	27·4	30·0
	0·50	5·5	9·6	12·9	15·6	18·0	20·0	21·9	23·5
1·8%	0·00	1·8	3·5	5·3	7·0	8·6	10·3	11·9	13·4
gifted	0·25	1·8	3·5	5·0	6·5	7·9	9·3	10·5	11·8
	0·50	1·8	3·5	4·6	5·7	6·8	7·7	8·6	9·4

These figures show that the second case is complementary to the first, and vastly more encouraging in terms of the numbers of children who will be recognized as gifted. With zero intercorrelations and only four dimensions, a fifth of the age group will fall into the top 5·5 per cent on one or other of the dimensions; with eight dimensions, more than a third of the group will be recognized as specifically gifted. Where intercorrelations are higher, it is still the case that as many as a quarter of the group achieve at the level of the top 5·5 per cent, in some activity or other, and ten per cent at the 1·8 per cent level. At the same time, of course, the table cautions against easy adoption of the notion that 'everybody can be gifted at something'. For this to become true it is necessary to engage in the futile process of infinite subdivision remarked upon earlier.

It should be clear that the usefulness of these tables does not depend entirely upon general agreement about the underlying assumptions. They enable any individual teacher to state his own preconceptions with regard to both the number of activities which he sees as integral parts of his curriculum and the probable levels of correlation which occur among them. He can decide for himself what proportion might usefully be termed gifted on any specific dimension, and then compare the numbers actually recognized in his school with the expected frequency. Where discrepancies arise, it would not of course entail that recognition was inefficient; but an *a priori* case for a careful re-examination of the situation would be established.

In arriving at conclusions with regard to dimensions and their intercorrelations, a teacher need not remain at the wholly intuitive and subjective level. Relevant evidence related to these decisions is derived from educational research, and from the views of other teachers. Both kinds of information are important and require consideration in the present context.

Correlation between dimensions: research findings

It is unnecessary to make clear whether the dimensions envisaged in our curriculum model are parameters deriving from some preconceived 'structure of mind', or simply straightforward school activities. The implied dichotomy cannot in fact be maintained: intelligence, as assessed by any test or method, is a form of achievement (Pidgeon, 1969; Vernon, 1966); and as such is presumably a legitimate curriculum dimension. It is certainly not uncommon for the goals of (say) project learning to be expressed in such terms as the development of 'critical thinking', 'logical expression', 'thinking skills', 'concepts', and 'an awareness of common elements in problem solving'. Creativity too has recently been the focus of attention as a second major aspect of giftedness and must also be susceptible of development through teaching procedures. Confirmation as to the fact of its appearance as a school activity lies not so much in the too frequent use of the word, but rather in the case of a recent course of lectures entitled 'Teaching English to Gifted Children', wherein practically every suggestion put forward as a technique for enhancing creativity was derived from the creativity testing movement itself as represented by the Getzels and Jackson (1962) programme.

It is thus convenient to begin our examination of the problems related to dimensions and their intercorrelations by reference to recent work on 'structural' dimensions, and then to assess the generality of these findings in terms of the more usual 'attainments' or 'activity' dimensions.

THRESHOLD INTERRELATIONSHIPS

Summarily, it can be said that the considerable degree of disagreement which exists among psychologists as to the relative independence of intelligence and creativity is due perhaps very largely to a neglect of the idea of 'thresholds'. This term implies that the level of correlation found in one zone of a continuum may be different from that in another and from that which describes the interrelationship across the whole range. In terms of correlation indices, the presence of a threshold relation would be indicated by high correlations in lower zones and lower correlations in higher zones. Representative findings are given in table 1.4.

These figures suggest that in above average IQ groups 'structural' inter-

Table 1.4   Creativity and intelligence correlations

(Haddon) IQ	r	(Ogilvie) IQ	r	(Yamamoto) IQ	r
70–135	0·480	70–140	0·540		
115+	0·076			130+	0·04
100+	0·164	108–140	0·195	110–130	0·08
100–	0·512	70–107	0·492	100–	0·31

correlations are likely to be quite low. How far is this true of 'attainment' dimensions? A tentative answer appears in table 1.5.

Table 1.5   Intelligence and attainment correlations

(Entwistle) Mean IQ	Boys VRQ (r)	Perf. IQ(r)	Girls VRQ(r)	Perf. IQ(r)
115	0·434	0·220	0·515	0·286
85	0·592	0·446	0·557	0·345

(Ogilvie) Mean IQ	Weight(r)	Concepts development Volume(r)	Float(r)	All(r)
114	0·09	0·05	0·27	0·001

Taking the two tables together it is apparent that the 'threshold' phenomenon is likely to be widespread in the curriculum and occurs even with regard to those activities like mathematics and language which have traditionally been regarded as 'intellectual' and heavily loaded on 'g'. One striking implication of this situation, in so far as it is true,[3] is that those who argue from the fact that 'slow learners' need and receive special education to the idea that the highly intelligent should also receive special treatment, take too simple a view of the situation. Whereas the former will tend to appear as a group, regardless of which particular dimension or dimensions are used for purposes of identification, this will be far less true with regard to the latter. Reference back to the effects of different levels of intercorrelation in the table on p. 13 will make this matter clear. It needs to be stressed of course that the argument being put forward goes only against a permanent grouping of 'gifted' pupils and not against more temporary groupings for specific purposes. It is in any event vitally necessary to consider teachers' views on the number of dimensions and their interrelationships before the previous analysis can be accepted; and it is to this evidence that attention may now be turned.

Teachers' views: the number of dimensions

As is well known, the Plowden Report (1969) argued for 'flexibility' in the curriculum and having listed 'broad areas such as language, science and mathematics, environmental study and the expressive arts', went on to suggest that, 'for young children the broadest of divisions is suitable. For children from 9 to 12 more subject division can be expected . . .'. The committee also stressed that 'children's learning does not fit into subject categories', but they nonetheless found it necessary to discuss 'experiences and ideas within the traditional subjects', and to 'give examples of work at most stages of the school'. The report in fact discusses eleven aspects of the curriculum separately, but not all these can be seen equally readily in developmental terms, and not all would in any event be generally thought of as legitimate dimensions of giftedness.

The Gittins Report (1967) follows its immediate predecessor fairly closely, and having again suggested four broad divisions goes on to consider a further breakdown of some dozen units. The most recent discussion of the problem is probably that contained in the Schools Council's own Working Paper 42, *Education in the Middle Years* (Evans/Methuen Educational 1972), and much of that document is highly relevant background to the present inquiry. Space permits only brief reference to statements of particular importance at this time:

1   This is an argument not for a narrow standard curriculum but for identifying common curricular elements that ought to be in every school. (p. 19)

2   The focus of schooling having moved from subject content to the learning process it is necessary to design a programme of learning which owes as much to the logic of the learning process as it does to the logic of the subject-matter. The discipline of the step-by-step analysis of the subject-matter has to be supplemented by the discipline of a step-by-step analysis of the learning process in relation to that subject-matter . . . the material must be sequenced to maintain interest, to be logically consistent, to be cogently comprehensible and to provide a 'map' of the subject. (p. 22)

3   At the more detailed level the pedagogical organization will seek to provide a logical sequence of appropriate and meaningful learning experiences, reinforcement, appropriate practice, and adequate evaluation. (p. 23)

The writers of this report obviously do not see the development of an 'integrated' programme and the extension of 'undifferentiated' learning as entailing the reduction of the primary school curriculum to a single 'dimension', and this conclusion is manifestly important for the recognition of giftedness. At the same time, their investigation showed that 'there is a general vagueness about many curriculum terms' which inevitably translates itself into questions regarding the recognition of outstanding capabilities. Some eighty-three different headings were produced by twenty headteachers, but 'many of these were of a similar nature', so much so, that they are reduced to about ten in the curriculum programmes reported by the study groups.

STUDY GROUP EVIDENCE

The present enquiry asked what probably amounts to the same question as that posed by the middle schools groups, but couched it specifically in terms of giftedness, thus: 'It seems generally to be accepted that all children should be educated according to age, aptitude and ability. This cannot be taken presumably to mean that teachers must try to develop any and every type of talent or achievement, otherwise the production of a highly creative telephone kiosk thief would be a laudable goal. Can the study group formulate a short list of the kinds of talent and achievement which it thinks ought to be provided for within the education system somewhere during the primary years?'

Despite some minor differences in terminology, the responses of our eighteen study groups can be analysed as in table 1.6.

It is mentioned that two groups report only approval of a 'broad curriculum'. The remainder provide views which closely parallel those expressed elsewhere and reported briefly above. The position may thus be summarized by saying that teachers see the primary school curriculum as comprising some eight or ten major activities which provide for the development of coincidental and concomitant gifts. It is however proper to point out at once that the totals in the right-hand column cannot be interpreted as showing the relative importance which attaches to the various activities. It was earlier noted (p. 10) that to conceive of some curriculum dimensions as being more obviously expressive of talent than others was entirely compatible with the model, and the totals on the right show that teachers entirely agree with this view. It is impossible to imagine that most groups do not attach great importance to elements designated 'moral/religious' and 'social studies'; the difficulty is simply that, in these areas, the development of giftedness is not quite so clearly a goal of instruction, and such activities are not ordinarily thought of quite in such terms. That they can be, however, is not likely to be an urgent issue.

EVIDENCE FROM QUESTIONNAIRES

Our information regarding teachers' views on curriculum interrelationships and the structure of children's abilities derives largely from responses to certain items on the questionnaire and the study group notes. The responses from the questionnaire are considered first and an analysis of replies is juxtaposed with each question below for convenience.

A.2   Children can be gifted with a high general intelligence or in specific areas of activity—music, history, sport, mathematics, etc. Which is more common—the general or the specific ability?

Table 1.6 Major curriculum activities as proposed by study groups

Curriculum dimensions	Study groups																Totals
	1	2	3	4	5	6	8	9	10	11	12	13	14	15	16	18	
Language	x	x	x	x	x	x	x	x	x	x	x	x	x	x	x	x	16
Mathematics	x	x	x	x	x	x		x	x	x	x	x	x	x	x	x	15
Science	x		x	x	x		x			x		x		x	x	x	10
Social studies	x				x												2
Moral/religious	x				x												2
Aesthetic and art	x		x	x	x	x	x	x	x	x		x	x	x	x		13
Music	x	x	x	x	x	x	x	x	x	x	x	x	x	x	x	x	16
PE and games	x	x	x	x	x	x	x	x	x	x	x	x	x	x	x	x	16
Intelligence		x					x						x				3
Foreign languages			x							x							2
Dance and movement			x	x		x	x	x	x			x		x			8
Drama			x			x	x		x	x		x		x	x		8
Craft and construction work				x				x	x	x				x			5
Gymnastics								x	x	x							3
Swimming								x	x	x							3
Social leadership										x	x	x	x	x			5
Observation skills													x				1
Totals	8	5	9	8	8	7	8	9	10	12	5	9	8	10	7	5	

Note: Study groups 7 and 17 did not specify activities but proposed only 'a broad curriculum'. There is no significance in the order and grouping of dimensions in the table.

Table 1.7 Analysis of responses to item A.2 of questionnaire ($n = 370$)

Response	n	%
General intelligence more common	149	40
Specific ability more common	135	36
Qualified replies	33	9
No response	53	14

Note: The proportion shown as 'no response', here and in the following tables, is artificially inflated by the presence of thirty students in the group who omitted some questions, and twelve teachers who did not receive questionnaires through the post and only duplicated the items from no. 6 onwards. About ten teachers thus left the item blank.

Table 1.7 shows that there is no consensus in the group. A substantial proportion of teachers would seem to hold to what may be termed the traditional view as to the all-pervading nature of intelligence. At the same time an almost equal proportion are more impressed by the occurrence of specific gifts. Further light is shed on the nature of both views by an examination of the responses to items A.4 and A.5 of the questionnaire.

A.4 Is it your experience that children gifted in any or all of these specific areas are also of high general intelligence?

A.5 Is it your experience that children of average or below average intelligence can be gifted in any of these areas? If so, which?

It is useful to consider both sets of data together, and they are thus conjoined in table 1.8.

Table 1.8 Analysis of responses to items A.4 and A.5 of the questionnaire

Response	Item A.4		Item A.5	
	n	%	n	%
Affirmative	81	22	289	78
Negative	33	9	9	2
Qualified reply	197	53	12	3
No response	59	16	60	16

The findings for A.4 suggest that perhaps a fifth of the group maintain strongly that high intelligence is a necessary, if not sufficient basis for giftedness in specific fields. Only some ten per cent feel able to give a categorically negative response, and it is clear that in the opinion of most teachers only a qualified reply is possible. The nature of the qualification most frequently made is revealed to some extent by the responses to A.5. Here no fewer than 78 per cent state that children who are average or below average can be gifted in at least some area of the curriculum, and only 2 per cent deny the possibility entirely.

It would appear therefore that despite the difficulty of framing unambiguous questions regarding the threshold concept, whilst at the same time avoiding any suggestion of such a possibility within the questions themselves, the evidence quite strongly supports the proposition that the great majority of teachers do in fact conceive of intelligence as providing no more than a possible basis for giftedness in some activities. It is apparent from the figures that even some of those who replied to question A.4 with an unqualified affirmative intended no more than that it is usually the case that specific giftedness is accompanied by high intelligence. Confirmation of this interpretation is found by an examination of individual questionnaires which shows that by far the most common qualifications made are of the form exemplified in the following quotations:

A.4   (i) Possibly but not necessarily.
      (ii) Often.
      (iii) Yes—with the possible exceptions of painting, games and athletics.
      (iv) Not necessarily—but a specific gift can develop further if accompanied by high intelligence.
      (v) As a generalization (if one must) this is the case but there are many exceptions, e.g. footballer, pop singer.
      (vi) Some, but not all.

A.5   (i) Yes—the creative artist, the imaginative actor and speaker, the athlete—where no logical intellectual thinking demanded as essential to the specific area.
      (ii) Yes—particularly art and craft and movement.
      (iii) Yes—craft and constructional work, games, athletics, movement and drama.
      (iv) In art, craft, games, and movement children of average intelligence may shine; only rarely do children of much below average intelligence.
      (v) Yes—painting, movement, drama, games, music.
      (vi) One boy with a flair for French at 10–11 had an IQ of about 90. Although I encouraged this and was delighted that he did so well, I shall be surprised if he develops to a very high level.
      (vii) Yes—music/painting/craft/construction work/games and athletics/movement/drama/spoken language.
      (viii) Yes most definitely in the specific areas mentioned in question A.3 with the possible exception of mathematics.
      (ix) Yes—many children have manual skills.
      (x) Yes—music, painting, craft, games, athletics, drama, spoken English.

Rather more examples have deliberately been included with regard to Question 5 in order to show which curriculum areas are typically regarded by teachers as having the lower IQ thresholds. These, predictably perhaps, relate mainly to activities requiring outstanding levels of physical co-ordination, but it is noteworthy that some activities of an intellectual type are included. More evidence, equally relevant, is contained in case study material to be cited later, since these cases include some profiles showing considerable variation even among the intellectual components. But the point is important, and therefore some additional very brief and pertinent case studies are cited below in exactly the form in which they were received from study groups:

(a) Considerable speed of thought; independent thought and action; ability to become absorbed in work; musically gifted; socially acceptable; well-balanced personality; no good at art.

(b) Exceptional mathematical gift but no apparent interest in anything else; unco-ordinated.

(c) Alive and stimulating; inventive; musical; needed to be accepted by fellows; emotional problems but a marked sense of humour.

(d) Considerable depth of thought; ability to express orally; creative, particularly verbally.

(e) Exceptional mathematical ability; speed of thought, particularly numbers; alive and stimulating but not apparently outstanding in other ways.

(f) Boy, 10 years of age; this child has a talent for mathematics which is sufficiently great for the mathematically minded teachers on the staff to regard as a gift. He grasps new concepts with ease and is prepared to develop his interests by working on his own. Since some researchers have suggested that an unusual degree of mathematical ability may be a specific ability and not necessarily linked to overall performance or to high 'intelligence', it is interesting that this particular child seems much less able in other curriculum subjects.

Summarizing the evidence from all three questions taken together, it is clear that although teachers may not explicitly postulate the existence of thresholds, they nonetheless implicitly believe in them. Some thresholds, particularly those related to more physical and aesthetic elements in the curriculum, are seen to be lower than others, such that pupils of average and perhaps lower than average intelligence may become gifted in specific fields; further evidence for this may be found on p. 46. The locations of the various thresholds for different aspects of more intellectual work would be the subject of considerable disagreement, and it is unfortunate that our investigation is not more helpful here.[4] It has nonetheless to be remembered that any research into this problem needs to take very careful account of the learning environments concerned. Attention was earlier drawn (p. 7) to the possible effects of artificial constraints in a curriculum, and the point is so vital as to bear constant repetition. Artificial ceilings on achievement must serve to reduce levels of performance, both for individuals and groups, and thus to increase levels of intercorrelation among the various types of activity. Thresholds are therefore no more than apparent and are likely to be higher than would otherwise be the case in any circumstances which tend to retard the development of individual differences. The general point under consideration here is well put by one of the study groups as follows:

The emergence and recognition of talents among children who are not clearly seen to be of good general ability is a hope which has yet to be justified and waits upon the provision of opportunity, i.e. the 'responsive school environment' [which] is itself the principal diagnostic tool for this purpose and we must apply it before we can evaluate the needs it may meet.

The attitude reflected here may be too pessimistic when related to the other evidence presented in this section, but the problem itself is ably described.

ADDITIONAL CONFIRMATION

The evidence from the other study groups confirms the general position described above. The following quotations from reports are included in order to substantiate further previous findings, together with the relevant entries on one questionnaire which is of particular interest since it was completed as a group task by one of our teams. It too presents much the same picture as previous evidence.

Group 3   The group felt that the highest level of success in a particular field was more likely to come from an individual where special skill was coupled with a high level of general intelligence than from an individual possessing only special ability and an average or below average intelligence. Examples of this can be seen in sport, music, drama, etc.

17   Is there a 'halo' effect in giftedness? . . . the group felt that there wasn't and that giftedness tended to be specific . . . the concept of IQ had a very limited value in identifying giftedness.

5   The child's gift may be intelligence, but certain gifted children may be lacking in high intelligence,

15   . . . it was often the case of . . . teachers saying 'there is something special', [going on] to illustrate it by describing a child . . . with an IQ score 100 whose English was nevertheless regarded by all the staff as brilliant . . .

16   The term 'gifted' may be used to indicate . . . children who show some outstanding ability in a specific field but who do not necessarily have a high intelligence.

Group entries on questionnaire

A.2   General: 9 (the most common form of giftedness)
Specific: 5
Don't know: 6

The panel commented that often high general intelligence is easier to recognize because facilities for recognition by the teacher and for expression by the child of specific ability may not exist.

A.4   Frequently but not invariably.

A.5   Children of average intelligence may be gifted in games and associated activities; art; craft; music (a few perhaps but high intelligence of a specialized kind is a sign of the really gifted musician); drama; movement.

CONCLUSIONS

On the basis of the definition of giftedness adopted here, the curriculum model derived from it, and the whole of the preceding discussion, three major conclusions, which are of the utmost importance for the consideration of giftedness, may now be drawn:

1   Actions which tend to reduce the extent of intercorrelation among curriculum activities hold out the promise of a greater number of children experiencing outstanding success. Actions which increase these intercorrelations will reduce the numbers.

2   The more disparate the activities, and the larger the number available, the less likely it is that talent will remain undetected and undeveloped.

3   Problems of giftedness form a part of the total of those concerned with individualization.

The professional views of teachers on issues related to these propositions are clearly of interest and receive consideration in the following section.

'General' or 'special' education? Study group responses

Stress has been laid on the need to avoid constraints on individualization and to minimize intercorrelations among curriculum activities. A first question immediately arises therefore as to the extent to which teachers are prepared to encourage the development of talent regardless of other considerations. The present study approached this problem by asking study groups to examine a number of interconnected statements and questions which, as a preliminary step, are conveniently taken separately:

2.11   In formulating its list of activities can it be taken as axiomatic that the group intends such activities to be organized in such a manner as to ensure that any child possessing exceptional gifts would have the opportunity to develop them to the utmost?

Ten of the study groups reported specifically on this item, and their comments are very briefly indicated by quoting only the most salient points below:

Group 2   We do not take it as 'axiomatic' that any child's talent should be fostered 'to the utmost' in the primary stage . . . it is important for all talented children that their talent should not be developed to such a point that it isolates them socially and emotionally from their peers . . . [but] the level of 'general education' offered in that area in which he is talented may for him be inadequate.

8   . . . it was taken as self-evident that such activities could be organized in such a manner as to ensure that any child possessing exceptional gifts would have the opportunity to develop them to the full . . .

9 Yes—provided only that this is not to the detriment of their general education.

11 . . . if a child showed a particular gift then it was important that attempts should be made to develop it . . . problems arise over the degree of concentration on a child's gifts . . . a child of primary age should receive a full general education.

12 The group was in full agreement with the point put forward in this sub-section . . . it should not lead to a talent being developed at the expense of an all-round education.

13 As far as possible these skills should be able to be developed within the framework of the child's normal school life.

14 All socially accepted talents should be supported during the primary years.

16 . . . the all-round development of the gifted child is important if a child is being prepared for life . . . the term 'utmost' is too strong.

18 Yes—otherwise there is no point in listing the activities, but we must keep a balance—swimming ought not to occupy too much time.

So far it would appear that the only considerable constraints on complete development of any talent stem directly from the need to develop skills which are socially acceptable. The above responses do, however, envisage some restraint arising from the requirement that every child shall receive a 'general education', and it is necessary therefore to consider how far teachers envisage education outside school as important for the development of talent. It was the aim of item 2.12 to elicit information on this point.

2.12   Where the group finds itself including in its proposals certain kinds of activity which it believes cannot, or should not be included in the curriculum of the ordinary school as part of a 'general' education, but which nevertheless ought to be available within the child's educational environment, broadly defined; an indication to this effect, together with, if possible, an outline of the principle underlying these decisions would provide important data.

As a preliminary to the examination of the reports, it is useful to draw attention at once to the failure of our study groups to state any principle of division as between curricular and extra-curricular activities. The comments are nevertheless cited because of the importance which is attached by teachers to extra-mural activities, even in the context of a 'general' education: a concept which again receives approval, and as now interpreted renders the term 'extra-curricular' superfluous.

Group 2   Where a child is not able, by virtue of his talent, to benefit from the 'general' education offered by the school, he should be withdrawn from it for special instruction . . .

4 The child with exceptionally high IQ should be segregated . . . if such selection is not possible, then peripatetic aid is needed . . . music and sports were catered for by outside groups and peripatetic teachers; for music and movement (ballet) ideally the authority should provide area schools . . .

9   We would include iceskating, rock climbing, horse riding, obviously this would depend on geography and expediency—we would look for evidence of unusual ability and interest in such pursuits at an early age.

11   . . . 'technical' subjects such as photography and subjects such as gymnastics, instrumental tuition and ballet, which are of limited applicability, should be specialist activities catered for outside the 'general curriculum'. The subjects requiring individual attention are by necessity forced out of the general curriculum.

12   Opportunity for the development of certain activities (not part of a 'general' education) should be provided, but usually out of school time.

13   . . . these skills should be able to be developed within the framework of the child's normal life, but where this is not possible the school should direct other possible lines of assistance.

14   Primary schools can and must provide sufficient extension for the gifted child in most cases with specialist facilities available as required.

15   There must be some provision over and above the normal school programme.

16   . . . areas such as dance, music, ice skating, are often taken care of by the parents outside the school activities.

18   . . . there would have to be additional opportunities outside the school— music, astronomy, ballet.

Here then is clear evidence of strong support for the deliberate extension of 'general education' into extra-mural activities. It thus becomes essential to consider the principles which should underlie support from public monies of some activities rather than others; a question put to us, it will be remembered, by one chief education officer (p. 4, 8). It has already been shown that there exists a strong body of opinion supporting the encouragement of all socially useful or acceptable talents. Where, however, as was bluntly stated by one panel, 'we recognize that economic constraints might prevent the needs of all types of giftedness being met in this [extra-mural] way', we are faced with what turns out to be, from the evidence cited below, a peculiarly intractable problem. Item 2.22 was an attempt to provoke views upon it, and the responses are given here in brief:

2.22   Is there any consensus of view in the study group on these matters? In more concrete terms, would the group support a proposal to assist a potential football 'star' or 'Olympic' swimmer in some way over and above the provision made for average children? Would it support a talented musician but not a footballer? Can it suggest where a line should be drawn between those gifts which should receive special support and those which should not? Or should no talent be specially supported during the primary years?

Group 2   An important adjunct to an interest based curriculum is the use of clubs. These must however be based on teacher strength so that there is knowledge and enthusiasm at the top.

4 The group was not prepared to put an order of importance to the different gifts.

6 Under the present educational system there are more opportunities for a child talented in sport than for a child talented in any cultural subject.

8 Most teachers would endeavour to ensure that provision was made for the potential Olympic swimmer, footballer . . . without suggesting that any one gift is of greater importance than another.

9 We cannot draw a line here; any gift not socially undesirable should be supported if this can be arranged locally and without too much disturbance of the school.

11 . . . it is difficult to assess activities, e.g. football and music for their relative degrees of social utility.

12 Every type of talent either inside or outside of school should be developed.

13 We would support the footballer, 'out of school'. [*but no principle of division proposed*]

16 The group would support a proposal to assist a potential footballer if the child is given a general education. [*again no principle suggested*]

18 The comparison of musician with footballer was . . . unfair, the former being general whilst the latter is specific.

It is apparent that not a single panel of teachers is prepared to state a principle of guidance which might be used to justify support, from public funds, of some extra-curricular activities rather than others. This is a finding of no little importance which will have to be borne in mind in any evaluation of provisions for the gifted. For the moment, it will be sufficient to point out that the difficulty is derived in no small measure from the fact that today it is far harder to distinguish the 'cultural' from 'leisure' or 'vocational' activities. Such differentiations are being progressively blurred, and have now reached a point where they are of little help to the curriculum constructor faced with a need to select. Unless our findings are translated into being a good solid argument for maintaining the *status quo*, which of course they are not, some other solution will have to be proposed.

Item 2.3 asks teachers to turn their attention to the problem of concentration on a particular gift already anticipated in some of the responses to previous items. If the concept of a 'balanced' education is pressed, in the context of limited time, then clearly there may be massive constraints on the pursuit of excellence in any one field other than that of 'g' itself. It was considered necessary therefore to obtain some knowledge as to how teachers looked at this particular aspect, since it had already been anticipated that they would ordinarily stress the virtues of a 'balanced' curriculum. The responses given below are conjoined with those from item 2.31, since they overlap considerably and can be examined jointly:

2.30 To what extent does the group feel that the interests of an apparently talented youngster will best be served by some degree of concentration on his particular gift? Some teachers argue that such concentration removes the child's freedom to decide his own future; others argue that refusal to develop such potential similarly restricts the child's freedom of choice.

2.31 What is the group's view regarding special schools which, whilst providing exceptional opportunities and tuition in one particular area, also provide, or purport to provide, a good general education? How do the group members relate their attitudes towards 'special' schools to the suggestion that provision for gifted children can and should be made in the ordinary school by means of special programmes of tuition? In regard to either system is it important whether the apparently talented youngster maintains his outstanding position in later life or not?

Group 1 The panel would not wish to see special care in one aspect of education at the expense of overall development . . . most members were concerned lest special schools for the very gifted might warp the child's natural development . . .

4 There should be some degree of concentration on the gift . . .

6 Some degree of concentration on a gift should be available . . .

7 . . . the special abilities of pupils could be recognized and arrangements could then be made for enabling these abilities to be developed . . . it may be useful to consider the possibility of arranging single purpose groups of pupils and the assistance of peripatetic staff not only for music . . . but also for other subjects.

8 . . . a talented youngster would be best served by some degree of concentration on his particular gift . . . it could be arranged for the child to have extra tuition . . . during lunchtimes or even as out-of-school work. Some teachers felt, however, that it could be to advantage to devote the bulk of the time to the development of the specific gift in an endeavour to draw from this interest and move out into other curricular activities.

9 There should be concentration on a particular gift as far as this can be done without interfering with general education . . . only exceptionally gifted children would benefit from segregation in special schools catering for a specific ability . . . by exceptionally talented we mean of such endowment that only say a dozen could be found of a given age in the country . . . it is not considered important whether an apparently gifted child maintains his position in later life.

10 Opinion within the group was much divided about the value of special schools . . . at the primary age the primary child [should receive] a very general education in addition to the specialized concentration upon one particular gift . . . the group found it impossible to generalize . . . It was the view of some that it would be better to provide for the 'part-time' coming together of gifted children.

11 . . . for a child in a poor area any concentration on a gift would provide a widening experience not a narrowing one . . . the group was against total segregation . . . the less talented children needed the influence of a pace setter [but] . . . gifted children needed contact with other gifted children [and] . . . there was considerable underdevelopment of talent in schools . . . various forms of segregation might be acceptable [but] it was of great importance that the gifted child of primary age should not be cut off from the normal school environment . . . problems in the use of partial segregation were adverse reactions on the part of

children and parents, which talents should be given special attention, and who should decide which children should be selected . . . a special school would be considered . . . the authority should also set up experimental tutorial groups . . . during the years of schooling the development of a child's talent was important in itself.

12   Special schools for special talents are acceptable if a general education is also provided.

13   Special schools for particular talents could be an answer . . . in talents that could not be accommodated by other means . . . the group stressed the social problems of such segregation.

15   [We are] against the idea of special schools for young gifted children and prefer the idea of special programmes of tuition in 'enrichment centres' . . . some [agree] that it was worth encouraging giftedness for its own sake, leaving the future to take care of itself; others felt that we should have failed if the outstanding qualities of giftedness were not carried over into later life.

16   Where a child has a specific ability and there is a failure in all else, then a school should be provided.

17   Special schools were in general regarded favourably. By offering scholarships . . . they seemed to offer the gifted a chance of working with their peers by age and aptitude, so meeting their social and intellectual needs more effectively . . . it was regretted that many local authorities provide peripatetic specialists in music and drama [but] such services are almost universally the first to be axed in times of financial stringency . . . the 'outstanding position' which might be attained in later life . . . was felt to be of minimal importance beside ensuring his personal sense of fulfilment.

18   . . . special schools were able to give a good general education [since] they were usually boarding establishments and the pupils worked longer hours . . . it was not considered important that the gifted child should maintain his outstanding position in later life; extra support should be given when the special gift is recognized.

These responses show that the study groups are by no means concerned to press the concept of a 'general' education too far. They constantly return, throughout the whole of their discussions, to the importance of a good general education, but they also express an equally strong desire to see no talent remains undeveloped. They are thus prepared to view special schools with favour for some gifted children; they applaud the idea of encouraging some real degree of concentration on a particular gift, as against a mere introduction to an interest; they propose a number of ways whereby a child can both 'generalize' and 'specialize'; and they regard the development of a talent as vitally important, whether the child will pursue it specially in later life or not. Several groups imply a strong awareness of the importance of success in some field to the child's self image, and the relationship of the latter to the prospects of achieving a good general education. One group makes particular mention in this connexion of deprived children, and in view of the comments in correspondence cited earlier (p. 4, 3) it is clear that our examination of present provisions ought to consider how far the talented are in danger of being neglected, paradoxically enough, in the educational priority areas.

Before attempting a survey of the preceding paragraphs it will be useful to consider briefly a concept frequently mentioned in the study group reports in connexion with a general education, namely, the concept of 'balance'. A careless application of this notion could obviously be a source of constraint on the development of individualism, and hence on giftedness; even in the context of a general education as described above.

'Balance' versus 'integration'

It is easy perhaps to see a need for balance in the curriculum. Society's general goals and values commit schools to maintaining, however uneasily, a balance among the following[5]:

(a) The goals themselves: the transmissive, the adaptive and the developmental all have a fundamental importance *and are interrelated*. Thus each must have legitimate status, no one can be neglected.

(b) The several growth dimensions: the cognitive, the affective (emotional, social, aesthetic, and ethical), and the motor physical, all have fundamental importance *and are interrelated*. Thus each must have legitimate status; no one can be neglected.

(c) The values of the various political levels.

(d) The spread of the disciplines.

(e) Learning methods.

(f) The immediate and the ultimate.

The second of these areas is the one which most concerns present issues, and the important point here is that the elements amongst which balance is to be achieved are themselves interrelated. But they are interrelated not within the school so much as within the individual person. This means that attention to one can have benign as well as malign effects; that balance within an individual may be achieved by means of imbalance in terms of exposure to different curriculum elements. It means too that an enforced external balance may in reality produce nothing more than ill-disguised imbalance within the personality.

It is here therefore to be argued that the concept of 'balance' may usefully be applied to a curriculum; it is far less usefully applied in relation to an individual. Its use is indeed positively inimical to a person's growth as an individual. For this reason, the concept of 'balance' must be replaced by a concept of 'integration' in discussions of giftedness. The former permits us to envisage only a relatively narrow range of personality profiles, especially if it is conjoined with a demand that everybody shall follow a broad curriculum. In these unfavourable circumstances the development of outstanding ability by different individuals in different fields would surely be severely inhibited.

Summary

Summarizing now the previous discussions on curriculum dimensions it is clear that teachers do not wish to prevent children from concentrating upon activities in which they show special aptitude. They do however see certain constraints arising, many of which spring from the need for every child to have a general education, but not all. Some derive from difficulties associated with segregation, for example:

1 The child's own social development may suffer.

2 The intellectual development of his peers may require his presence as pacemaker.

3 The reactions from parents of children not selected may be adverse.

Others derive from practical problems of organization and provision which, having received incidental and cursory recognition above, can be more conveniently discussed in Part II. At this point attention must be turned to certain viewpoints, an examination of which is now fundamental to further progress since they are related directly to the needs of gifted children.

Notes

1 This general philosophical position is further described by King and Brownell (1966), especially chs. III and V.

2 Kallen (1951) says 'the history of systems no less than of people shows that plurality occasions unification but that unification never overtakes, only pushes on, plurality'.

3 Other interpretations of this kind of evidence are proposed. Gallagher and Crowder (1957) found in a sample of thirty-five 150+ IQ children that 68 per cent were 3+ grades ahead in paragraph meaning, 58 per cent were 3+ grades in science, 27 per cent were 3+ in arithmetic reasoning, 3 per cent were 3+ grades in arithmetic computation. They then say the explanation 'would seem to lie in the construction of the tests themselves'. Against this, Professor Bowker is quoted in an NAGC newsletter as stating that he found different levels of ability even within the different spheres of mathematics.

4 Views very much in accordance with what is implied here have been stated elsewhere, thus:

(a) Eysenck (1964) 'theories of linear dependence between cognitive and non-cognitive areas may have to be supplemented by theories stressing non-linear dependence'.

(b) Anderson (1960) 'we assume rather . . . that whenever we deal with a relationship between two factors that the relationship is one of correspondence throughout the whole range of the two variables'. And McKinnon estimates a threshold of 120 IQ for intellectual work (Vernon, 1963, p. 164) of some kinds. More work is needed before much can be said about schoolchildren and their curriculum activities with real certainty.

5 Inlow (1966) provides this list. Only sections relevant here are quoted in full; *italics are ours.*

2 The needs of gifted children

The correspondence cited in the last chapter suggests that some educationists are very prone to assume that an expressed interest in giftedness entails more than a mere interest in segregation: that a desire to recognize talent implies a wish to establish permanent groupings of specially selected pupils. One of the Schools Council subject committees was moved to state:

The fact that special consideration is being given to the gifted child seems to contradict the contemporary educational emphasis which is placed on such things as the integrated day, vertical grouping, non-streaming and non-selection.

The need for recognition

The extent to which teachers themselves feel a need to recognize the gifted child's ability, regardless of what particular organizational arrangements we may have in mind, is therefore an important issue which was posed as item 2.21(i) in the notes for study groups. The term 'segregation' was used deliberately in order to put this problem in its most tendentious form, and to enable those who wished to argue against any special need for recognition most readily to do so. A second section was appended to this question since it was also clear that some teachers expect real giftedness to emerge of its own accord. If this is true, then again 'recognition' becomes something of a false problem, and since the working party itself was already agreed that identification presupposes not any particular action, but certainly some kind of action, it further agreed that if teachers were not interested in recognizing a gifted child, then this must presumably be because they could envisage no useful action on the basis of such knowledge. Conversely, if a strong interest in recognition was evinced, then further study would become essential. The responses to item 2.21 are exemplified below:

2.21   Two issues arise in this general context:

(i) How far ought problems of recognition and segregation to be kept separate in discussions about gifted children? Some teachers argue that if there is to be no special segregation of any kind there is no point in worrying about recognition.

(ii) Some people, perhaps a great many, believe that gifted children are already sufficiently advantaged not to need any special attention of any kind either in the ordinary primary school or elsewhere. Not infrequently there is coupled with this attitude the view that 'giftedness' will emerge regardless of environmental conditions, and an implicit definition of 'giftedness' which is somewhat circular in that it is taken to indicate a level of talent so high as to ensure that nothing but death can prevent its emergence.

Group 1   We had conflicting comments on the question of identification . . . one view is that if undetected a gift may be lost, the other . . . that a genuine gift would emerge whatever the circumstances.

2 (i) Recognition and opportunity (which implies some degree of segregation) are interdependent.

(ii) Rubbish!

3 . . . unanimously agreed that early recognition of special skills is both advisable and desirable.

4 The group completely disagreed with the statement in 2.21 (i) and generally disagreed with (ii) although they felt giftedness could possibly emerge.

5 The reservoir of talent in the working class does not emerge. . . .

7 Giftedness in the physical subjects may need to be recognized very early.

8 . . . with some children giftedness would probably emerge regardless of environmental conditions, but it could not be said that this would apply generally.

9 (i) . . . recognition cannot be separated from segregation, one follows from the other. *But* the segregation is not necessarily a physical segregation. We do not think gifted children should be simply left to get on with it.

(ii) It was generally agreed that it was important that a teacher should recognize the gifted child and provide him with help.

12 It is essential to recognize giftedness . . . [it] may emerge [but] further encouragement is needed.

13 . . . special treatment was needed with highly gifted children but [the group] hoped that the climate of schools would be such as to accommodate children's individual needs anyway . . . there was disagreement about the ability of giftedness to 'emerge' regardless of environmental conditions.

14 . . . without special attention and opportunities gifted children often become frustrated.

16 (i) 'Segregation' was considered too harsh . . . the gifted child should be integrated.

(ii) The statement does not take into account the disturbed and maladjusted gifted child . . . if the giftedness of a child is not recognized, difficulties may occur.

17 (i) Members found that they had not in practice been able in the past to identify more than a very occasional child as in any way 'gifted'.

An examination of these statements leaves little doubt as to the attitude of teachers towards the need for recognition of giftedness. Although some tend rather to think in terms of latent talents, waiting as it were to be spotted in a sort of all-or-nothing way, others have more of a continuum in mind; all are concerned that the teacher should be in a position to assess the child's capacity.

Additional information on this derives from an analysis of some of the items in the questionnaire, which is undertaken in table 2.1. The items are these:

A.7 (i)   It is important to recognize the highly intelligent child
A.7 (ii)   It is important to recognize the highly creative child
A 7 (iii)   The early detection of exceptional talent is vitally important
A 7 (v)   Early specialization is unimportant for the development of exceptional talent (If you disagree please indicate which areas, in your view, require early specialization)
B 2 (x)   Failure to recognize potential giftedness [is a condition possibly harmful to the development of giftedness]

In table 2.1 and the following tables, the five columns ranging from emphatic agreement to emphatic disagreement represent points on a scale on the original questionnaire (p. 205). Those replying were asked to tick one of five positions on the scale to indicate the strength of their feelings on the statement given; the middle column represents no particular opinion, while the second and fourth columns show moderate agreement and disagreement.

Table 2.1 The need for recognition: analysis of responses to items A.7 (i), (ii), (iii), (v), B.2 (x). $n = 370$

| | No reply | | Emphatically agree | | | | | | Emphatically disagree | | Qualified reply | |
	n	%	n	%	n	%	n	%	n	%	n	%	n	%
A.7 (i)	24	6	287	78	49	13	5	1	1	0	2	1	2	1
A.7 (ii)	26	7	269	73	67	18	6	2	0	0	1	0	1	0
A.7 (iii)	28	8	150	41	126	34	46	12	11	3	4	1	5	1
A.7 (v)	34	9	78	21	97	26	56	15	70	19	29	8	6	2
B.2 (x)	9	2	193	52	128	35	24	6	14	4	0	0	2	1

Note: For interpretation of the format of this and the following tables see above.

The table shows that it is important to recognize the creative as well as the intelligent child, and the general failure to qualify these questions tends to confirm that teachers see them as interrelated according to the threshold theory put forward earlier. Early detection is apparently less urgent, however, than recognition at some stage in the primary years, and one reason may be that teachers do not believe in early specialization if this means taking up much of the time available for general education. As we have seen, there is widespread support only for 'some degree of concentration'. The areas mentioned in A.7(v) as requiring early specialization were usually music, ballet and physical activities such as gymnastics and swimming.

Further needs: study group evidence

In order to discover what might be thought to be the further needs of children once it is accepted that they require to be recognized, study groups were requested to state their views in response to item 2.4 (page 212). The following selected replies summarize what was reported:

Group 1 Gifted children certainly need contact with their more ordinary peers and it is most helpful if they can meet similar gifted children.

2 Their needs differ largely in degree. They have a particular need for goals, for challenge and this is most frequently missing . . . social and emotional development needs to be specially safeguarded. All children need contact with others at their own level of ability.

4 He must be stretched within his group.

6 Listed: Freedom to develop at rate which suits him.
   Encouragement from teacher and parent.
   Social training—integration in society.
   Acquisition of basic skills and tools, and simple techniques . . . these apply to all children [but] the limits and range of ability were greater . . . [hence] more attention for their needs.

9 . . . probably less direction . . . contact earlier with specialist teachers . . . access to more advanced books, apparatus and facilities . . . to be stretched but not overstretched . . . emotional stability and social development should keep pace . . . contact with others similarly gifted.

11 . . . for sympathy and tolerance as these children are often under greater stress than average children . . . more academic approach and greater depth of treatment of subject . . . social contact with their intellectual equals . . . emotional stability and social development was seen as self-evident . . . a humbling experience may be provided through competition . . . (also need) width as well as depth . . . contact with other children in the ordinary school environment . . . if they are not stretched or challenged they may become bored or naughty.

12 Any special attention however should be on a pro rata basis . . . not [to be] set apart . . . a distinct need . . . to have a place 'on their own' where they can . . . cut themselves off occasionally . . . imperative for these children to meet and talk to other adults (rural schools).
   Generally agreed that
   (i) gifted children ought to be stretched and challenged.
   (ii) treated exactly as other children.
   (iii) a little intellectual growth can be sacrificed in order to allow for a proper social development.
   (iv) there does exist a real need for contact with similarly gifted children.

13 More than the average child [they] need provision for continuance of study and opportunity for depth of enrichment . . . contact (adult or other) with others of their own ability.

18 . . . to pass quickly through elementary stages . . . pursue own lines of research . . . a form of counselling, this may be needed by parents too who may find it difficult to understand or help.

It is probably well to examine the study groups' views by first stating two rather obvious truisms:

(a) Gifted children are only children and their needs can only differ in terms of degree.

(b) On the basis of our definition, or indeed any definition, it is difficult to generalize since a child's needs clearly relate to the nature of his talent, his background and his personality. As one study group put it:

Further help must be influenced by the personality of the child, for this will be the determining factor in deciding both the level and direction of achievement ... some may be blessed with persistence of motive and effort, have confidence in their abilities and ... great ... force of character ... their very versatility may make the guidance of them more difficult; some may need the stimulus of being with other similarly gifted individuals: some will thrive in a secure settled environment, others may need the challenge of 'irritants'.

All this is true. We are only concerned to state it in order that what follows is seen in clear perspective. The generalizations made below, far from being useless in terms of applicability to any individual child, are of the essence of individual treatment. To say that gifted children need competition, for example, is not to say that some will not need it more than others, or that the not so gifted do not need it. It is to say that if those conditions necessary for competition are absent, then the proper needs of some gifted children (and possibly others of course, who are not here our concern) are not being met. Or again, if there is no Saturday orchestra meeting, and we state that there is such a need for gifted children because they need to be challenged, this cannot be taken to imply that all gifted children should attend regardless of individual circumstances, or even that only gifted children will benefit. It is to say that the needs of some gifted children are not being properly met; and it is to say that in the absence of such provisions, talent cannot flourish as it otherwise would. These then are the kinds of generalization which we take our study groups to intend in discussing the needs of gifted children. Attempted refutations based on an argument either that all children's needs are the same, or that gifted children differ so much amongst themselves that generalizations are impossible, are themselves insubstantial generalizations which are singularly unhelpful. They reveal only a misunderstanding of the intent of the study groups and a misinterpretation of the whole import of the present study.

The primary needs of gifted pupils as they appear from an examination of study group reports may now be listed:

1 Contact with their average peers
2 Contact with children of comparable levels of ability
3 To be stretched and challenged even to the point of experiencing failure and humbling experiences
4 To be guided rather than directed through a more academic approach to a greater depth of treatment

5   To avoid being set apart but to have opportunity to set self apart on occasions
6   To pass rapidly through elementary stages and use advanced resources
7   To pursue their own lines of research
8   To be exposed to some form of counselling—and their parents too
9   To be treated like other children.

More detailed needs can be derived readily from this list but these will arise incidentally in discussing present provisions. Only two further needs might usefully be added here and these appear in response to items in the questionnaire, as below. An analysis is shown in table 2.2.

B.1 (ii)   Gifted children need contacts with teachers who are similarly gifted.
B.2 (vi)   Lack of opportunities to exercise specific talents [is an important condition possibly harmful to the development of giftedness].

Table 2.2   Analysis of responses to items B.1(ii) and B.2(vi). $n = 370$

Item	No reply	Emphatically agree——————————disagree					Qualified reply
	n %	n %	n %	n %	n %	n %	n %
B.1 (ii)	7 2	142 38	131 35	47 13	29 8	10 3	4 1
B.2 (vi)	14 4	252 68	87 24	12 3	5 1	0 0	0 0

Findings here suggest that it is likely to be helpful to state specifically in any list of needs both of the following elements:
10   Contact with teachers gifted in similar fields
11   Abundant opportunity and encouragement to exercise specific talents.

The unanimity of view with regard to the final statement is quite remarkable, and clearly draws attention to what must become one of the major criteria for assessing any educational system's provision for the gifted. Before proceeding to an examination of the views of subject committees it has to be pointed out that study groups did not feel a need to discuss small schools separately. In general, the opinions expressed were to the effect that they each had advantages from a gifted child's point of view. Observations were forwarded from individual members but are not considered here since space permits only reference to views which are seen to command some kind of general support within the groups.

The views of subject committees

One final possible source of evidence regarding the special needs or otherwise of gifted children are the papers presented by the Schools Council subject committees. Relevant comments are cited below, though it should be noted that these are selective and do not necessarily represent any committee's total or unanimous view.

ART

We would not recommend that there is any particular form which any such activities should take, except perhaps for providing the gifted child with the stimulus and material which is a little more demanding than is often found in the primary school situation.

MODERN LANGUAGES (FRENCH)

Children with certain abilities of a high order require teachers of comparable ability, and despite the fact that the limited supply of such teachers is bound to necessitate the withdrawal of some children from school for specialist tuition, it is essential that these withdrawals should be neither too frequent nor too lengthy . . . [gifted children] are dissatisfied with the lack of breadth and intellectual rigour . . . they wish to go beyond the vocabulary of the audio-visual course . . . they feel deprived because they receive few or no guidelines for generalizing what they have learnt orally and because there are no, or limited, means of pursuing the subject on their own through the printed and written word.

ENGLISH

. . . the generally acknowledged view that too early or extensive specialization is regrettable has to be reconciled with the fact that some . . . are very precocious in one direction and perhaps below a good average in others. . . . How far should the developing process be taken in training and offering of facilities and how far should the effort continue to stimulate all-round interests in every child? . . . It should not be too difficult to provide literature which is continuously satisfying and stimulating . . . but . . . this would quite early demand, in exceptional cases, more wide and special knowledge of literature than some trained . . . for the primary range possess . . . even if . . . they had English as their main subject.

HISTORY

Some members doubted whether the special treatment of 'gifted' children was necessary or justifiable at the primary stage . . . in terms of the teaching or study of history, it seemed questionable whether special arrangements could or should be made and indeed how exceptional gifts in this field might be identified.

MUSIC

The need for early recognition received special consideration and the committee comments, 'delay may prevent the natural unfolding of a creative or executant talent, on account of the complexity of the skills involved in musical expression, and the consequent need for acquiring them very early in life'. Other general needs are implied by the following statements which derive from the Music Committee's own small investigation undertaken on our behalf, but entirely by its own decision:

(i) The home is of paramount importance and the mother's influence the predominating one in early music experience.

(ii) The earliest recollections are important and are often connected with the mother singing or playing, and with home music making.

(iii) Opposition sometimes registered (by the father in particular) is over-ridden in the desire to follow a musical career.

(iv) These students had begun their chosen instruments between seven and ten years of age, or even earlier.

(v) Encouragement by a good private teacher when one could be found was important.

(vi) In some cases . . . the decision (on a musical career) had been confirmed by some tangible success, such as a very good Associated Board result or a school award.

(vii) Some secondary schools appeared to have been discouraging where choice of a musical career was involved.

PHYSICAL EDUCATION

To provide special facilities by coaching or other specialization at this stage carries the danger that the child's talents might be channelled into the wrong specialism and might lead to a narrowing of the whole physical education experience. Whatever special arrangements in the arts and music are made for children showing evidence of gifts, this should not preclude full participation in the normal activities of the school, including physical education . . . too much reliance should not be placed on the home for stimulation of particular interests since this may apply only to the few.

MATHEMATICS

. . the gifted child may be an extremely vulnerable phenomenon. The statement that able children can take care of themselves is misleading: it may be true that mathematically such children can fend for themselves better than less able but this does not mean that they should be entirely responsible for their own programming; they are not sufficient unto themselves—they need guidance, encouragement and the right kind of opportunities and challenges to fulfil their promise. . . . What should we bear in mind in the case of the gifted child?

The following are some suggestions:

(i) Compared with the ordinary child his learning needs to be greatly accelerated and progressively intensified as he develops. He usually has a hearty appetite for work that interests him; he will not tire and lose interest as quickly as the less able when his attention is thoroughly roused.

(ii) His intellectual nourishment should be much richer, broader and deeper in content, than the normal school course.

(iii) He should be given as much freedom in his work as is compatible with a sound comprehensive mathematical development: mathematics is a cumulative study with a broad developmental structure; this certainly means building up but it does not mean that mathematical learning has to follow a prescriptive linear programme. The able child has a catholic taste and an avidity for new ideas, and should be introduced to broad and complementary areas of mathematical activity.

(iv) He should be exposed to excellence and given the experience of rubbing shoulders with his peers. It is desirable for the gifted child to spend some time at periodic intervals in special activities with his equals under the guidance of a mathematically cultured and sensitive teacher. A half day or a full day a week at a centre with such a teacher might not be unreasonable, for a child in the later years of the junior school.

(v) The gifted child needs a balanced general education. Despite his mathematical brilliance his development in other respects may be quite normal. Physically, emotionally, etc. he may be a very ordinary fellow and for this reason it might be unwise, even if it were possible, to segregate him completely from children of his own age and ordinary endowment.

In the past the very bright child in mathematics has been put to work with older children or has been given a leading role in mathematical ventures in his class. But the abler and older he becomes the greater is the gap between him and other pupils. His mode of thinking will have become much more mature mathematically and, if this is not appreciated by his teacher, he will become bored and frustrated with a consequent dissipation of his talents.

GEOGRAPHY

Some talents can only be adequately developed outside the school even though they may be recognized within the school and referred to parents and LEA officers such as music and drama advisers . . . the gifted child may wish to pursue some line of enquiry on his own.

RELIGIOUS EDUCATION

Though a child can be identified as 'gifted at art', or any of the specific abilities . . . one would not expect a child to be 'gifted at religious education' . . . the teaching of RE makes deliberate use and explicit connexion at some time or other with all aspects of primary content and method.

These brief and to some extent highly selected comments are sufficient to show that the subject committees agree on the need for gifted children to be recognized. Other stated needs parallel those already suggested, and it seems clear that the list of needs described above would receive wide support from this source. It is unnecessary to prolong the consideration of the findings of the subject committees any further at this point since, in the main, they deal with the needs of gifted children indirectly by discussing present provisions. It will thus be necessary to examine them more closely in Part II, and our enquiry into the needs of gifted children as seen by teachers may be concluded by noting that a similar list derived from the literature, mostly American, would contain some of the items, but by no means all. It would also include statements which would require very heavy qualifications if they were to be found consistent with our evidence: thus Hildreth (1966) asserts:

Undifferentiated programs of schooling are wasteful of time and talent. Each student needs an optimal program in which he begins at the point he has actually attained and then proceeds at his own pace. (p. 175)

This may usefully be compared with the reasoned suggestions put forward by our Mathematics Committee above, for example.

3 Recognition: how efficient?

All the evidence presented so far insists that the first need of the gifted child is recognition of his level of ability; and it thus becomes urgent to ask how efficient recognition in fact is. But in some sense the question is unanswerable: as Kellmer Pringle (1970) argues, we cannot know the size of the problem; and a number of teachers have suggested that since we never become aware of the negative instances—the 'gifted' who never reveal gifts—there is not much point in asking whether many go unrecognized. The position to be adopted must depend upon the consequences. If rejecting the question leads to inactivity and complacency, then it seems better in fact to ask it, even in the face of obvious criticisms. The case for putting the question is further strengthened in the present instance since the 'size' of the problem has to do with more than mere hypothetical numbers. If, for example, it can be shown that children recognized as able are not seen as being as able as they really are, then this amounts to a failure in recognition: or, again, if different teachers fail to agree substantially in their judgements regarding the ability of the same children, other things being equal, then this too is suggestive of the attention required. Finally, a theoretical model has already been proposed which is at least some guide to those who are prepared to make decisions on certain basic assumptions.

How efficient then is recognition? It seems arguable that intellectual prowess presents no problem anyhow. Surely the characteristics of such children are so well known, and so obvious in the child possessing them, that recognition is only difficult where there is maladjustment. Before considering how far this is true, it needs to be asked whether teachers themselves believe it to be generally true, bearing in mind the self-evident fact that it is undoubtedly true in some cases, as exemplified by the various studies on the following pages.

Teachers' views: the questionnaire

Professional opinions on this issue were sought from items A.7 (iv) and B.2 (x) and the findings are presented in table 3.1.

A.7 (iv)   Many gifted children probably go unrecognized in school.

B.2 (x)   Failure to recognize potential giftedness [is an important condition possibly harmful to the development of giftedness].

Table 3.1   Efficiency of recognition: analysis of items A.7 (iv) and B.2 (x). $n = 370$

	No reply n %	Emphatically agree				Emphatically disagree		Qualified reply n %
		n	%	n	%	n	%	n	%	n	%	
A.7 (iv)	28 8	87 24	92 25	63 17	73 20	27 7		2 1
.2 (x)	9 2	193 52	128 35	24 . 6	14 4	0 0		2 1

The results for item B.2 (x) would seem to imply that the vast majority of teachers take steps, or feel steps ought to be taken, to recognize potential, but that these are not as effective as they might be. This interpretation is confirmed only in part by item A.7 (iv) which shows about half agree that many gifted children probably go unrecognized in school. Perhaps a quarter just are not prepared to guess, and the remaining quarter feel that recognition is probably fairly good. Taking the two items together, it is reasonable to conclude, tentatively, that in the professional opinion of most teachers there is a risk that intellectual giftedness will remain unrecognized unless great care is taken; and certainly that there is an *a priori* case for looking closely at the situation in the light of evidence from other sources.

Study group opinions

The study groups provide a first such source, in response to item 2.5 of the notes:

2.5   There is evidence to suggest that when teachers are asked to nominate intellectually gifted children from amongst those in their charge, they omit, perhaps, fifty per cent of those who are, by other criteria, undoubtedly gifted and usually they include a few who are not. Thus, in response to a request to indicate intellectually gifted children, a group of teachers omitted nearly a half of those with measured IQs of 130 plus and included several below 110. One nominee had an IQ of only 84. [Information kindly supplied by Professor Tempest—see p. 45.]

2.51   Can the group comment on this situation? If it is true that a sizeable number of very able children are not recognized as possessing very high potential it seems likely that such children are not sufficiently encouraged to move forward at rates commensurate with their capacities. (The children involved above were seven years old.)

Group 2   We are not familiar with the evidence for this extraordinary statement so we cannot comment . . . the suggested explanation of non-recognition is . . . perhaps because teachers do not feel any need to worry about bright children.

4 The group was surprised that the incidence of omission was as high as fifty per cent, but thought that teachers probably assess on attainment and therefore miss the highly intelligent child.

7 Some members felt that it may be unwise to test intelligence at an early age, e.g. before the age of seven. Reference was made to a child whose intelligence quotient was 140+ in the infants, but who never came up to expectation in the junior school.

8 The nomination of intellectually gifted children is obviously difficult because of the various criteria used. It is not surprising that the response in 2·5 was so. . . . Why the assumption that any 'intelligence' test is a measuring instrument for intellectual giftedness? . . . they offer the opportunity to compare and relate pupil performances in certain prescribed circumstances . . . many 'gifted' children could go unnoticed—missing out in school and home completely. Those who achieve are seen to achieve, but those who failed may have been overlooked or even ignored . . . most teachers agreed that it was their own subjective assessment of pupil potential that was valued most. Test scores were only of interest if they supported the teachers' own assessment of the pupil's ability or capacity.

9 . . . on occasion a child with a high IQ reached only a middle position in a class. This was not necessarily due to lack of encouragement. . . .

11 It was generally agreed that the exceptionally gifted child would stand out and that there would be no difficulty in recognition. However . . . there was a major problem in the recognition of [those] whose gifts are hidden by poor background, emotional disturbances and personal problems . . . in 'good' areas some children's gifts were overemphasized as social pressures encouraged them to 'keep up with the Joneses' . . . a survey of all children would be interesting to see how many scored well in IQ tests.

12 . . . this paragraph could not be discussed satisfactorily because it is not known:
　(i) how these children were tested.
　(ii) the size of the sample.
　(iii) how long the children concerned had been known to the teachers.
. . . most teachers try to encourage and stimulate all children to progress at rates commensurate with their abilities.

13 . . . recognition of gifted children is difficult sometimes when the child comes from a deprived environment . . . judgement is so often made on ability to communicate and social adjustment . . . there are known to be some missed if there is not some good objective testing.

14 . . . the accuracy of such a test (IQ) . . . cannot be assumed because:
　(i) results can differ in two similar tests.
　(ii) children develop at different rates.
　(iii) some environments assist in raising the individual test scores.
　(iv) the health of the child at the time . . . bearing on the result.
　(v) . . . tests are standardized on selected social groupings and . . . show bias towards these groupings . . . the most reliable method . . . was a series of intelligence and creativity tests . . . given over a period of time. [The group probably

took it as self-evident that reading disabilities are a common source of error on verbal tests.]

16   The ability to recognize or not recognize a gifted child can be linked with the recognition of the influence that the home environment can play on the child. There must be correlation of home and school.

18   Doubts were expressed on the reliability of intelligence tests, particularly for seven-year-olds. There was general agreement however that it is likely, indeed probable, that in our classes there will be gifted children that we do not recognize.

The complexity of the problem is reflected in these comments. They suggest that:

1   Whilst admitting the difficulties involved, teachers still feel that they are quite good at recognizing high ability.

2   That intelligence tests are no better, and may be worse, but that teacher opinion needs checking against objective assessments.

3   That 'underachievement' is a real phenomenon, and the problem is how to deal with it when the causes are extra-mural.

4   The oft-mentioned danger that teachers will 'hang an IQ round a child's neck' can be very largely dismissed.

It is not the function of this report to review all the literature relevant to these views. Much of it is American anyhow, except of course the extensive coverage of 11+ selection procedures, and British teachers would not consider that our school conditions are necessarily at all comparable to experience elsewhere. There is need however to consider at least some relevant evidence regarding the effectiveness of recognition, and we shall content ourselves therefore with a brief description of, first, the 'classical' American findings; secondly, the experience of researchers at Liverpool University; and finally, the materials presented to us by teachers themselves. Teachers responsible for the latter information would not claim that their research was anything more than indicative, but the indications are not without interest.

American findings by Pegnato and Birch

These researchers gave an individual intelligence test to 1400 children in one high school, and selected 91 as having an IQ of over 136 (i.e. c. 2 per cent of random group). The findings are stated in the following figures, as given by Gallagher (1964).

It can be seen that American teachers nominated only 41 of the 91, and Gallagher comments:

In comparison group achievement tests and group intelligence measures identified much more of this gifted group even though they also 'misidentified' a large number of students.

Table 3.2 Effectiveness of different measures of identification of gifted children in junior high school (USA)

Method	Criterion	Number identified	Correctly identified	Mis-identified	Over-looked
Teacher judgement	Mentally gifted	154	41	113	50
Group achievement tests	Three grades over grade placement	335	72	263	19
Honour roll	B average or better	371	67	304	24
Group intelligence	Otis B—IQ				
	115 plus	450	84	366	7
	120 plus	240	65	175	26
	130 plus	36	20	16	71

Teachers, however, might well stress that, with a cut-off point of 130+, group tests identified only half as many as they did, and it is necessary in fairness to point out that Pegnato in the end recommended the use of more rather than fewer criteria for the recognition of giftedness. Hoyle (1969) reviewing this evidence concluded that:

Intellectual giftedness is usually associated with a fairly high measured intelligence but after a certain threshold point the channelling of this capacity . . . will be partly dependent upon factors of personality and interest . . . the intelligence test is a useful tool for identifying the gifted . . . but informed opinion recommends the use of a range of techniques.

Research at Liverpool University

Professor Tempest reports as follows (see also p. 170):

Seventy-two children in all were nominated by their teachers and, of these, twenty-four obtained IQs of 127 and above on the test used (Young, D., *Non Readers Intelligence Test*, ULP, 1966). Of the remainder, nine were not tested by the Young Test, and this left thirty-nine with IQs below 127. Seven of these had IQs below 110, one child scoring 84. Finally, of the top thirty children selected after further individual testing, fourteen or about fifty per cent were nominated. It must be remembered however that the children were only in the last term in the infant school, aged about seven, and much younger than those in the Pegnato and Birch enquiry. Identifying the gifted among them was therefore more difficult, but it is surprising that the two children whose reading age as measured by the Schonell Word Recognition Test was six years above their chronological age were not nominated by their teachers as gifted.

Individual assignments in the present study

In view of the importance of the issue, and the possibility that there might be widely differing opinions as to the effectiveness of teacher recognition, it was felt that the present study should attempt to encourage interested teachers to undertake their own investigation of the problem. Item 2.62 was therefore included in the notes for study groups, and the following details were among those received as a result:

SCHOOL A (HIGH SES AREA WITH FEW LOW SES)

The following note was sent round the school:

Would you please write down the names of any children at present in the school and either in your present class or in previous classes you have had whom you would consider to be gifted either generally or in one particular field. It is important that you do not confer with other members of staff, look up records or ask me for a further definition before putting down your names please, i.e. first impressions are essential.

Seven teachers forwarded fourteen names, categorized as follows:

General ability:	8
Artistic ability:	2
English expression:	1
PE:	2
Soccer:	1
Total:	14

These numbers may be compared (i) with the school records which show fifteen children with IQs of 130+, and (ii) with the theoretical expectations of our model on four dimensions which predicts 5·7 per cent (16 children), with the toughest criteria, and 20 per cent (55 children) with the weakest. One further fact emerges, which may or may not be significant, namely that no child is mentioned twice in the lists. The headteacher expressed the view that some teachers were less ready to appreciate giftedness in children living 'on the wrong side of the track'.

SCHOOL B (44·2 PER CENT IMMIGRANTS)

The table on pages 48–9 shows the results of a similar investigation in the form of comparative comments by members of staff on children considered by their class teachers to be in some way gifted. This type of presentation is particularly valuable in that it shows how difficulties of recognition derive from genuine differences of view about a child, and have little to do in many cases with mere differences of definition.

SCHOOLS C, D, E AND F

These four schools were asked to supply information about the gifted children in the schools and the numbers to be expected in a normal sort of population. The responses were then checked against information supplied by the county psychologist regarding IQs (Young), and the results are tabulated below, with the headteacher's accompanying remark where necessary:

School C
I see no gifted children here at the moment, but would expect 2–3 per cent normally. None would score 130+ on IQ tests in my view.

Test results
1 eight-year-old, IQ 140
1 nine-year-old, IQ 129
1 ten-year-old, IQ 131
1 eleven-year-old, records missing.
    The infants are not included as IQs are not taken at that stage.

School D
We have no gifted children in school at present and I would expect none in a normal population. None would score 130+.

Test results
2 eight-year-olds, IQ 130 and 135.
1 nine-year-old, IQ 128
1 ten-year-old, IQ 135
1 eleven-year-old, IQ 129
    Again infants excluded from consideration.

School E
The number of specifically gifted could be quite a few. We have twenty intellectually gifted (7·3 per cent).

Test results
These were only available for 116 children in the school and totalled:
4 eight-year-olds, IQs 137, 140, 129, 133.
5 nine-year-olds, IQs 134, 140, 139, 133, 134
2 ten-year-olds, IQs 133, 132
i.e. 9.5 per cent altogether.

School F
This was the fourth school in the group, and the only one to provide details of the kinds of talents recognized. The headmaster writes:

I have judged giftedness as an estimated score of 130+ assuming it would be possible to measure it, or a very subjective assessment that I think that particular achievement would be of a very high calibre (top 2–3 per cent).

Continued on p. 50

Table 3.3 Children considered gifted in some way by the class teacher (School B)

Children	Teachers' views		
	a	b	c	d
1 Boy 11 yrs	Above average intelligence. He is an all-rounder who takes interest in academic work and games. He is extremely good in chess.	Scientifically enquiring mind: has a real ability to follow a problem through. Enjoys maths and science problems. Fascinated by formulae. Brilliant chess player.	Maths problems: has the ability to think round a problem and to look through to a solution not apparent at first sight.
2 Boy 11 yrs			Ability to see 'models' in 3D form. Can translate pictures into 3D models. However gets bored easily and rarely finishes anything.	
3 Boy 11 yrs	Drawing: seems to have a very good imagination which he projects in his drawing ability		Art: can 'copy' any drawing. When interested works in great detail.	Artistic: very imaginative boy. Can reproduce anything visually (i.e. picturewise) that comes into his imagination and can also copy excellently.
4 Girl 11 yrs			Athletic: has developed quite recently. Possesses a brilliant 'crawl' stroke but is inherently lazy.	Beautiful stroke and leg action allied to physical power and economy of effort.
5 Boy 11 yrs	Seemed a fairly good athlete in second year.		Athletic?	
6 Boy	Did not show any signs of giftedness within the classroom.	Games: if he didn't have difficult home conditions he would have had a better record of achievement.	Games: good aggressive player. Probably not gifted.	Natural eye in ball games, cricket, football. Also good co-ordination in PE. Natural flair for position.
7 Boy 10 yrs			In my view he is very good at 'copying' a picture or drawing that he can see.	Artistic: has the ability to reproduce anything accurately; eye for detail and has technique.

Teachers' views				Totals Gifted?		
e	f	g	h	Yes	No	Maybe
Good brain and enquiring mind. Capable of logical thinking.		Maths: did not reveal this facility in the third year.		2	1	3
		Not outstanding in my experience		1	1	1
				2		2
		Games, needlecraft: has always shown much ability and originality in art and needlecraft.		2		2
			Gymnastics: excellent control of movement. Shows courage and co-ordination	2	1	1
				2	3	
Artistic: obviously an outstanding artist.	Exceptional artistic ability.	Art: most meticulous, good eye for detail. Copies rather than creates. Work greatly admired by children as well as adults.		4		2

Giftedness in particular aspects in this school at present

Activity	Number
Mathematics	0
Reading (3 years above CA on Schonell G. W. list)	4
Imaginative writing	2
Accuracy of expression	1
Natural science	1
Music	1
PE movement (innate agility undeveloped)	1
French (oral)	3
Art/craft (colour sense and creativity)	2
Accuracy of recall	1
(8 children)	16

and continues:

An interesting feature, at least to me, is that it involves eight children. Two appear in three activities, one in two, and five children in one area only. Of the two with the widest attributes one has an IQ of 130+, I would estimate, and the other tests at 120+ only . . . [4 children test 130 in school] . . . I believe [two of] them to be inflated scores.

Since this school has a roll of 100 the number of children concerned also gives the percentage. Given the information above we can apply the curriculum model using two per cent and eight dimensions with $r = \cdot 50$. The expected proportion is 9·4 per cent, which approximates reasonably well with the headteacher's eight per cent. This may be thought a nice illustration since the teacher concerned had failed to recognize his own gifted son, and had to be told by an educational psychologist of the child's high level of ability. It may be that this headteacher is now more proficient than most of us at recognizing talent in children!

SCHOOL G

Here the headteacher reported four children in his school (roll 400 plus) as being gifted as follows:

D.M.: reported as high English ability;   IQ 130+
G.P.   mathematical ability;   IQ 134+
J.S.   physical ability;   IQ 104
P.H   artistic ability;   IQ 115

Children in the school with measured IQs above 130+ numbered five. The headteacher comments:

The three . . . not rated as gifted would all unhesitatingly be said by the staff to be able.

and it is apparent that this school staff defines 'gifted' certainly as 'within the top two per cent'. Nonetheless, the application of our model reveals a massive discrepancy since even taking 1·8 per cent, only four dimensions and a correlation of 0·50, some twenty-three pupils ought to be recognized as gifted, i.e. six times the actual number.

It is important to state that the staff involved here were quick to draw attention to what they themselves clearly felt to be a very high cut-off point to adopt. Their note reads

There is a possibility that we are setting our sights . . . too high but we have tried to distinguish between a talent or a special ability and a genuine gift . . . by those standards these four children are the only possibilities.

These teachers, who have clearly considered the problems involved in recognition most carefully, would perhaps be the first to concede that their standards of recognition are, in all probability, higher even than they had thought.

SCHOOL H

This school was visited by the project director who, having been informed that there were no gifted children in the school, was provided with lists of reading ages. This information revealed that:

	RQ
One child in the first year (first term) had a reading age of 11·8	157
Seven children in the second year (first term) had a reading age of 11·2+	161
	163
	140
	134
	130
	135
	131
Six children in the third year (first term) had a reading age of 12·2+	165
	150
	161
	133
	131
	130

These results can only be interpreted as suggesting that some pupils are more outstanding than the teachers realize, even if a very high level is indicated by the term 'gifted'. Although careful records were being kept, they were used mainly to detect children needing remedial reading tuition.

SCHOOL J

This school was specially visited by the director of the project as being of particular interest in that its staff has a great deal of experience in dealing with very able but maladjusted adolescents. (The term 'maladjusted' is here used in a very general non-technical sense.) The important question for the moment relates only to information regarding records of recognition and achievement and these are given below:

Number in group = 33

Mean IQ	129·6
Mean Mental Age	17 yrs 7 mths
Mean Chronological Age	14 yrs 8 mths
Mean Arithmetic Age	13 yrs 2 mths
Mean Reading Age	13 yrs 7 mths
Mean Spelling Age	12 yrs 11 mths

Comments

1   In comparison with average mental age all 33 children underachieved in all subjects   (100%)

2   In comparison with average chronological age 20 children underachieved in all subjects   (60%)

3   One child only had attainment age level above chronological age in all three subjects   (3%)

Age when first perceived to be 'bright':
Primary school—27 children   (81%)
Secondary school or later—6 children   (19%)

The fact which is immediately striking here is that despite a large measure of underachievement within this group, primary school teachers contrived to recognize no fewer than 81 per cent of these children as 'bright'. Perhaps they were not seen to be quite so bright as individual intelligence tests suggest they are; perhaps they were seen to be bright towards the very end of primary schooling. Their measure of underachievement might indeed support such views; but, as was noted earlier by a study group, teachers do not always feel able to remedy situations even after they have efficiently diagnosed what is wrong. It is therefore a most remarkable finding in the face of all the difficulties, some of which have yet to be commented upon, that the teachers in contact with these children should have performed their task of recognition so well. It is further important to remember that the children originated in widely different parts of the country, and were taught in quite unrelated primary schools.

The evidence also shows that six of the group, a not wholly insignificant proportion, apparently went through the whole of their school lives without anyone appreciating their level of ability. More fundamental still, of course, is the simple fact that educational provisions were somehow inadequate for every single child involved, excepting that they each contrived somehow to develop 'intelligence'. Without pressing the matter, it is perhaps fair to say that potential was hardly matched by performance, and it is necessary to do no more than refer to the work of Kellmer Pringle to show that the findings here are repeatable elsewhere. Certainly the headteacher involved in the present investigation is prepared to state:

I believe that quite a large number of able children are getting into trouble. . . . I am convinced that they form a bigger proportion than is generally supposed . . . [estimation is difficult] because of the absurd distinction between 'maladjusted' and 'delinquent'.

Clearly the problems of maladjustment and recognition are closely inter-related. If a child is recognized as gifted only indirectly, in that he arrives in front of an educational psychologist as maladjusted, and is consequently found also to be highly intelligent, then a dangerous situation arises quite apart from the obvious implication that recognition itself is inefficient. In the first place, it may become accepted that nobody is highly gifted unless he is mal-adjusted, and that therefore recognition is in fact highly efficient: the argu-ment runs thus: those we miss become maladjusted, so we don't miss them at all; we only wait a little while for some of them.

In the second place, it might happen that children may be transferred to (say) private schools recognized, unofficially, as catering well for gifted children, on the grounds that they are maladjusted in the ordinary school which is failing to provide for their needs. In such a case, public monies would be available since it would be treated not as 'special' provision for a gifted child, but as one of 'proper' provision for a maladjusted one. It would be culpable *naïveté* not to imagine that some parents might encourage symp-toms of maladjustment (temporarily) in their highly intelligent child if this seems to be the only effective method of obtaining a transfer of school, or state aid with private school fees.

There is no evidence in the present study to enable further useful comment to be made with regard to the second point. As is already apparent, some authorities and schools will not admit to doing anything 'special' for gifted children as such, so conditions are not such that our speculations can lightly be brushed aside. It has to be understood that the present enquiry has revealed cases where children designated 'maladjusted' have been transferred, on the further grounds of high ability, to private schools. The point being made here is not that such transfer is improper; it is simply that such transfer was probably urgent to the child's well-being *before* he became maladjusted. In some educational climates however, it could be virtually impossible even to envisage this kind of action, much less actually to make some sort of proper provision. There is thus a need for research into the various types of assistance which are being extended to children designated 'maladjusted' and 'gifted', and into the methods of recognition relied upon.

It is also urgently necessary to investigate the incidence and type of maladjustment experienced in private schools. If there are cases of gifted children becoming maladjusted in the private sector, and the headteacher of one of the schools visited assured the project director that he had indeed experienced one occasionally, then these might provide invaluable comparisons with those who appear similarly in state schools. The findings, needless to say, would benefit all schools regardless of type.

Individual cases

The experience of individuals can only throw indirect light on the problems of recognition. They are nonetheless extremely valuable in pinpointing some of the difficulties which must be faced in setting up an acceptable system of detection and provision, and one or two are described below. Where the case is of interest from several points of view, and not merely illustrative of recognition problems, it is quoted at length. The main source of information regarding the study is indicated.

CASE STUDY I (PARENTS)

By his fourth birthday he could read easily and do quite a lot of sums and number games; I taught him for a short while each day as he seemed so keen to learn . . . we decided to start P at the kindergarten when he was 4½. His class teacher was herself a trained psychologist with four children . . . she surprised us by saying she thought P was far more intelligent than her own and guessed his IQ to be around 165. This was the first inkling we had that he might be a 'gifted child'. He loved school and settled down happily into a group about a year older than [himself] and was quickly learning to do addition and subtraction, writing stories and poems, telling the time and reading anything. Because he was interested he also learnt his tables himself.

At five, after much insistence on his part, P started violin lessons which he took to with great enthusiasm and an obvious ability as he progressed rapidly. He was a quiet child, not very sociable or out-going but very happy and completely absorbed in whatever he did, whether it was writing stories, designing maps or playing in the sandpit with a plastic truck.

We [had] to move again when he was 5 years 11 months and on the advice of his former teacher (who felt a state school would not be adequate to cope with him) started him at a pre-prep school. This proved to be a mistake: he could cope with the work and was indeed moved up so many times that after a year he was with boys of 8½ and he still came top in everything. However, it was a very formal school with no facilities for games or sport or even adequate playing space and no importance attached to arts subjects at all and we felt he was becoming far too much of a book worm; he was now wearing glasses and seldom wanted to do anything other than the three Rs. Moreover, he did not *enjoy* school.

We were recommended our local primary school which we went to see and were immediately impressed by the headmistress and the whole informal yet working atmosphere of the school. As soon as we transferred P we noticed the difference in him; he became far more sociable, keen to play and participate in physical activities, learned to play chess and joined the thriving school orchestra. It seemed as though everything was attempted at the school and P was delighted to have so much to interest and occupy him. The headmistress gave him extra English and there were always plenty of interesting projects on hand for him to work at with a wonderful choice of books in the school library. Children were always free to come and use these books and were constantly moving from room to room or popping in to see the headmistress. There was an atmosphere of busy activity everywhere. The head herself talked to us about his intelligence and at this point we decided to join the NAGC (having read about it in the *Guardian*) although we had no problems at all.

Unfortunately we had another move. . . . After our happy experience with the primary school we automatically sent P and his younger sister to our nearest primary school. Before we moved, however, we visited the headmaster and told him that P's previous headmistress wanted to send a report and a personal letter about the child and his ability. The head agreed to get in touch with her before term started and we did make the point that P was doing more than most of his classmates although still kept with his age group.

However, some weeks after term started at the new school, because of increasing apathy from P and general unhappiness at home, we went to the school and asked to see his form teacher She never seemed available so we went to talk to the head teacher. He had not written to the previous school and said we were making a fuss as the child was perfectly all right. At the parents' evening the form teacher told us P was a good, quiet boy, no trouble at all. We asked again if he could have rather more stimulating work or if he could bring his own books to read; we inquired if there was a chess club or any music group; football or swimming—but there seemed to be no 'extras' at all. He was doing hundreds of simple sums and expected to get 60 right at a time, otherwise he had another set—work he had been doing at five or six. We were pleased to hear a class newspaper was to be started for which P was a writer but when he produced an article on Vietnam, he was told that sort of thing wasn't suitable for children.

At home he did nothing. He became quiet and morose, lying in front of the television, not reading or writing or taking an interest in anything.

We had another useless interview with the headmaster who thought we were making a lot of fuss over nothing and told us that there were 'several' children in the class as bright as P so the work was quite adequate and stimulating enough. We then went to see an education officer who agreed that P must be seen by an educational psychologist and have his IQ measured. P enjoyed this immensely—one of his 'best days'—and the result was found to be over 170 (Stanford-Binet) and just below 160 on the WISC. We then met the headmaster and education officer together to discuss how his work could be made more

G.C.P.S.—3*

interesting. The psychologist had suggested he be moved up a year but this was turned down as being quite impracticable because of the fuss which would be made by other parents. Nothing new was suggested at all and we felt to continue like this would be disastrous.

Very reluctantly we decided to consider a private school. The headmaster tested and interviewed P and took him the following term, putting him in a higher class at once. Immediately the change was obvious: he came home smiling, rushed to do homework, chatted enthusiastically over tea about all the sports and team games, house competitions etc., and then started to work on projects in his bedroom. Now he takes part in everything. He learns French, Latin and science, plays several games, goes swimming, plays his violin with the choir, belongs to the chess club and the work is sufficiently difficult to keep him interested. There are some bright boys in his class and he certainly doesn't come top in everything but this is a very good stimulus for him and he seems to thrive on competition. The educational psychologist has visited the school and agrees that, although formal looking and old-fashioned in some respects, it is certainly far better for P than the primary school he so hated.

CASE STUDY 2 (PARENTS)

Agencies involved in recognition
    (*a*) Parents, especially mother
    (*b*) Teachers
    (*c*) School doctor
    (*d*) Child psychologists

Behaviour leading to recognition, type of gift
    No particular gift has been revealed.
    Extremely lively and active baby; always alert.
    Boisterous and unco-ordinated toddler, very aggressive towards children of his own age. Difficult to control. Excitable. Quick to learn.
    At school, which he attended 3 mornings weekly from the age of 2 years 9 months, his teachers found him to be 'a firework', 'clumsy and noisy', and a child who 'won't conform'.
    His behaviour continued to give the impression of an undisciplined background to his teachers, who advised that he did not respond in class and that there might be some physical defect. This led to:

Age at which recognition became fairly certain
At the age of $5\frac{3}{4}$, having been to the school doctor, a child psychologist tested his IQ and [he] was rated at 147 (Terman-Merrill ?). At a later test, given privately by another psychologist, at the age of $6\frac{3}{4}$, his IQ rating was 170.

Educational difficulties: hypothetical causes
    (*a*) Difficult to control and discipline. Possible cause: his excitable and emotional temperament.
    (*b*) Difficulty in learning to read. Possible causes—dyslexia (yet to be examined), inability to concentrate arising from lack of interest. As the child

could read well by the age of 6¾ I would not wish to over-emphasize this problem, but he was certainly well behind the rest of his class in this, and in writing ability.

(*c*) Difficulty in concentration. His teachers have all found that he does not attend to general instruction, possibly because he is easily distracted. He responds to and prefers individual attention.

(*d*) Difficulty in mathematics. His teacher reports that 'he won't obey the necessary rules' of number. He makes a meal of simple arithmetic. Possible cause, boredom or lack of motivation.

(*e*) General difficulty of underachievement. This is most irritating to his teachers who have questioned his intelligence in the past, although they have tried to find an answer to this problem.

This child demonstrates the immense problems involved in both recognition and provision. Almost the only evidence of ability resides in IQ test performance. But the performance, it seems, is repeatable; and the teacher's comments,

1   It is difficult to believe a child of his alleged intelligence could be so apparently 'clueless', and

2   that he is highly intelligent is not in doubt.

reveal the extent to which a conscientious teacher may be driven to near distraction by having to face evidence which so plainly contradicts his everyday experience.

It is tempting to suggest that the tests are wrong, but a knowledge only of classic cases like Albert Einstein, Thomas Edison, W. B. Yeats and Winston Churchill, cautions against so obvious a conclusion. There is here demonstrated a very clear need for cases of this kind to be re-tested, not only independently and by unusual methods, but also in the presence of the teacher. There is perhaps an esoteric mysticism about IQ testing which requires examination, but the effects on the teachers of not sharing the psychologist's experience can only be detrimental to the activities of both. The parents too who 'realize that a solution of the problem provided by gifted children is yet to be found', are in need of more than sympathy when they state that their first requirement of the system is,

. . . for positive advice from educational advisers and child psychologists. Apart from the knowledge that the problem has been recognized we, the parents, have learnt nothing which might help us in deciding how our son should be educated.

CASE STUDY 3 (PARENTS)

Agencies involved in recognition
Swimming instructor suggested we had IQ done. Made an appointment with local educational psychologist who did an IQ test.

Behaviour leading to recognition
Early interest in numbers, reading and precocious use of language.

Age at which recognition became fairly certain
About 4 years.

Educational difficulties and hypothetical causes
We are not aware that he has any educational difficulties except perhaps that he does occasionally complain of repetitious and boring school work.

Facilitating or inhibiting influences
Since he is an only child he both demands and gets a great deal of his parents' attention.

The main interest here is that there appears to have been no awareness of the child's very high ability on the part of the school. Only an observant swimming instructor anyhow thought it worth while to suggest an IQ test, and the boy was almost certainly not being fully stretched. But the child did not of course show symptoms of maladjustment, and there was thus no cause in school to have him checked by the psychologist.

CASE STUDY 4 (PARENTS)

His IQ is 147 on the WISC test and 152 on a different test; which I think was the Stanford-Binet, but I'm not quite sure on this latter point.

He attended a small primary school, but not in the country. We deliberately selected this school because of its homely atmosphere, which we felt would give him security. Even so, he did not willingly attend, and we had particular difficulties after week-ends and holidays in getting him there at all. Once in the building, however, he seemed to be happy enough, and we were not able to discover his objection to going. With hindsight, we realize that he found the work very easy, and that he may have been bored, although he did worry about things which he did not understand.

Regarding the fact that his abilities seemed to go unrecognized, it may have been because we had no means of comparison with other children. Indeed, in the home he has appeared forgetful and dreamy.

He was small as well as timid, but grew appreciably in his tenth year. He is not now so timid but I think he is still the smallest boy in his class, although he is also the youngest, of course.

Parent/teacher contacts did occur and the teachers did recognize that he was bright. The problem in school seemed to be his immaturity, and only in the later stages of his primary school career did he play a full part in oral work, drama etc. Teachers commented that he would not volunteer answers in class, for example, but a change was noted in his last year at school. The school's objection to a transfer at the age of ten was on the grounds of the immaturity, and we were worried about this ourselves and balanced it against the risk of disillusionment with a repeated final year in the primary school. We have been relieved to find how happy he has been in secondary education, and he has never once shown any unwillingness to attend.

Here again there seems to be a degree of partial recognition, but no true appreciation of the level of ability actually possessed until quite late in the primary stage. This description should be compared with that presented by the composite list of traits given below. Although very few criteria appear to have been evidenced there are without question one or two.

CASE STUDY 5 (SCHOOL)

Agencies involved in recognition
No tests involved—assessment has been based on our own observations of the boy in school. Detailed notes nave been kept by each teacher who has had care of him from the time he was admitted to school. From that time his curiosity and powers of invention when playing games or doing constructional work were always in advance of his age. We were fortunate in that during the boy's first term at school we had the services of a 'mother-helper' in his classroom who was a trained child psychologist. We found her observations most helpful.

Age at which recognition occurred
During his first term in school.

Type of giftedness involved
Mentally gifted. It is difficult to single out a special field at his age; I feel more specific fields will become apparent as he matures. At present he rates high in most aspects of school life. He is lively and energetic, self-assured, and has an excellent command of language. He is able to structure his thinking when solving both oral and practical problems. He is an acknowledged leader [with] the other children.
Comment by a below average child, when asked why he liked building in the brick corner with him: 'He makes up good games for us to play and thinks of smashing things to build'.

Educational difficulties experienced if any
His verbal ability far exceeds his written work. He tends to lose interest quickly in the written aspect—but any oral explanations he gives are of great value to other children who may be involved with him.

In this case no scores from IQ tests are available, and assessment is based directly on teachers' observations. Two aspects immediately stand out:
1 An educational psychologist was accidentally available.
2 More than one teacher had the opportunity to observe.

There is no doubt that this child is well adjusted in school, and the question as to whether he should be subjected to an objective test is one that needs raising. It is interesting to compare a sample of this child's written work with that of the following case where an objective assessment is also lacking:

I am 7 years old and my brother is $1\frac{1}{2}$ years old. He some times goes up stairs on his own when nobody is looking and once he tried to go up stairs with a dustpan and brush but before he could get up stairs mummy caught him and put him in his playpen. I like exploring caves and once I went to the blue john mines and when I was in them I saw a piece of blue john it is a very dark blue and looks just like a piece of coal. As well as going in the blue john mines I went in the peak cavern and I saw the place where an underground village used to be and the people who lives there made rope and there is still some of the paths and machines left. Sometimes I get my army toys and make an army camp. I made trenches and I covered it with grass and a german wagon fell in. At home I made a layout on a piece of card board and I made some feilds for my farm animals and once N nearly got it. At home my favourite thing is listening to my daddys radio and some times he lets me turn the dials. In school best I like playing with S and he is Mrs. — dog and I have not got a dog but I would like one. I cannot have a dog because it is to dirty but I am going to get a hamster and this will be my fourth. When I grow up I want to be a naval diver.

CASE STUDY 6 (SCHOOL)

T is recognized by his teachers as being 'very bright'. To what extent he can be described as 'gifted' they are not prepared to say, since they are aware of the need to compare with children in other schools. A sample of work (age 7 years) is given as follows:

The Knight and the Griffin
Once upon a time there was a very brave knight who had won many battles. Now in a bog near the county of Dublin there was a terrible griffin and every night he came in to the county and stole a cow and two sheep from farmers. Now one day the knight was riding along a country road, when he saw the griffin rising up in front of him and the horse he had been riding bolted in fright. But the knight didn't panic, he just stood and looked up at the griffin. It suddenly did something very strange. It lifted its head and said 'I wish I lived where you live, it looks ever such a nice little place tucked up in that little nook over there'. It was very nice to have your village spoken of very well. But the knight said, 'I cannot take you into the town but I can come and see you every day.' 'That will be fine but could you bring something for me to eat as well as seeing me?' So every day the knight came to see the griffin and brought him some sweets as well. So the dragon and the knight lived happily ever after and believe me the knight brought the griffin his sweets every day.

These examples will be referred to again later (p. 181) together with the following sample from an older child:

CASE STUDY 7 (TEACHERS)

This particular example (age 10 years) is included to illustrate the possibility that not all outstandingly good writers score highly on group objective tests since his performance falls within one standard deviation from the mean. Most teachers however would have no hesitation in stating that the child is probably gifted, and the case illustrates quite beautifully one reason why teachers cannot rely too heavily on objective tests:

About my school

It is a summer evening, and everyone has gone home. There is an air of serenity about the school, and all is quiet except for a door banging in the wind. The playground, once swarming with merry children, is now quiet, and the wind whips up little whirlwinds of dust and leaves and blows them across the asphalt.

In the hall, the climbing ropes swing idly at rest, and in the swimming baths the water slops restlessly over the sides onto the grass, still warm from the last lesson.

A last wisp of smoke puffs out of the boiler chimney, and a last drain of water gurgles from the kitchen into the drain, on its long journey to the sea. The cloakrooms are empty, the classrooms are empty, their chairs all neatly placed on desks. Not one light is burning, and the warm glow from the fires gradually gets dimmer and dimmer. Every door is locked, every window closed. All the bright charts and paintings are gone, and the walls are utterly bare. The caretakers car disappears up the drive. The school is alone. The Summer Holidays have started.

The preceding case studies, together with the previous evidence from both research and the various assignments, have shown that the recognition of gifted children by teachers may not always be as efficient as might be hoped and expected. It is unnecessary to press the point further by going into details with cases such as:

1 The B-stream primary child who wins a scholarship to study computer science at University.

2 The child in a B stream with a known IQ of 130+.

3 The well known fact that teachers do not contrive to make proper age allowances when assessing children's intellectual abilities.

4 Biographies of famous people—Churchill, Einstein etc.

All this is to be found in literature critical of 11+ selection procedures (see for example Heim and Watts, 1957, and various authors, 1954), and in any event it has been shown above that many experienced teachers are aware of the difficulties involved. It is thus apparent that any action which can be taken to increase the teacher's skill in evaluating abilities will amply repay the energy expended.

4 Individual differences and the behavioural criteria of giftedness

There can be little doubt, in the face of evidence and teacher opinion reviewed so far, that there is some truth in the statement by one study group that the recognition of gifted children is the 'biggest gamble in the whole educational sphere . . . [it is] so dependent on luck'. They had in mind the unevenness of provision with regard to facilities of course, but not only that. The character of the teaching staff in terms of experience received special attention, thus:

It is only through experience that a teacher can establish any norm of behaviour or attainment . . . some teachers obscure the possession of giftedness with an obsession with neatness . . . the boy's ability was not recognized until he had a more experienced teacher, and did not show itself fully until he was noticed . . . in secondary school . . . to join a special class in electronics.

The inescapable conclusion is that we must, somehow or other, concertina and concentrate experience; and the construction of a list of cues and pointers is at least a beginning. With this possibility in mind, the study groups were requested in item 2.53 of the notes to list the behavioural criteria by which talented or potentially talented youngsters might be recognized. In response to this proposal most study groups first made the following points:

    1   The younger the child, the more difficult it becomes to make a sensible list of traits.

    2   Gifted children differ so much amongst themselves that any list of behaviours could be misleading if not interpreted very carefully.

    3   Such lists are not useful therefore as 'selectors'; they can only be helpful aids to teachers.

A further caution, which is of the utmost importance, was that lists formed from studies of high measured IQ children are certain to be culturally biased. Thus 'voracity for reading' is a trait which invariably comes high on American descriptions, and it is perhaps difficult to imagine a gifted child who does not read a large number of books. The fact remains however that, in some families and subcultures, books as such are not important even to the very able, and it is naïve to imagine otherwise. Without pressing this point, attention may be drawn to Laycock's (1957) check list for teachers which contains several items (e.g. 8, 17, 18, 19) that are almost certainly culturally loaded against 'deprived' children; and which, interestingly enough, do not appear directly in the list below. Much the same might be said of the list given by Hildreth (op. cit.), another set of items frequently presented in courses for teachers at the present time as descriptive of the traits of giftedness. There is thus a clear need to construct not one list but several; each related, as well as may be, to given backgrounds. Clearly educational priority areas provide a first case for inquiry, and in the meantime a list, backed by brief case studies, should be of assistance, since the teachers involved represent experience in extreme ranges of educational environments including immigrant populations.

A list of behavioural criteria

The list that follows is compiled from the observations of the study groups, in response to item 2.53 of the notes.

1   Display of extraordinary initiative: singleness of purpose
2   Intense curiosity, sometimes in only one direction
3   Day-dreaming through boredom: possibly idle and can't be bothered with mundane tasks
4   Divergent, or even delinquent behaviour: independent
5   Highly imaginative forms of expression
6   Exasperation in the face of constraint
, 7   Contempt for adults of less ability: supercilious
8   Above average dependability
9   Ability to rationalize about lack of achievement
10   Highly developed sense of humour
11   Lively and stimulating conversation: not keen on writing everything down always
12   Ability to be absorbed in work for long periods
13   Suggestion of associated musical ability
14   Exceptional speed of thought
15   Exceptional depth of thought which shows itself, *inter alia*, in:
    (*a*) their power to organize material
    (*b*) ability to see the need for many different words to express shades of meaning
    (*c*) their power to make and understand analysis
    (*d*) their power to use images
    (*e*) their capacity for adopting methods for unusual purposes
    (*f*) attention to truthful detail
16   Finding no need to labour the practical approach; jumping to the abstract
17   Finding it necessary to listen to only a very short part of the explanation given; will withdraw if compelled to listen further
18   Interests—sometimes may seem unhealthy or precocious.

19   Questions—may be tiresome and difficult to answer: asks a lot of 'might' and 'maybe' questions
20   Bossy or cocky attitude—means of defence because they feel inferior in (say) games or handwork
21   Fear of failure—doesn't like to be proved wrong or inadequate
22   Dissatisfaction with own efforts and contempt of approval for work of standards which they realize are very ordinary
23   Perfectionism; mental speed faster than physical capabilities permit in action
24   Impatience—sometimes difficult to control—intolerant, pernickety
25   Less conformity—does not always do well; will opt out
26   Uneasy relationships with other children sometimes
27   Sensitivity and highly strung behaviour
28   Acute awareness of verbal puns etc.
29   General preference for sharing ideas with older children
30   A tendency to direct others in play and project situations
31   Alertness; often too observant for comfort
32   Good memory, frequently, but not always for 'facts'—for the way things 'work' or are related; often forgetful of 'minor' matters
33   Keenness at collecting ('rubbish' sometimes)
·34   Humility about their achievements; not necessarily anxious to shine
35   Inclination, sometimes, to be self-centred or aggressive; attention-seeking
36   Lack of enthusiasm about group activities or group games
37   Appearing not to need a massive amount of sleep
38   High achievement in some line(s) or other

Observational aspects of case studies

Several study groups implied that perhaps the soundest way to help parents and teachers to recognize ability would be to recount relevant parts of case studies. This is therefore attempted below, and references to the above check list are indicated by the numbers in brackets. Studies from both teachers and parents are included in order to demonstrate incidentally the possibilities of conflicting views arising. IQ scores are in several cases unknown but the present study is not confined merely to such pupils as happen to have been tested.

CASE STUDIES 8 AND 9 (PARENTS/TEACHERS)
Both C and M had:
   shown responses such as head raising at 5 weeks old.
   been able to stand at 5–6 months.
   been absorbed as infants in manipulating objects such as bottles and their tops.
   C at 1 year had been able to recognize and play simple melodies on a piano.

At age 3 years M had been able to play gramophone records without supervision but paradoxically had refused to use a knife and fork. C at the same age
made four structures from large pieces of wood and had succeeded in pulling
her larger brother into a tree by means of a pulley devised herself. Neither child
seemed to require as much sleep as would normally be expected (37).

Both had learned to talk at 1 year and at 2 years possessed extensive vocabu-
laries, M inventing words for unfamiliar objects. C had started school in
Germany at $4\frac{1}{2}$ years; by $5\frac{1}{4}$ years had been fluent in German and by $5\frac{1}{2}$ years in
French.

Both were reported to have had social difficulties. They had been inclined to
be self-centred, aggressive towards those not sharing their interests (35) . . .
impatient and sarcastic (24) . . . subject to extreme moods . . . had refused to
conform . . . and had disliked group activities (36) . . . their parents had not
recognized their potential . . . C's frustration had caused a partial breakdown
in mental health after a year in school . . . while M initially rejected and rejecting
(26) only finally came to be accepted at about age 7 years.

CASE STUDY 10 (TEACHERS; 7 YEARS OLD)

Excellent sense of humour (10), sees a joke even against herself and laughs at it.
Very highly strung (27). Bossy with her two brothers and playmates (20). Not
too popular as she always want to take the lead (30). Plays with older children
when they will let her (29). Does not play at 'make believe'—likes toys etc., to
do real things. Knits with needles tucked under arm [and] gets frustrated if she
makes a mistake (23). Exceptional memory—father reads stories every night.
Later she can 'read' whole story from memory. Extraordinary memory for
music (13). From age 4 she began to 'pick out' tunes with one hand. At five
using both hands—vamping with left—can play tune on piano in natural key
after first hearing.

CASE STUDY 11 (INFANT TEACHERS)

When he commenced school he was able to read and was eager to do so. He
read words such as 'rhinoceros', 'hippopotamus' with ease. His number work
was exceptionally good for his age (38). His paintings and illustrations were
detailed and colourful and he became absorbed in whatever he was doing (1).
His general knowledge was good, also his vocabulary—he showed a great interest in all class activities. Academically his work was good, but practically he
was very slow, i.e. dressing himself, washing hands and tidying away; he was
quite prepared to let someone else do it for him, without making any attempt
himself (3). He was forgetful of items such as gym shoes or articles of clothing
and left his scissors, paint brushes and other tools wherever he had been using
them (32).

He reads fluently—on sight— and his reading covers a wide field of subjects
(38). He reads much more complex material than any of his peers and with
understanding and retention of content (15). He is completely absorbed and
oblivious to anything or anyone when he is reading and this applies also to a
lot of his work, painting, maths, investigation etc. (1). His vocabulary and

spelling are very good and he has an interest in derivation and a feeling for words (28). He can write well and at length but only when he really wants to (25). His attitude seems to be that he wants to absorb and discover and rarely does he willingly want to impart his findings (36). His general knowledge is excellent and he learns rapidly and easily. He is curious and observant, has long concentration spans and therefore must not be overscheduled (1), (2), (12).

In painting and drawing he is original and imaginative, has excellent colour sense, perspective and form (5). He has recently become fascinated by maps and the *Reader's Digest Atlas*, and arising from this he has painted, freehand, large maps of England, the world, Africa and Australia—the latter two from memory. These have been remarkably accurate, on a large scale and he has inserted towns, rivers etc., afterwards (32). His maths work is very good—not purely in computation but in application of principles (16).

He is immature in some ways, i.e. dressing, in play, in accepting responsibility (35), but it often appears that he is really oblivious to ordinary classroom instruction (3). He responds more appropriately and on smaller clues to given stimuli than the rest of the children in the class (17). His reading age was assessed in January as 11·3—his chronological age then being 6·9.

CASE STUDY 12 (INFANT TEACHERS AND PARENT)

In lots of ways he is a charming and engaging child. He is lively in class and seems to enjoy all class activities (8). He is obviously intelligent, this showing in his conversation, vocabulary and general awareness (11). He demands and seems to need a lot of attention (35).

His great interest lies in mechanical factual things. He is very keen on building and making gadgets and machines (2). At home he makes things with bulbs, batteries, wires etc., with surprising accuracy and understanding. In class he will build from Lego attaching strings and cords on his models to make them function. His imagination in this field is very ingenious (5), and he can often be seen with a small group around him explaining things and answering questions (30). He himself asks questions incessantly when his imagination has been aroused, and won't rest until he knows the far end of everything (19), (31). He particularly enjoys science lessons with peripatetic teacher (2). In other work he is disappointing. He lacks motor control and does not try very hard, although he has shown some improvement (25). His reading is only fair (Blue *Gay Way*). He spends much of creative activity time in Wendy House play.

He has a good vocabulary, can describe and explain verbally but seems unable and unwilling to record anything. He has poor motor control but he also lacks the urge to improve (25). He has an interest in the infant science work, i.e. circuits, magnets etc. and can work well in this field with the proviso that he has plenty of attention and appreciation.

He is very immature for a child with the obvious ability to progress further. His reading is 'on demand' and again his slow progress would appear to be due to his own lack of ability to concentrate—in fact he appears to have a lazy attitude to work (3), (25). It is difficult to tell whether he actually needs more personal attention or whether too much obvious attention has held him back

(35). Certainly he must acquire the basic skills to enable him to use the undoubted ability he has.

When tested with the Burt (re-arranged) Word Reading Test his reading age was 6, yet he could give the meaning of words: projecting, nourishment, trudging, emergency and binocular.

His parents came to see me today at my request. We have discussed his progress at various periods of his school life and they felt that he had improved in ability to produce legible writing. We are still concerned that his written work, both in form and content, is below the average of his class. They described his absorption in electrical and mechanical objects saying that one morning he got up at 5.30 a.m., put on his clothes and played for two hours with these gadgets before anyone else was up; the surprising fact is that his father is completely uninterested in this field and has no knowledge along these lines. He bought a set of electrical equipment for him at Christmas because he had shown interest and read the book of instructions so that he could, if necessary, give him some help. [The child], however, unable to read the difficult instructions, accepted no help and worked out a bell and bulb circuit on his own.

CASE STUDY 13 (TEACHER)

He entered this small two-teacher village primary school at 5 years. On entry he talked fluently and with ease (11), had an excellent vocabulary and his general knowledge was far above average (38). He would not play with toys and had no desire to do any manual creative work (2). His sole object was to master the skills of the three Rs as quickly as possible. By 6½ years he was reading and writing fluently, delighting in increasingly skilful literary expression in story writing.

During his first year in the junior form, aged 7, it was evident that he was developing in a far more outstanding way than other children of his age group, pursuing a very wide range of interests with an exceedingly lively enquiring (19) mind. He was enthusiastically learning and pursuing all he could find out in every field of knowledge, especially history. Everything concerned and connected with this subject filled him with a tremendous desire to discover and learn more and then this thirsty mind developed alarmingly as he sorted out and stored all this knowledge (31).

At 8 years he was at least 2 years in advance in the ordinary skills of maths, but disliked this subject until he went to [public school] (38). He was very keen on sport but being in a small school competition was limited. Before leaving at 9+ he had begun to create some geographical, but mostly historical models. This always leads to so much research for absolutely correct detail (15) that unless carefully watched he did the research while the other boys carried out his instructions (30), (1). Although so outstandingly intelligent he was a great favourite in class, and an unassuming boy with no airs of 'I know it all', even though he was by nature very self-confident (34). It was also this child's home background which helped so much in his early formative years. The parents were ever ready to discuss all matters of interest with him. He grew up in an atmosphere of intellectual conversation and discussion.

CASE STUDY 14 (TEACHER)

He is a hardworking (12), thoughtful boy, with a good level of attainment in all subjects (1). His examination position this term is second in a class of 37 boys and girls (38). He is talented in art and his interests are football, chess and reading. He shows leadership and initiative in group activities within the class (30). He is mature in outlook for his age and has a well developed sense of responsibility (8). He is Head Boy of the school and also serves on the school magazine committee.

CASE STUDY 15 (INFANT TEACHER)

(High score on verbal IQ, performance IQ only about 120).

He lacks perseverance. He only works when he can shine in a group. He is spiteful, antisocial (35), obviously very intelligent, disliked by other children (26). He lags far behind his peers in manual dexterity and is channelled at home into learning somewhat superfluous precocious general knowledge (38). All 'play' must have a purpose at home. At school he uses his intelligence to escape work, and to get his own way. He will cheat readily and put the blame for his own misconduct on others with wide-eyed innocence (4). Once when reprimanded he calmly stated that he did not know how one determined right from wrong (15). All written work is produced unwillingly (3), (25).

CASE STUDY 16 (PARENT/TEACHER)

Slower to talk (and walk) than his brother but whereas his elder brother began with recognizable single words, he completely omitted this stage and began with phrases of several words. He has always had—and used—a wide vocabulary.

Showed remarkable aptitude for handling toys requiring reasoning—fitting shapes, jigsaws, etc. Always very contented, rarely required entertaining, could concentrate for a longer period than most children on something that interested him (12).

Interests and Hobbies

Making models, painting, drawing, inventing puzzles and games (5), collecting interesting objects (33), activities connected with school, e.g. finding information for projects. Shows a great interest in figures and statistics (38). TV does not interest him if he has some more interesting work on hand. Is very selective in his viewing (1).

Character

Well-balanced, contented and affectionate at home. Neat, tidy and methodical. Mixes well, enjoys the company of his friends, most of whom tend to be slightly older than he (29). Is never bored or unhappy long—can always occupy himself (4). Extremely modest—never parades his knowledge, though will, if asked, assist his brother (1st year Grammar school) in English and spelling if requested. Was once observed dictating an English composition to elder brother! (34), (29). Generous in praise of other children's achievements. Is intelligent enough to realize how much he has to learn.

Independent (4). Is often impatient of help because he feels he must do things alone whenever possible (24). Strict sense of fair play, and transparently honest even when testing himself, e.g. he amused himself recently by attempting to find 100 words from CONSTANTINOPLE. When mother suggested 'contest', he refused to write it down although he had previously thought of it himself, because he could not satisfy himself it was all his own work. Refuses help in homework or model-making, even where teacher obviously would not object (8). Anything he achieves, or has achieved, has been done without any assistance at home, not because parents are unwilling, but because he insists upon independence, which trait augurs well for future study habits.

The following 'snapshot' studies are included in order briefly to exemplify trait combinations not already indicated; they are all supplied by teachers:

CASE STUDY 17
Considerable speed of thought (14); independent thought (4); and action (12); musically gifted (13); socially acceptable (30); well balanced personality. No good at art.

CASE STUDY 18
Exceptional mathematical gift, but no apparent interest in anything else (1), (38); unco-ordinated (23).

CASE STUDY 19
Alive and stimulating (11); inventive (5); musical (13); emotional problems (25), (24), (26); marked sense of humour (10).

CASE STUDY 20
Once wrote about: 'The sex life of a ping-pong ball' (18).

These case studies, together with those recounted elsewhere, sufficiently illustrate the observational criteria listed above.

Evidence from questionnaires

Attention may now be turned to the somewhat less spontaneous observations of teachers, as these are suggested by an analysis of item A.1 in the questionnaire. Again it must be remembered that teachers frequently draw attention to the fact that 'none of these characteristics is sufficient by itself to indicate giftedness; a combination of any might do so'.

The findings in table 4.1 are of interest from a number of points of view; it seems, to begin with, that intelligence tests are not the most popular method for assessing giftedness. Teachers are more impressed by the observation of an intense curiosity, a wide vocabulary, and imaginative writing. This is perhaps a little surprising, if only because the evaluation of these behaviours might be thought to be quite difficult, and certainly less objective than the

Table 4.1   The indicators of giftedness: analysis of item A.1 in questionnaire ($n = 370$)

Item	%
(i) Display of extraordinary initiative	48
(ii) Intense curiosity	65
(iii) Day-dreaming	18
(iv) Delinquent behaviour	1
(v) Divergent behaviour, i.e. unusual and original but not delinquent	45
(vi) Memorizing reams of poetry etc	8
(vii) Inability to understand aggression in others	6
(viii) Imaginative writing	56
(ix) Rapid reading	48
(x) Wide vocabulary	65
(xi) Extraordinary perseverance	36
(xii) Extreme independence	36
(xiii) Extreme unpopularity	5
(xiv) High achievement test scores	38
(xv) High intelligence test scores	53
(xvi) High creativity test scores	21
(xvii) Rejection of school work	6
(xviii) Exasperation in the face on constraint	28
(xix) Exceptional physical characteristics	9
(xx) Any others	21

Note: The figures indicate the percentage of respondents who marked the item as a reliable indicator of giftedness. Qualified replies were received from 1 per cent of respondents for each of items i, iii, iv, v and xvi.

intelligence test itself. Achievement tests too are not mentioned as frequently as might have been anticipated, and it may be that there is among teachers a healthy scepticism about tests, any tests of the pencil and paper type. Remembering the previous comments of our study groups, however, it seems more likely that many teachers are dissatisfied with the 'convergent', or what they believe is the 'convergent' content of most standardized tests at present available. Thus whilst accepting the value of intelligence tests for 'convergent' giftedness they are less happy about their value in recognizing the more divergent pupils.

A second feature of the findings is the apparent stress on verbal facility. Rapid reading, imaginative writing, wide vocabulary, and intelligence tests themselves are clearly loaded verbally; and all are important indicators for a good proportion of teachers. This suggests that able children from 'non-verbal' backgrounds, or of a cognitive style different from that envisaged in this collection of traits, are more likely to be underestimated or missed by teachers. This is not merely a result of the initial item selection process; see next page.

Viewing the sequence of negative or rejected traits, it seems clear that the gifted delinquent is almost certain to be missed. The child who opts out and rejects school work will also seldom be considered very able, as will the child who is unpopular. On the other hand, the imaginative child who displays unusual behaviour of an acceptable kind, who is highly original in his products and ideas, is very likely to be remarked as gifted. This will be especially true if the child shows initiative, independence or perseverance.

It is perhaps noteworthy that about a fifth of these teachers are prepared to consider the results of creativity tests, although a number expressed disquiet concerning the results of such instruments. There can be little doubt that most professional people would view such evaluatory procedures as no more than interesting experiments at the present time. They would not, however, reject such experimentation out of hand, and this is of great importance in that it demonstrates the sympathy many practising teachers have with any attempt to improve our recognition procedures.

The fact that no one characteristic received more than a 65 per cent 'recognition rate' suggests that the vast majority of teachers do not anticipate that giftedness reveals itself invariably in any one type of behaviour. 'Giftedness' is a complex concept, and it is perhaps not surprising to find that teachers expect it to be displayed in complex combinations of behaviours rather than in any simple form.

Finally and predictably from what has been said, a fair proportion of teachers do not consider the proposed list as being complete. The table shows that 21 per cent add further characteristics to those given, and inspection of the questionnaires shows the following to be among those most frequently added:

(xxi) Selection and discrimination
(xxii) Perception of analogies
(xxiii) Creation of images and perception of relationships
(xxiv) General enthusiasm and co-operation
(xxv) 'Butterfly' behaviour due to rapid absorption of facts
(xxvi) Desire to excel
(xxvii) Exceptional energy.

The results from A.1 support and reinforce the findings from previous sources, and show that there is some degree of real consensus amongst teachers regarding the most probable characteristics of able children. It would be misleading however not to repeat at this point the caution that the patterns of behaviour indicated in the findings described above are generalizations. They are guides which will serve no useful function in the hands of the unwary.

Pointers towards specific talents

The preceding discussions have tended to be conducted in terms of intellectual giftedness without being exclusively devoted to that area. It is necessary now to redress the balance and consider those behavioural features which might be associated with more specific talents. As an introduction it will be helpful to consider the responses of study groups to item 2.52 of the notes which asked for opinions about the degree of difficulty involved in recognizing talents such as music, soccer, and swimming.

In general, the study groups expressed the view that intellectual giftedness was more difficult to recognize than the types of talents mentioned in 2.52. They made one very obvious but nonetheless vital proviso, namely that the child must have the opportunities and facilities necessary for his talent to show. In other words, in many of the more specific activities, the problem of recognition is coupled with the problem of provision. But there is more to this problem than that, as may be seen from the perspicacious comments on the recognition of physical giftedness given in the following extract from study group 7's report:

It would appear to be much easier to recognize physical giftedness than intellectual giftedness because:

(a) In individual sports such as athletics, swimming, and cricket, every performance, even in training, can be measured (stop watch, tape measure, averages), and very quickly a picture of ability will emerge.

(b) In gymnastics and diving, exercises are graded and the marking is standardized and includes a tariff system.

(c) In team games such as soccer, rugby and hockey a high degree of skill is comparatively easy to appreciate.

However these assessments are not really measurements of natural ability or giftedness but measurements of achievement—which is a combination of talent and effort. In my experience it is unwise to assume that any rate of progress in physical abilities will be maintained, and yet it is perhaps a fair assumption to make that any real giftedness should be of a permanent nature, and if this is the case I would suggest that it is much more difficult to recognize physical giftedness than intellectual giftedness. . . . I know that I have been proved wrong far too many times in my original assessment of permanent ability. There are so many factors involved that can retard progress, e.g. lack of growth, lack of strength, loss of suppleness, emotional problems, or even lack of interest.

Having concluded that it is difficult to recognize the above average in physical ability, I would say that it is relatively easier to recognize the exceptionally gifted because they often have physical characteristics peculiar to their particular sport, which sometimes puts them in the 'freak' class, e.g. distance runners with a pulse rate in the thirties, or high hurdlers with exceptionally long legs.

These points serve as a useful introduction to the views on recognition expressed by the Council's Physical Education Committee:

[There is] in physical education no clear definition as to what [is] meant by a 'gifted' child. Children who are gifted might manifest themselves in different ways, at different ages and in a variety of activities. In the primary school it is evident that development in physical achievement among children is uneven, depending as it does on the experience and maturity of the child, and it could be hazardous to predict that any child who showed evidence of talent at about the age of 10 years would continue to do so as he approached maturity.

As was noted earlier, the profession is agreed that the future performance of an outstanding child is not of primary importance in the context of provision for his present needs. It is essential that provision be matched to present capability, and it is the latter therefore which requires recognition. In an effort to ascertain the kinds of behavioural evidence which teachers would tend to accept as probably indicative of outstanding performances, a number of fields were suggested in item A.6 of the questionnaire. Here teachers were asked to write in those characteristics which they thought most commonly formed the basic ability syndrome in relation to each activity. Since physical education has already been under general review, this aspect is considered first.

PHYSICAL EDUCATION (GAMES AND ATHLETICS)

The characteristics most frequently noted include the following:
   (i) Intuitive 'ball sense'
   (ii) Appreciation of the use of space
   (iii) Ability to play (run) 'off the ball'
   (iv) Agility and grace of movement; joy in performing
   (v) Speed of movement
   (vi) Awareness of the possibilities and limitations of what his body will achieve; self-confidence in ability
   (vii) Skill in execution
   (viii) Imagination

MUSIC

In music the features given below were noted:
   (i) A sense of rhythm
   (ii) Rapid learning of an instrument; skill and facility in execution
   (iii) Aesthetic appreciation of tonal quality
   (iv) Ability to sing in tune
   (v) Sense of 'pitch' and harmony; aural perception of high standard
   (vi) A musical memory
   (vii) Imaginative tune making
   (viii) Rapid adaptability to new rhythms
   (ix) Spontaneous improvisation
   (x) Feeling for melody and phrasing

It is to be observed that here particularly a very large number of our teachers failed to respond, and pointed out that they had neither the knowledge nor the experience in music to be able to recognize levels of ability, high or low. This fact has obvious implications for the consideration of provisions, and points to the need for experts in the field to draw up the criteria of recognition which might help teachers to decide whether an adviser should be consulted. One such commentary, for which we are indebted to Dr A. Little and his ILEA colleague, is reproduced here.

There is no simple answer to the somewhat complex questions which you have posed.

As I see it there are two basic factors in the performance and perception of music—pitch and rhythm. It is my experience that the second factor is present to some degree or other in most children and is capable of being developed to a fairly advanced standard. Pitch however appears to be more of what is loosely described as a 'gift'. Like rhythm it is capable of development though at widely differing rates, the confusing factor here is the ability of some children to perceive differences in pitch aurally without being able to recognize them, perhaps through physical limitations.

Aural perception also embraces the recognition of varying timbres (e.g. difference between orchestral instruments). This talent is sometimes present in children as young as 3 or 4 years of age.

Side by side with the above are other factors which can often be determined at an early age: musical memory (the retention of themes or the reproduction of patterns) and dexterity in performance on a musical instrument. The latter presupposes, in addition to muscular and mental co-ordination, hereditary traits, etc., the presence of parental support and a sympathetic environment; especially with regard to contemporary attitudes to 'pop' or classical music.

It has also been my experience that there is a considerable correlation between musical ability in children and general intelligence though this is not invariably the case and should not of course, for example, be used as an argument to deny less able children the opportunity of taking up an instrument as there are cases where below average children have shown remarkable progress not only on an instrument (however primitive) but also, by transfer, in other spheres of activity where formerly little progress has been shown.

It will also be useful to relate one or two case studies which are of particular interest in the context of recognition of musical talent. They are chosen so as to reinforce further and amplify the preceding account of the problems involved in recognizing talent.

CASE STUDY 21 (SCHOOL)

D is believed to have some degree of giftedness in trumpet playing. Presented with an instrument for the first time at the age of 8 + he could immediately pitch different open notes. Within a couple of days he was able to play two simple hymn tunes without any further guidance from the teacher. Recognition of this (potential?) talent was brought about by one factor only: the provision and opportunity of attempting to blow a brass instrument. [It was noticeable that the boy] . . . revealed quite a degree of self-confidence—he rather enjoyed other children watching him later. This same pattern [has been observed] in other [specific] gifted children, e.g. PE, swimming, and French.

An extraordinarily similar case was drawn to the attention of the project director on one of his visits to schools. Here again, the provision of a brass instrument for the child was wholly fortuitous. We are not here suggesting that more brass instruments are required by primary children. Musicians apparently do not agree on their suitability and more investigation is required. At the same time these instances are a warning against making any so-called 'authoritative' statement that such provision is unsuitable for primary children just because they are 'primary'.

CASE STUDY 22

She had no interest in academic learning in spite of being highly intelligent. In order to awaken in the girl, who was extremely pleasant-mannered, some desire to use her abilities her experienced teacher concentrated on her fine voice. An experienced musician himself, he brought the girl's singing to a fine level of performance so that she became the soloist in the school choir. This was quite a distinction as the choir of that time contained some very competent singers. The music organizer on a visit to the school was so impressed with her singing, he invited her to join his choral society. She did not accept the offer.

At fifteen her singing voice was obviously one of excellent quality and her teacher was most anxious to help in developing what was unquestionably a talent. No contact could be made with the home which did not surprise the school staff. The whole talent was lost once the girl left school.

The case has been stated to show how all the efforts of experienced and eager teachers are brought to nothing by a home environment. Here a 'gift' was recognized at 13+, developed to the girl's obvious enjoyment and justifiable pride, then lost.

The question has not been raised as to why the girl's potential was not recognized before 13 years of age, although the implication is that there was no music specialist in the junior part of the school. Nonetheless we have here very clear evidence of what teachers do achieve against even the most adverse home circumstances. Two further points arise from this study:

(a) Our study group findings show no support for the view expressed above that 'all the efforts are brought to nothing' when a talent fades or is neglected in after-school life.

(b) Continuation of the exercise of a talent after school ought to receive more active consideration than is implied in any pious expression of woe and regret.

CASE STUDY 23 (SCHOOL)

7+ Picture Test 100: 8+ Sentence Reading 126:
8+ English Progress 135.

Placed in J.3 at age of 8 years. Able to adjust to higher age group.

Began learning violin 1965. When teacher left was sent to neighbouring school one afternoon a week until parents, and head, objected to him losing half a day's schooling for half an hour's violin lesson. Resumed study when new teacher appointed.

A quiet self-contained boy, regarded as a 'character' by other children, as he disliked games and preferred to play or even read about music. With assistance of ordinary music teacher composed and harmonized, and passed grades 2 and 3 violin exams.

Passed entrance exam to special music school, being under age. Immediately placed in junior and then senior orchestras. When school changed to music school accepted as LEA place holder. Sent twice weekly to College of Music under the Professor.

Musical director of school describes him as 'very gifted'. He says he has been 'coerced' into learning piano in addition, but needs building up in personality. Shows great technical achievement but is too self-effacing and lacks confidence as regards public performance. Is one of the youngest boys in 4th form.

Ranks 3rd musically. Plays in quartet and orchestra with older boys.

This case is of great interest from several points of view. Apart from showing how relatively 'unbalanced' and yet well 'integrated' this boy is, despite or because of his acceleration to a higher group, there is evidence of the possibly oppressive effect of parents and teachers. Here they combined to prevent the child from spending one half day per week in another place to pursue a fairly obvious talent. Insufficient information is available for us to question this decision: it was no doubt wise in all the circumstances of the case. There is a clear need, however, to stress the implications for provision at this point; they are twofold at the very minimum:

(a) School staffing must be on a team basis so that all essential expertises are represented, even if peripatetic help is required to complete the team.

(b) Extra-mural provision will minimize the need to place 'general' and 'special' aspects of education in contradistinction and competition.

It needs no imagination to appreciate that without an adaptive and robust temperament, coupled with an enduring interest in the violin, we have here a case where talent could so easily have been destroyed. Had the child been average at 'ordinary' school work, one cannot help wondering whether his musical talent would not have gone by the board altogether. This of course raises the question as to how far schools which have special facilities for musical education should require high academic standards of entry in addition to outstanding musical prowess. If they do, then conditions would be created under which provisions that purport to be aimed at the maximum encouragement of the growth of talent, actually work to prevent its development, except as it occurs in a particular form, i.e. allied to high verbal ability.

The project director raised this point during his visit to the Yehudi Menuhin School and found that pupils of considerably less than outstanding verbal capacity are in fact accepted. This policy might with profit be considered anywhere in connexion with any talent, despite the obvious attraction of the alternative to the particular school concerned. From the conversations which the director had with teachers during the enquiry it is apparent that many teachers view the idea of 'special' schools for (say) music with some degree of suspicion. They wonder how far such schools might not be, or become, thinly disguised grammar schools, when they as teachers feel committed perhaps to the comprehensive ideal.

This is not the point at which to do more than simply raise the question; attention must now be turned to another vital element in this same case study.

It will have been noted that this particular child did not begin to learn the violin until he was ten years of age. Before pursuing this further it will be useful to outline a short series of other case studies which also have similar implications. Apart from the first, these are highly curtailed in the interests of brevity[1].

CASE STUDY 24

The earliest contact with musical education that I can recall was a short series of private piano lessons when I was six years old. Although I was not forced into these, by any means, they were short-lived and came to nothing. It was probably an interest in practising and theory which was lacking, rather than an interest in music, for I continued to play about on the piano, without having any actual lessons.

At this stage, the thing that made the most impression on me was my first hearing a Gilbert and Sullivan operetta at the school an older brother was attending. This became an annual event, and before each one I would take out the musical score from the public library to go over the words and music—the latter of which did not mean very much to me.

Music at the primary school consisted of hymn singing as far as I remember. There was no opportunity for instrumental music whatsoever. The only exception was one particular year (I was about ten years old) when we had a young and enthusiastic teacher, who formed a choir, taught us part songs and motets and gave us the chance to perform before an audience. This teacher also 'discovered' that I had quite a good voice and often had me singing solo parts.

On the results of the 11+ examination I went to a secondary modern school and was placed in the 'grammar stream'. As far as music was concerned here, the emphasis was again on class singing. As for theory of music, I learned nothing in the first couple of years of secondary education. At this time my rather vague and undirected interest in music took various forms. I tried to compose 'operas' —(I would make up stories, often in verse, and put tunes to them, although I

could not actually write the music down.) The tunes were in my head and I could manage to play them by ear on the piano—the melody line only, of course. I also tried taking the piano to bits to see how it worked!

By now, we had a record player at home and I was beginning to hear a few of the more familiar classics.

Eventually the music teacher began to form a small orchestra, and I discovered that a boy in my class was going to a music class and he suggested that I should go with him. This was in the evenings and was run by Mr ——. On my first visit they lent me a violin so that I could practise at home. I was then fourteen years of age.

This actual involvement with music-making led to a widening of my interest, and my first visits to concerts and operas.

During the following year, I realized that music was my main interest, and asked to do the O level music course. Since music was not taught as an academic subject, I had the benefit of some individual tuition, which gave me the chance to make up for lost time. At this time I joined the Schools Orchestra, and, on the recommendation of my music teacher in school, was accepted in the Youth Orchestra. I toured Germany with this orchestra, giving three or four concerts in different cities. This involvement with these two orchestras introduced me to many musicians, professional and amateur, whereas previously I had known hardly any.

During my studies for the O level music, the music teacher left the school, and I was left more or less stranded. However, I continued my studies alone and gained the examination.

Unfortunately, I had not passed sufficient O levels to transfer to a sixth form, so my family decided to let me spend another year in the secondary school. By the end of this second year I had gained seven O levels, and was transferred to the sixth form of grammar school.

Here I received the main stimulus to my musical interest, as there was an extremely active music department, which involved me with opera, chamber music and orchestral playing, as well as the normal class studies leading to A-level music. With this sudden change of the situation, however, I found myself lagging behind the others, whose musical backgrounds had been less turbulent than my own, and I realized that it meant I would either have to 'pull out all the stops' so to speak, or give up. However, with the encouragement I received I managed to catch up and finally gained three A levels with a B for music and was accepted for the Bachelor of Music degree course at two universities.

As for my progress at university, it is difficult for me to assess, but at the end of my first year I was accepted for the Honours Degree course. There are about 150 music students in the university and I have been chosen to play in the orchestra on several occasions. This year, one of the professors asked myself and three other students to form a string quartet, and he tutors us in his own home. I have also been chosen to play in a concert for —— when he comes to officially open the new Music Centre at the university.

In my first year I was recommended to do the performer's degree, but have since changed this to the writing of a thesis, which I think will be of more value to me.

This year it has been suggested that I do research—assuming that I obtain a First at the end of my third year.

Looking back, it seems that I had an interest in music from an early age, but for some reason, probably lack of opportunity, I was unable to communicate this enthusiasm to others—(even learning to play the violin was someone else's suggestion!) or to transform it into any sort of conventional music-making. My interest was probably not nurtured in the right way from an early age—for instance, I did not see a concert or professionally produced opera until I was fourteen—the age at which I also began violin lessons.

My main instrument now is, of course, the violin, with piano lessons as an integral part of the degree course, plus three modern foreign languages.

If my life seems to have revolved around music then I have given a wrong impression, for I had little contact with it for many years. Before I was sixteen, I never considered myself primarily as a musician. I had other ambitions and was extremely interested in English literature, and had practically decided to go in for teaching. Nevertheless, some of the earliest things I can remember are connected with music, and for as long as I can recall I have had particularly strong feelings of affection and fascination for music.

This study is recounted here as an outline autobiography of a young musician who has not yet completed his education.

CASE STUDY 25

Instrument: 'Cello.

Standard: County Major Award.

School contribution: Secondary: not much, advised not to take music at O level; member of choir. Primary: musical experience in singing and recorder playing; had little influence on musical interest.

Home influence: Father a violinist; family contact with other musicians. Private tuition on 'cello from seven years on.

LEA contribution:

(*a*) Loan of instrument?	No.
(*b*) Assisted tuition?	No.
(*c*) Saturday Music Centre?	Yes.
(*d*) Youth orchestra?	Yes.

CASE STUDY 26

Instrument: Organ.

Standard: Mus.B., A.R.M.C.M., A.R.C.O., etc.

School contribution: Secondary: followed A level music course. Primary: musical experience here nil. 'Nothing whatsoever observed or brought out.'

Home influence: Mother is musical, plays piano. Private tuition at ten years of age on piano. Changed to organ at 15 years.

LEA contribution:

(*a*) Loan of instrument?	Yes—violin.
(*b*) Assisted tuition?	Yes (in a group).

(c) Saturday Music Centre?   Yes, but run by a student and didn't work:
pupils withdrew.
(d) Youth orchestra?   Yes.

CASE STUDY 27

School contribution: Secondary: Orchestra, but not a member; joined jazz group—bought instrument at sixteen years—no lessons, self-taught; private lessons at 17 years. Primary: Played recorder; created mild interest.

Home influence: Mother plays piano; father 'musical'.

LEA contribution: Nil. But ultimately became a member of local chamber music groups, etc.

The extent of primary school influence on six further case studies can be summarized as follows:

1   Two schools only appear to present a rich musical environment. In one the headteacher taught the piano at lunch-time; in the other there was both choir and orchestra.

2   The loan of instruments by LEAs helped in two cases.

3   The ages at which instrumental tuition began were varied: 5 years, 6 years, 9 years, 10 years, 10 years, 15 years.

This summary might usefully be read in conjunction with that given above (p. 37), where the need for an early start was stressed. There are clearly very wide individual differences in relation to this particular need. A case was cited where one brilliant student was actually 'thrown out' of a youth orchestra! Perhaps he possessed some of the characteristics of the following boy:

Big and boisterous, untidy and frequently slipshod, but intelligent and able. Keen on football and other games, though often rough and sometimes uncouth. Learned to play violin well, though not a dedicated musician.

Showed interest in maths and science, but not indicating any great giftedness beyond general high standard of work.

Could be unruly—and in fact could be called a normal rough talented boy. Went to grammar school.

O levels—English language, Latin, French, German, maths, physics with chemistry, Russian.

A levels—maths (A2), physics (A2), chemistry (A)

Awarded place at university to read physics.

However this may be, it seems clear that whatever is meant by 'an early start' needs considerable qualification if it is to be of help in deciding the kind of provision needed during the primary years. The evidence adduced so far is inconclusive in that the age at which formal instrumental tuition begins does not seem to be crucial; some outstanding musicians start early in the primary years but others begin quite late. On the whole, however, it is surely dangerous to take the line that some form of early specialization is not necessary in the absence of far more information than is at present available. We know that the home background is, under present conditions, the vital factor, even without Suzuki's striking demonstration of what young children achieve on a violin[2]; and teachers who believe in equal opportunity can hardly view that situation with anything but dismay. Those teachers (75 per cent) who responded to item A.7 (v) by agreeing that early specialization is unnecessary might usefully begin a review of their basis for that opinion with a consideration of the following piece of written work by a child of 10 years 2 months:

I like flowers very much and I have a little patch of soil in the little path that runs down the side of a house. There is a little fir tree that is about forty five cm high I grew it by myself. I hope to get some Irises to round for they are my favourite flowers. I am very interested about music. My favourite composer is Mozart. I play the violin and piano and I am in grade three in both. I have some musical friends from the same family J and R play the violin and M my best friend plays the cello we have little quartets together every Saturday night we usually go to bed very late because the quartet takes such a long time last Saturday we went to bed at two oclock in the morning. D and I are very alike in the ways we think we often say the same thing at the same time. We both made the game Running at the same time this game we play every time we go home on the bus you have to get of the bus and run past the first tree before the bus passes you. D and I are very alike in the things we do except D is an artist and I am a designer. I am very quick D is very slow so it gets madning when we have to do things together at the same speed. My family and I often play games on Sunday but I am hopeless at most the games we've got so I rarley win. In between my practises I have short scampers which is running about for a while usually I say to mummy 'I am going to have a short scamper' but I make it as long as possible.

I used to live in America when I was young. One day I bit my own finger and mummy said 'Cry and it will make it better' not meaning it at all after that she wished she had never said it because I set a great big howl hoping my finger would get better. We have a very beautiful pussy who acts like a dog he comes along with us to the passage and waits with us till Mr B comes and when we get at the bus pussy is waiting for us at the top of the road. I think this is really very funny. Of all the things I like violin playing is my favourite thing.

It is doubtful whether this child would be described as specializing in music; but that such activities are receiving far more emphasis than might appear at school, or indeed could appear in some homes, is undeniable. Similarly, a case has been described to us in the following terms:

Chance exposure to musical opportunity revealed this boy's talent . . . [the] child is so eager, he rises at 5.30 a.m. before the family is up in order to practise instruments before breakfast.

Again it becomes clear what kinds of mechanisms in the home serve to facilitate the development of outstanding capability. If the school system is to act as a compensatory factor in any real sense with regard to musical education, then something must be done to encourage the kind of emphasis which is permitted in the good home for a child of talent.

In concluding this section on the recognition of musical talent it may be helpful to present a list of the distinguishing marks of the musical child prodigy, as proposed by G. C. Kop (*Mens en Musick*, J. Muuses, 1958)[3], which may be compared with what has been discussed above:

Distinguishing marks of the music prodigy

1   Abnormally keen ear (for intonation and other factors).

2   Phenomenal musical memory.

3   The child listens, sometimes for a considerable period, to a particular instrument and then expresses a strong desire to play it (examples include Casals and Menuhin—one might add Jacqueline Du Pré).

4   The child plays fluently, and even performs in public with distinction, before he has learnt to read notation. (cf. the Suzuki method, and note the possible converse—that early ability to read notation may not indicate outstanding musical talent so much as general intellectual endowment.)

5   A high degree of talent for an instrument is sometimes shown by facility in playing without looking for the notes (playing in the dark or, like Mozart, with a cloth covering the keys).

6   The child prefers his chosen instrument to any other plaything or occupation.

7   He becomes completely absorbed in making music, so that his instrument seems an inseparable part of his personality.

8   He is self-possessed in performance and does not suffer from stage fright.

9   He improvises spontaneously.

10   Genius is shown not merely through complete technical mastery, but through the creative ability with which the child interprets the music.

ART

There would in all probability be general agreement with the proposition that art is an indispensable component of a general education for every individual. A similar measure of agreement might greet the further proposal that our educational goals include the development of artistic talent wherever it may be found. From that point on, disagreement and dissentions arise; and progress is halted in the face of one apparently quite intractable problem, namely, that of constructing a developmental dimension, or dimensions.

Closely connected with this primary difficulty is the frequent failure to reach any consensus on what constitutes a 'better' artistic product as distinct from a 'worse'. The strange paths into which attempts at the evaluation of art can lead us are indicated by the following comments:[4]

An orang utan which recently won a Kansas painting contest was competing only against children aged between four and eight. He must by now be astounded by his own moderation. Why did he aim so low? What now is to arrest a glitter-

ing career—New York, London, Paris; the Young Contemporaries, the Bienn-
ale, the I.C.A.?

Nor is this question wholly frivolous. The judges in this contest were looking
for 'freshness and an uninhibited quality'. These attributes are what most art
critics and juries seem to be looking for these days. Who better than an ape to
supply them? A capacity for deep thought or feeling; the ability to advance by
experience and self-criticism; great technical skill, the ability to reproduce in
paint or by other means, what is seen, felt or imagined; good taste; a profound
insight into God, man or nature; a profound or intuitive knowledge of art itself:
all these are or may be inhibiting factors, inimical to freshness. A stranger to
them all, the ape is thus peculiarly fitted for success in an art-world which mis-
trusts, despises, fears or even hates civilization. No noble savage so savage, or
thus so noble, as he.

One must sympathize, in the face of such events as this, with the teacher
who would limit his goals in the teaching of art to the therapeutic effects
associated with mere engagement. The development of talent can then be
disregarded, and problems associated with it can perhaps be ignored.

The briefest reconsideration of the working party's definition of giftedness
makes it clear that the intention was to consider, *inter alia*, giftedness in art.
It was essential therefore to explore the views of experts in the field as to how
far giftedness could be recognized, and for this evidence we turned to the
Schools Council Art Committee. In view of the complexity and importance
of the point at issue, two statements received from the committee are
quoted in full.[5]

Statement one : the artistically gifted child
Many experienced teachers would not accept the view that judgements cannot
be made about what constitutes good child art, especially if the view has arisen
from a confusion between the state of the world of adult professional art and
child art. There is no reason why judgements about child art should be subject
to the same restrictive fear of subsequent inaccuracy which prevents critics from
saying what constitutes good professional art. The art of the primary school
child is very dissimilar to the sophisticated mature expressions of the trained
artist, in spite of apparent superficial similarities.

The laudable and valid philosophy of most teachers of art which claims that
no child should fail, ought not to lead us to the view that as no child fails, therefore all children succeed equally. Such a blinkered view of the mechanics of the
relationship between a teacher, a child and the materials of education, could
lead not to universally acquired heights of attainment but to an easily accepted
set of lower standards, both through a failure to recognize different levels of
ability as well as different levels of usage of the language of art. If the teacher
fails to recognize these different levels and fails to provide varied materials,
varied problems, varied inter-class and group relationships because of them,
then there could be much difficulty for children and certainly less success.

Child art is a very complex subject and different art educators describe
different constituents. More agree, however, that it is a form of language, or

recording, of personal statement and a method of expressing ideas. Being a language it depends for its expression on a mixture of the accretion of experience, of an innate mental ability to have ideas and to make imaginative projections, and a physical co-ordination and dexterity to bring ideas into a communicable form. There is also one very important constituent where the quality of insight is such that the child communicates a feeling or an emotion, and perhaps this is an ability which though not possessed by all children is possessed by many and, more than other constituents, does cross the ability range.

These are skills which, like those of other languages and arts, are subject to both innate ability, sensitivity, and the degree of acquired experience.

To distinguish the potentially creative artist from the rest, experienced teachers would want to single out a number of different but closely related abilities. One would certainly be the ability to draw, paint or make in some other form, an analytical representation of an observed object. Another would be a readiness to have ideas related to art. Another—an unusually inventive approach to solving design problems. Another—the ability to represent characteristics and qualities. And another to describe, in visual terms, a feeling or emotion. Sometimes a teacher would be excited to find a child who possessed all or nearly all these abilities and would then say that he had discovered a potentially creative artist.

A child who possessed potentially creative artistic gifts would not be easily inhibited by a negative environment. A characteristic of such a child would be to tend to survive such an external influence. On the other hand his gifts could be enlarged by a combination of stimulating influences and a demand, from the teacher, for the living use of the language of art.

A workshop atmosphere where the activities themselves provide stimulation alongside some deliberately contrived inspirational material would be developmental.

It is possible to over-stimulate as well as produce too rich an environment, but we in schools are at present less at risk from this phenomenon than we are from the lack of stimulation or the ill-conceived classroom environment. Besides which the child is not only subject to the influences educators arrange. What he discovers, delights in, and is excited by outdoors, is also an influence compensating one way or the other.

This elegant statement requires no comment beyond noting that the project director discussed these propositions with a number of teachers and art advisers and found only substantial agreement. Whilst accepting the difficulties involved in judging artistic creations, teachers are not prepared to give up the goal altogether. The logical consequences of a failure to distinguish the difficult from the impossible are too costly for the teacher of art to contemplate.

The psychological consequences cannot be neglected by teachers either. The project director was privileged to visit a Saturday Morning Art Centre, and in conversation with one eleven-year-old pupil discovered that she was much happier doing pottery in the centre than when she was similarly engaged at school; the main reason being that whatever she turned out at school was invariably described as 'very good' or 'excellent', whereas at the centre objects which she herself recognized as in need of improvement were almost always constructively criticized. The dangers inherent in adopting a complacent attitude towards the notion that provided an inexpert teacher takes on the limited role of giving 'general encouragement', then all is well, are clearly demonstrated here. The actual result of 'encouragement' turns out to be discouragement for this sensitive artistic child who is anxious perhaps to emulate the work of the masters.

Statement two

It was generally agreed that it is difficult, if not impossible, to formulate a satisfactory definition of what is meant by 'giftedness in art'. At the same time, it was agreed, there are some aspects of the matter which can be evaluated, and some manifestations of the child's art activities which can be assessed.

Take for example colour, a significant, perhaps *the* significant, element of art. There is no mistaking the fact that some children, even as young as three years of age, handle colour in an exceptional way. They may use it with exuberance, with poetic delicacy. Alternatively, they may display selectivity, or show powers of orchestrating, or organizing colour. We contend that it is possible to discern with certainty when a child is sensitive to colour. The child who is not sensitive to colour will not be capable, except accidentally, and this can be checked, of making artefacts which demonstrate that he possesses sensitivity to colour. In other words it is possible to say 'this child is exceptionally sensitive to colour'.

Sensitivity is the key word.

As with colour, so with the other main elements of art, viz. 'line', 'texture', 'pattern', 'two-dimensional shape', 'three-dimensional form'. It is possible to say with certainty that a girl or boy has an exceptional sense of pattern, or line, or texture; is in fact particularly sensitive to any of these qualities.

But sensitivity to one or more of the elements of art is only one facet of the matter. It is the passive component, a matter of sensual experience.

Sensitivity alone is unlikely to produce any manifestation of giftedness in the form of 'works of art'. For sensitivity to be productive there must also be additional active components.

The active components are equally observable. They consist in (i) the handling of tools and (ii) the practice of the basic skills in various 'media'. It is possible to tell at a glance which of the girls or boys has more than normal ability and delicacy with a needle; which boy or girl has an instinctive grasp of the dynamics of the hammer. Consider the lino-cutting tool, the pencil, the pottery turning tool, the tjanting, the scissors. The presence or absence of skill in manipulating these tools *is* discernable. Some children have highly sophisticated skill in the control of tools, and sometimes this is coupled with an advanced degree of muscular-visual co-ordination.

In much the same way, it *is* possible to say positively, 'he has a remarkable ability in lino cutting', or 'making pressed dishes', or 'printing with silk screens', or 'manipulating paint', or in 'tie-dying', or 'batik' and the rest; or building structures in wire, paper, steel or wood.

We would say that a child who demonstrates sensitivity in one or more of the elements of art and who combines that with mature and skilful ability in the manipulation of tools and also shows mastery in the grasp of basic skills in any of the media, that child can safely be assessed as 'gifted in art'.

No mention has been made in this letter of the use to which the child may put his sensitivity and his mastery of tool and medium.

Sensitivity to the elements of art develops as a result of exposure to those elements within the environment and as a result of cumulative subjective action and re-action.

When a gifted child, or adult, is triggered into creative action by significant aesthetic or other experience then his giftedness may become the vehicle of genius.

Giftedness is less than genius.

We submit that we can identify the lesser quality of 'giftedness in art'.

This letter has been agreed by the Art Committee with the exception of one member.

Here again it would be impudent to comment further. The implications of the positions outlined in these statements are what must be of interest, and these will be taken up in chapters 5 and 7. For the moment it will suffice to point out that an indispensable element in anything that justifiably warrants the description 'an enriched art environment' is a teacher with some real expertise in this field. One study group stressed this, especially, by first describing the important behavioural elements.

(i) A highly developed sense of spatial relationship
(ii) An ability to visualize three-dimensional forms
(iii) A sense of design and balance
(iv) An original colour sense
(v) A feeling for line and pattern.

And then they added the rider, 'These qualities are not always perceived by the teacher.' This is surely true; and the good teacher is no doubt the first to make such a comment. To object is vainly to translate a statement of unpalatable fact into a criticism where criticism is neither intended nor possible.

SCIENCE

The signs indicative of scientific talent overlap those given earlier for giftedness as such. Teachers generally list the following:

(i) Keen powers of observation
(ii) Intense curiosity about natural events
(iii) A logical and experimental approach to problems
(iv) An ability to 'leap in the dark'

(v) An ability to connect and exploit relationships
(vi) Ability to classify materials; to select significant elements.

One case study in particular demonstrated the way in which science 'catches' some gifted children beyond all else; and as this child illustrates circumstances of wider importance than simple recognition, considerable detail is provided.

CASE STUDY 28 (PARENTS)

Agencies involved in recognition (in date order)
Hospital doctors—from birth to 3 months
    Parents
    Paediatrician at Child Welfare Clinic (child aged $2\frac{1}{2}$ years)
    Teacher at school
    Family associates in medical and educational fields
    Educational psychologist
    National Association for Gifted Children

Behaviour leading to recognition
(Selection from notes and diaries kept over the years—still available.)
Alertness and focusing right from birth
    Smiled at 3 weeks 6 days
    Let the side of her cot down (both ends) at 6–7 months.
    Continually undoing the screwed nut sun-canopy on pram during the summer.
    Able to manipulate tools, knife, fork, before 2 years. (This early dexterity was noticed by doctor during routine visit to clinic with brother; suggested we take her to university for testing. Child aged $2\frac{1}{2}$ years. Offer not taken up owing to pressure of domestic work and another very young baby.
    Once able to talk—an endless flow of questions: no childish chatter.
    At the age of 3 years she made her first 'invention' which kept her occupied for the next 18 months. This contraption was of the Emmett type although she had never seen any of his models or drawings. It was basically a kitchen-type chair which she had in her bedroom to which she would add any length of pipe, string, wire, plug etc. she found. It became in turn a washing machine, aeroplane, rocket etc., all with sensible working explanations. It slowly disintegrated when sister became mobile and she was by then at school.
    She practically taught herself to read and write.
    Facility with numbers and shapes.
    Absolute fascination for all things of a mechanical or scientific nature. No interest whatsoever in dolls or the usual girls' toys and pursuits.
    By the time she was 5 years of age, with two other younger children in the family, we felt that there was a certain 'something' in this child.
    She started the local, newly built, well-equipped, state primary school at 4 years 10 months. She never went to any nursery school or play-group as there were no such amenities available at that time where we lived and she was always fully occupied and content at home and did not seem to want or need the company of other children.
    The headmaster and reception teacher remarked after the first two weeks on

the unceasing questions which were disturbing the continuation of the lessons. Questions to which they themselves admitted they did not know the answers. 'How does the light work?' 'What makes the chalk squeak on the blackboard?'

She would not play with other children in the playground. She told us they were 'babies'.

By now she was becoming a compulsive reader (which she still is). Very bored at school as she had covered the first year's reading and arithmetic by the end of the first term. The headmaster had shortage of staff difficulties and could not stream off the more advanced children. We decided to send her to a private school to work at her own speed. She was then 5 years 10 months. The private school was a coeducational school where she remained for 3 years. During this time teachers remarked that she was rather unusual in her talents for a girl. We then moved to another part of the country and she attended a new junior school.

Six weeks after starting the new school her form mistress, a mature and very experienced teacher, told us on parents' evening that she was one of the most unusually talented girls she had ever had, with interests and aptitude quite uncharacteristic for a girl, i.e. her passion for Meccano, science, anything of a scientific, mechanical, and engineering nature, although her English and other subjects were well above average. But the teacher confessed that she was also one of the most difficult children to teach as with the child's unquenchable thirst for knowledge, given the chance she would stop any lesson with endless questions and would only concentrate and listen when it suited her. She told us that she thought there was a streak of brilliance in her and was very much aware of the child being 'different', and the underlying deep sensitivity which could so easily be upset by a chance careless remark or the lack of understanding and appreciation of the child's needs.

Type of gift
[We are advised] that she has:
    (*a*) Spatial and mechanical ability
    (*b*) Scientific interests
    (*c*) Creative ability

Age at which recognition became fairly certain
Strong suspicions by 8 years; further confirmation from individual IQ testing at 11 years.

Educational difficulties and hypothetical causes
Our daughter, basically a very quiet and studious girl, has become by virtue of her own personality, intellect and uncharacteristic interests an 'outsider'. She is very stubborn and will not conform either in school or out of it. So far, persuasion, 'carrot and stick' method, have had no effect whatsoever. Academically she will do only what she wants to do and consequently has no mental discipline.

Boredom in class makes her withdraw from it and coast along, thereby underachieving. Any pressure to 'do better' either from the teachers or by us will produce no improvement in her work—only more stress.

Lack of appreciation and interest among her classmates and also teachers of her mechanical constructions, chemistry experiments, writings, original ideas etc., make her even more unsociable.

She cannot accept things on authority. She questions the bases of all information. The answers are not always forthcoming but she is not prepared to continue until she is satisfied—lessons proceed without her.

After one year at the junior school our daughter entered a new class and because she could not establish a rapport with her new teacher she continued to turn to her previous teacher who was always willing and ready to discuss her activities with her even to staying after school hours. This teacher then left the school and our daughter had no one to go to as she said 'to demonstrate her models and talk things over'. Some members of the staff when informed that the child was unhappy at school were surprised and also totally unaware of the girl's needs and her capabilities in science. It is from this date that she started to 'opt out', becoming over the next 12 months very frustrated, irritable and withdrawn, underachieving in her studies, with the resultant outbursts of aggressive behaviour which appeared to culminate in bouts of headache and sickness. This school did not at that date have 'science' on the curriculum.

In school she was at times humiliated and embarrassed in front of the class when asking questions. This resulted in a great deal of stress which, with the other difficulties mentioned above, precipitated referral to an educational psychologist.

At her secondary school she started off well, bright, alert etc., as all the new subjects unfolded during the first week or so but soon acquired the tag of 'egg head' from her classmates as a result of her questions and uncharacteristic interests. Although this was meant kindly on the whole she had by now become over-sensitive and over-reacted to any remarks and as she has never been able to 'laugh things off' and takes life very seriously, she then became more withdrawn from the class and unwilling to participate. She was absent on several occasions with sickness and headache.

She was examined by our own General Practitioner who could find nothing wrong with her physically. Headache and sickness do seem associated with these stresses.

Aspects of environment other than school having a facilitating or inhibiting influence on development
Facilitating: House always full of books. Excellent and most helpful public library. Very understanding local chemist who supplies chemistry materials. Plenty of apparatus available as husband is an electronics enthusiast. Holidays spent abroad visiting places of interest. Many friends in university and professional fields always willing to offer 'enrichment'.

Inhibiting: She has never been able to play and mix with children of her own age. Very few children and classmates with whom she can get on the same wavelength. Loathes noisy entertainments and children's parties and social functions. For a girl, she has no interest in clothes, fashion, or the 'pop' scene. She is a quiet and serious girl who does not make friends easily among her contemporaries yet, on the other hand, with great perspicacity can quickly establish a rapport with someone with similar intellect, inclination, or genuine interest and understanding. Invariably this is an adult, male, with whom she can talk 'technicalities'. A condescending attitude makes her 'freeze'.

Steps taken to improve the position
At nearly 6 years of age because of the teacher shortage and large size of classes she went to a private school.

Contact with the NAGC; educational psychologist in liaison with the school; every help given at home with educational needs and facilities; friends to take her to universities, laboratories, museums etc.

This perhaps unusually complete case study was considered to warrant amplification, and the project director therefore put certain supplementary questions to the parents.

(*a*) *To what extent do the parents feel that they may be showing too much of an overt interest in the child's school day? Or is it that they just cannot stop this most intriguing girl from discussing her activities with them?*

We do have other children at school and do not consider that we show an overt interest in this particular child's school day. Rather the opposite is the case as over the years we have learned from experience that direct questioning of her activities will reveal nothing if she does not wish to be forthcoming or communicative. She 'closes up'. She will only comment on the day's events when and if she wants to. She has never been one for school gossip or girlish chatter. On returning home from school we can tell immediately from her expression and behaviour how the day went without our needing to say anything. Once out of school and homework completed she lives and breathes for science and therefore we just cannot avoid the continual questions from her or the experiments and paraphernalia lying about the house.

(*b*) *Do I assess the situation aright by saying that there may be dangers in teachers trying too hard to achieve a 'balanced' development in the case. The child's enthusiasm for scientific projects is presumably affecting the interest she can show in some other areas of the curriculum.*

The school's syllabus is rigid and although providing a very good broad education there has been no alternative choice or flexibility, i.e. being allowed to drop a subject, e.g. domestic studies, which she loathes to the point of making herself ill at the thought of a double-period lesson, and pursuing one of the sciences to a more advanced level, not with the intention of specializing but in order to satisfy her thirst for the subject. Her frustration and the lack of reciprocal interest in her hobbies and mechanical constructions do affect the rest of her work. She becomes unresponsive and unenthusiastic in all her lessons and withdraws into herself. Consequently the quality of her schoolwork deteriorates. She works only for herself and her own satisfaction and not for teacher approval. Also we feel that scientific hobbies pursued at home are not sufficient compensation for boredom during the actual school day.

(c) *It seems strange that some of the other teachers having contact with the girl failed to appreciate her worth. This would seem to be especially true where at least one teacher had in fact spotted unusual signs and would have mentioned them, if only casually one feels, in staff room discussion.*

Her first teacher in the junior school recognized the potential and capabilities and understood her. There was an excellent rapport between our daughter and this woman and she provided the stimulus and motivation and knew how to deal with her. When this teacher left the school, although the rest of the staff knew of our daughter's interests and worth, their own interests were not directly scientific and they did not realize or understand how necessary and in fact vital it was for our daughter to be able to communicate with someone with her deep interest in scientific subjects. Our daughter was looked upon as something slightly 'freakish' with her unusual interests and ability and had to contend with the daily diet of English, arithmetic, geography, history, domestic studies and games. There was no science on the timetable even of the most elementary type. There were no men on the staff. Our daughter is a nonconformist and no one would satisfactorily undertake to cater for her needs. Consequently she became frustrated to the point of opting out.

Our daughter has the rather unendearing habit at times of persisting in her questioning until she is satisfied with the answer and on quite a few occasions severely strained the patience of the teachers and at the same time badly threatened their status with her questions.

She was given a project to do on William Blake whom she regarded as 'soppy', poetic and to her totally uninteresting. During her research on him she became engrossed in the mechanics of his copper engraving and his use of chemicals. Because of this scientific link Blake was no longer dismissed. Having become involved in the subject the man became 'alive' and her interest was in fact widened beyond the narrow scientific. However, without the scientific nucleus this broadening of education would not have been possible. The poetry and language of Blake still hold no interest but she now appreciates and acknowledges the brilliance of the man himself and is now more willing to tolerate his works, whereas before he was rejected.

Although this child will turn any lesson into a science lesson if given the opportunity, this tendency is one which might well be utilized in reverse by teachers in the interests of a broader education.

It is appropriate, if a little out of context at this point, to consider how far it is true that gifted children present special problems to teachers. In the face of such cases as the previous one described, and of course others cited elsewhere in this report, it is hard not to conclude that they do; and that such problems are not confined to difficulties of recognition only. Obviously in some sense all children present special problems simply because they are individuals; but to state further that outstanding children present types of imbalance which require particular attention is hardly to detract from the worth of others who may not possess this kind of 'advantageous handicap'. In order to assess the sensitivity of the profession to this problem, and incidentally to strengthen the case for stating that there is a felt problem of giftedness in our schools, item B.1 (i) was included in the questionnaire. The results are given in table 4.2. Teachers were asked if they agreed or disagreed with the proposition that gifted children present special problems to teachers.

Table 4.2 Gifted children as special problems: item B.1 (i)

	No reply	Emphatically agree				Emphatically disagree	Qualified reply
	n %	n % n % n % n % n %					n %
B.1 (i)	8 2	183 49 138 37 18 5 15 4 5 1					3 1

It is possible to interpret the findings from this question as implying simply that all children present special problems to all teachers, and that this is why nearly everybody agrees with the statement. In our view this is to ignore the general context in which the question was asked and we conclude that the very great majority of teachers feel that gifted children present a certain class of problems which are worthy of study in their own right. That such study might have beneficial spin-off effects which benefit all children is clearly a point of some importance, albeit at a subsidiary level, and teachers were asked if they agreed that this was so. The results are tabulated in 4.3.

Table 4.3 Special attention and its spin-off effects: Item B.1 (vi)

	No reply	Emphatically agree				Emphatically disagree	Qualified reply
	n %	n % n % n % n % n %					n %
B.1 (vi)	11 3	68 18 140 38 90 24 45 12 15 4					1 0

In view of the relatively large proportion of teachers who were not wholly in agreement with this apparently straightforward proposition, the findings are analysed further in table 4.4.

This analysis suggests that the more responsible and more experienced teachers anticipate spin-off to a somewhat greater extent than those with fewer responsibilities and less experience. On the whole, however, it seems possible that a number of teachers have reservations akin to those of administrators quoted earlier as being somewhat sceptical of the appropriateness of 'special' treatment; and that this makes them reluctant to consider possible spin-off from policies which in themselves receive only qualified approval. However this may be, it is important to notice in conclusion that only a very small proportion of the group express positive disagreement and thus anticipate that no beneficial results would accrue to children of every type.

Table 4.4 Special attention and its spin-off effects: a further analysis by teaching experience, level of responsibility, type and size of school

		No reply		Emphatically agree/approve		agree/approve		disagree/disapprove		Emphatically disagree/disapprove		Qualified reply				Totals	
		n	%	n	%	n	%	n	%	n	%	n	%	n	%	n	%
Teaching Experience	No information	0	0	5	16	13	42	7	23	5	16	1	3	0	0	31	8·4
	0–4 years	6	11	7	13	18	32	14	25	7	13	4	7	0	0	56	15·1
	5–9 years	3	3	13	15	34	39	26	30	9	10	3	3	0	0	88	23·8
	10+ years	1	1	43	25	63	37	38	22	19	11	7	4	1	1	172	46·5
																(347)	
Level of Responsibility	No information	0	0	4	36	4	36	1	9	2	18	0	0	0	0	11	3·0
	Headteachers	0	0	17	22	40	51	17	22	3	4	1	1	0	0	78	21·1
	Deputy heads	1	3	5	13	17	14	9	23	4	10	3	8	0	0	39	10·5
	Assistants	10	5	42	19	67	30	58	26	31	14	11	5	1	0	220	59·5
																(348)	
Type of school	Infants	4	7	15	27	19	34	8	14	9	16	1	2	0	0	56	15·1
	Juniors	3	2	21	16	44	34	41	32	13	10	7	5	1	1	130	35·1
	Middle	2	9	2	9	10	43	4	17	3	13	2	9	0	0	23	6·2
	Infant/junior	2	2	29	25	42	36	28	24	13	11	4	3	0	0	118	31·0
	Preparatory	0	0	1	5	12	60	4	20	2	10	1	5	0	0	20	5·4
																(347)	
Size of school	0–99	0	0	7	25	15	54	5	18	1	4	0	0	0	0	28	7·6
	100+	1	4	5	19	7	27	11	42	1	4	1	4	0	0	26	7·0
	200+	3	3	15	16	37	41	18	20	15	16	3	3	0	0	91	24·6
	300+	3	6	9	17	18	35	14	27	5	10	3	6	0	0	52	14·1
	400+	3	3	16	17	33	36	20	22	14	15	6	6	0	0	92	24·9
	500+	1	2	16	28	17	29	17	29	4	7	3	3	1	2	58	15·7
																(347)	
Totals:		11	3	68	18	140	38	90	24	45	12	15	4	1	0	370	100

Note: (i) Category 2 includes one psychologist
(ii) Total group includes a set of students

The above comments form something of an interpolation within this discussion of scientific talent and its recognition. The fact that science seems often to fascinate very able children of certain types makes it imperative that the particular case study recounted here be examined in some detail with regard to its more general implications. It will be necessary to refer to it again: meantime sufficient has been said to demonstrate that problems of recognition and provision are very closely intertwined. Some teachers may well feel that this child's scientific bent is more a product of bias in the home environment than in any innate preferences, and that the school ought to compensate for rather than encourage such one-sided development. Without an awareness of the difficulties such children experience however, and regardless of the precise causes of their apparently one-sided interests, there is a grave risk that their problems can be shrugged off as purely parentally inspired. It is moreover, important to realize in this context that to warrant the term 'outstanding' as applied to any specific field almost certainly entails that the child can be accused of possessing a one-sided set of interests. The following description of the gifted child scientist can usefully be considered from this point of view:[6]

Provided that the child has been given a rich environment, at home and/or at school, I would expect a high ability in science to have become manifest by the age of nine, by some of the following signs:

(i) A natural interest and ability in mathematics, together with a high power of reasoning.

(ii) An intense interest in natural objects, mechanical objects, and/or natural phenomena, followed by the patience necessary to acquire mechanical skills in order to carry out investigations. The ability to initiate and complete investigations into problems.

(iii) An intense curiosity in a variety of living things, possibly followed by the perseverance necessary to collect and classify one or more of these groups. Patience in observing and recording behaviour of living things.

The ability to use books would be necessary for much of this work.

It is further interesting to compare what is said in general with a specific report from a teacher about one of his pupils showing an enthusiasm for science:

She scored 122 on an NFER V21 test administered in November. Internal school ratings gave her attainment as 123. Maths and discovery grades are better than English by an average of five points.

She tries very hard at *everything* she does—even games and PE which she finds most difficult. Some time ago she had surgical treatment to her left leg and was re-admitted to the infant department after a period of home tuition. She still experiences slight difficulty in movement due to her leg condition.

An outgoing personality, she shows a consistent mature attitude to her work. She is able to plan her own weekly timetable and stick to it! She is meticulous to a fault, becoming unhappy if everything is not as it should be—she likes to 'organize' other people.

Partly because of her slow movements she tends to be a 'lone wolf' from preference although she is fairly popular and could join various groups of girls is she so wished.

Her home background is working class. Her father is a mechanic, mother does not work. She is an only child; the parents encourage her without pressurizing.

The class had experienced relatively little work in science before this year. I believe that her success in this field arises from three main sources:

(*a*) She has an enquiring mind and enjoys asking questions and attempting to find the answers for herself—this often involves experimentation.

(*b*) She is very painstaking—nothing is too much trouble, and she is patient enough to wait for results.

(*c*) Choice of experience to further definite objectives has kept her interest and provided continuous challenge.

The parallels between these two quite independently produced descriptions, the one as an attempt at generalization and the other a portrait of one individual, are sufficiently striking to demonstrate the usefulness of both case studies and behavioural criteria check-lists in sharpening our powers of recognition.

ENGLISH

The comments of the Schools Council English Subject Committee serve as a useful introduction to this section on the recognition of able 'verbalists'. They write:

Pupils particularly gifted in the range of activities described as 'English' should, it was generally accepted, be catered for within the resources of their own schools. So many of these activities are highly individual that it should be possible to make available to the gifted child the range of reading and written work from which he is capable of benefiting. Another point which was made was that a facility with language implies a marked ability to organize and integrate experience which will show itself across many aspects of the primary school curriculum. It is not likely that a primary school child will be gifted in English alone.

It seems likely that 'English' is here interpreted as having a wider base than some study groups envisaged. They propose the following characteristics under the rubric 'English':

  (i) Verbal fluency and originality
 (ii) Verbal facility; a wide vocabulary
(iii) Memory and feeling for words
 (iv) Delight in words: capacity for analogical thinking
  (v) Absorption in books

(vi) Intellectual response to precision in the use of words

(vii) Linguistic ability

This list may be related to the following case studies which are selected as having demonstrated some kind of verbal ability and as being of wider importance.

CASE STUDY 29 (PARENTS)

Agencies involved in recognition

(a) Mother.

(b) Stanford-Binet test administered by qualified educational psychologist with 25 years' experience—IQ = 148 (CA—4y 8m; MA 6y 10m).

Behaviour leading to recognition

(a) Superior baby from the start. Just slept and fed for the first three months. Then later he was very contented as long as he was occupied when awake and he very seldom cried. Crawled at six months and so was never bored.

(b) Entered morning play school at two years two months but at three and half his mother realized he had derived most of the benefit he could from this source and she was worried how to extend his mind until school entry.

(c) Long periods of rapt concentration most marked.

(d) Determination and persistence to master situations.

(e) Mother finally took action when at three years seven months without prior teaching of writing (although he could read) he sat down and from across the room copied quite legibly a sentence written on the blackboard for his elder brother.

Age at which recognition becomes fairly certain

Three years seven months.

Educational difficulties and hypothetical causes

(a) No provision for a child when he is too old for play school mentally but chronologically too young for school.

(b) On school entry a fortnight ago (age at four years eight months) he was immediately abnormal for he was several (3) books ahead of the next brightest child in the school reading scheme but he has settled quite happily to reading children's books from the public library instead of the readers usually provided.

CASE STUDY 30 (PARENTS)

Agencies involved in recognition

Both my husband and I have considered our daughter to be a very intelligent child right from the time she was a few months old. Her teachers, too, have all been impressed by her academic ability.

Behaviour leading to recognition

Our daughter seemed to be born with the inbuilt idea that night was for sleeping (she slept 6 or 7 hours a night right from birth) and daytime for doing things. She slept little during the day but she did not cry when awake. We would often put her in the middle of the playpen (as we lived in the tropics and this was cooler than a carry-cot) and she would lie there watching intently all that was going on in the room. She sat up unaided at just 5 months, both crawled and walked round the furniture at 7 months and walked unaided at just 10 months. By her first birthday she was running around just as well as her brother, who is 18 months older than she is. She also started talking at about this time. The first real sign of precocity came at the age of 18 months, when she persisted in walking about holding a cloth bag containing letters of the alphabet. She kept repeating both her initial and her name while doing this so we undid the string and tipped out the letters, whereupon she selected the initial letter of her name from this bag of over 40 letters.

Age at which recognition became fairly certain
My daughter was two and a half years old when her brother started kindergarten and on his first day at school, she being used to his company seemed at a loss, so I offered to read to her. She brought me the Ladybird Book 1A and said she would read to me instead. To my surprise she read right through the book, but as I was uncertain whether she was reading or 'remembering words and pictures' from her brother's reading I went out and bought Book 1B which had only just then been published. This I knew had the same words but different pictures. She immediately read that right through! The next day we went on to Book 2A and then I bought Book 2B. She knew most of the book and in fact, made quite rapid progress through the series up to Books 9A and B, when the print seemed too small and the contents too mature for her. By the time she started kindergarten at three and a half years she was a fluent reader and her teacher said it was the only time she had had a class in which she could allow one of the children to read to the others instead of doing so herself.

Educational difficulties etc.
Our daughter is nearly 8 years old and has had no apparent major educational difficulties but she has been fortunate in that she has always been ahead of her age group. She was accepted by the private kindergarten at three and a half years though they normally prefer pupils to start at 4 years. She spent two terms in the nursery class and began formal lessons at $4\frac{1}{4}$ years. When she was $5\frac{1}{4}$ years we moved and she went into the top group of the top of two middle infant classes. She went into top infants at $6\frac{1}{4}$ and when she was moved to the junior department she was placed in the second year juniors instead of the first year. She is tall for her age and socially as well as academically advanced and fits in well. There are two or three other very able children of her own age in the same class. I feel it is only because she has been 'ahead' that we have had no problem with her. I can envisage considerable difficulties in trying to fit her into her own age group.

CASE STUDY 31 (SCHOOL)

Talent : Use of the written word both story-form and descriptive.

Manifested itself for example (i) passion for writing, (ii) reading advanced literature: Tolstoy's 'War and Peace' (9 years).

Criticism: I'm enjoying it but too many characters to keep track of. (My feelings precisely).

General academic ability—good.

Craft—restricted in imagination but well produced.

Physical—distinct lack of interest at the beginning of 3rd year. Great change at the end but talent limited. (He enjoyed the games period.)

Social: Apparent close friendship with boy who was a 'top boy' but an introvert. When this friendship broke up rather precious Frederick became Fred and much more socially acceptable to his peers. Previously his friends were girls who mothered him somewhat—although as he matured he developed an attractive personality and the attraction altered slightly.

English: Well above average—outstanding vocabulary. Very good descriptive writer—he developed a wonderful imagination. Consequently his stories were well written and full of interest.

Not a quick worker but his work was beautifully presented.

Well read, a good memory and sound general knowledge. Enjoyed drama—wrote extremely good poetry.

CASE STUDY 32 (PARENTS)

Firstly, she started to talk at a very early age, i.e. 9 months and by 12 months had a large vocabulary. She started putting words together and at about 15–18 months was using pronouns correctly. At 18 months I remember her asking for 'orange juice and whizzy water' and going to the soda siphon to get it. At 20 months she spent her first morning in nursery school and by this time was equal to any 3-year-old in being able to converse and make her requirements known; she was also able to use the nursery equipment, was never shy, had very little dependence on her mother as she had already realized the interesting things were in the places where mother did not go! At 2 years when she was going to nursery regularly she knew all the nursery rhymes but seemed also to understand the meanings of the words in them. She collected new words avidly and quickly put them into use but rarely got them in the wrong context. By the time she was reading fluently at 4 years it was quite obvious she had complete understanding of the words she was reading, as the expression she put into reading was remarkable. She never had phantoms, but for the last 2 or 3 years she has set up dramatic situations for herself at home, sometimes using dolls and toys, and occasionally and if available a willing younger sister. In these situations she carries out all sorts of conversations, using what she thinks is a suitable voice and suitable vocabulary for each participant. For example, she will set up a classroom and be the teacher as well as each child in turn. Sometimes the situation will be a foreign country and each participant has to have a name appropriate to the country, e.g. France and a lot of French names. This week it is India—know any Indian girls' names? These stories and dialogues are never written down, but are always spontaneous and spoken though never recorded.

For a long time, up till quite recently in fact, she would carry out long conversations after she went to bed and had no light at all. She called it 'playing her games'. This took the form of conversations between various people, especially the teacher and the children in her class, and she would use what she considered the appropriate voice and dialogue. She would not go to sleep until she had finished 'the game' which would last usually about one hour, sometimes two, and she became distressed if cut short or prevented from doing this.

Her written work, which is only done when compulsory, i.e. at school, has a very marked style, often controversial, and frequently intentionally humorous.

Without wishing to generalize in any strict sense from these few cases, it is nevertheless worth noting that children with high verbal ability are likely to find the ordinary school environment congenial, and it may be that here is the basis for the contention by some teachers that recognition is quite efficient. Children with verbal talent are not however always keen to write: they quite often prefer simply to talk. This could be the cause of difficulty in a number of cases and is exemplified in a very extreme form by the following instance:

It is understandable that from the previous child study there was some difficulty in reconciling what might on the surface appear to be contradictory facts. The following rather detailed account of the sequence of events is by way of explanation and clarification.

The first indication of writing difficulty was when we received the first completed writing book with teacher's comments. This would be near to the end of the first term in school. The class teacher assured me that there was nothing we could do to help him at home. Eventually another writing book appeared with more teacher comment.

About half way through the second term whilst seeing the teacher about another matter I enquired about the child's writing progress. This opened the floodgates. Having made the child sit alone on a table separate from his group she then refused to allow him to go into PE until he finished that day's writing, kept him in at break and finally sent him to the head teacher, with good and bad samples of work, to be reprimanded.

I felt this treatment was rather harsh for a child so young, after so short a time in school, but not wishing to aggravate the situation, refrained from any comment. I did also feel a certain amount of sympathy for the teacher, who complained of [the child's] frequent loss of belongings, particularly his pencil, and lapses into daydreaming, which can be very irritating. However, judging the child to be bright she concluded that he could write, as indeed he had produced good results on occasion, and interpreted his unwillingness as stubbornness.

Even though the child was having frequent attacks of vomiting at this point we did not connect the two. Shortly after this hospitalization was recommended and after two weeks of intensive tests and observations 'abdominal migraine caused by the stress of life' was diagnosed.

I should explain that over this period the child's whole personality was undergoing a change. He was gradually becoming more withdrawn and was finding it more and more difficult to mix socially with other children, both at home and in school. In the end he complained of being rejected by the children in the playground at school and at home wandered from window to window watching the neighbour's children play, but nothing would persuade him to join them. There had been no such difficulty experienced during the pre-school years.

After the hospital verdict we began to suspect a link between the writing difficulty and this violent stress reaction. However, we did nothing positive as there was no proof and we knew that attacks of this kind could be triggered off by many causes both physical and emotional. However we were still concerned, knowing that the child was not behaving normally.

Then, after visiting the school on parents' evening, we were informed that the child would be returning to the same class teacher the following year. It was this prospect that finally prompted me to consult a friend, who was an experienced educational psychologist, to find out if I was worrying unnecessarily. She assured me that there were grounds for concern and drew my attention to the fact that I could request the head teacher for referral to the School Psychological Service.

This I did and it was at this point that the head teacher, feeling resentful at the inference that the problem had been intensified by lack of understanding on the part of the school, turned the tables and questioned me on possible causes in the home. I considered her questions reasonable and answered as honestly as possible. Even expressing my own desire to find out if, in fact, the migraine could have been unwittingly caused by some home circumstance did not weaken her resolution against referral. The interview ended with the head teacher promising to reconsider in a year's time, if there was no sign of improvement.

Naturally, I considered the outcome of the interview to be unsatisfactory and that the welfare of the child was more important than the wounded pride of the head teacher, who was incidentally newly appointed and comparatively inexperienced. I, therefore, appealed to my friend to make a private investigation. It was this that revealed the child to be gifted, emotionally disturbed and that there was a reason for the writing difficulty.

In the face of this indisputable evidence the head teacher climbed down completely and offered help in any way possible. However, after due consideration we decided that it was important that the child had a fresh start away from an atmosphere in which he had been so unhappy. Our previous experience of the school had not given us any grounds for feeling confident about their ability to cope with the situation. By this time the child had been nicknamed 'slowcoach', and naturally this had been taken up by all the children. Transfer to another state school had been eliminated because of the local practice of zoning.

These comments by a parent were in response to questions put to her by the project director as a consequence of his reading the original case description. The child scores 167 IQ (Terman-Merrill L–M), but it will be remarked that the teachers concerned recognized this boy's ability and fell, very understandably, into the trap of assuming that ability in one or two fields implied that failure elsewhere could only be due to laziness. The teachers involved deserve, and should receive, nothing but sympathetic understanding: only the enthusiastic teacher who feels a strong personal engagement in her children's progress is likely to become involved in a case of this kind. These circumstances serve again to underpin what was said earlier about the possibility that able children can create very special problems of recognition and treatment, the nature of which might escape even teachers of long experience in the absence of close acquaintance. Since this must always, in the nature of things, be quite fortuitous, a vicarious introduction through the citation of illustrative case studies is urgently required (cf. p. 61).

As a conclusion to this section, a report from one member of a study group demonstrates that recognition of a talent in 'English' is probably more effective when not based on any assumptions about the generality of the capability being assessed. She writes:

One of the most interesting results came from a girl aged 11 years 1 month (tested on SRA P.M. Abilities). She scored very highly on Verbal, Perception and Spatial but in Number and Reasoning her results were only 72 and 86.
. . . On reading her teacher's assessment I note that he mentions spatial ability being above average and her reasoning to be shrewd and calculating. I know that this child has ability, is volatile and that her concentration and effort vary in intensity. She enjoys reading and writing [she is fluent] revels in words, and writes poetry even without realizing that she is doing so.

DRAMA

The behavioural features associated with this particular aspect of the expressive arts are perhaps the most readily evident to teachers. They almost always include the following:
  (i) Empathy with the experience of others
  (ii) A degree of exhibitionism or extroversion
  (iii) High levels of verbal expression
  (iv) Powerful imaginative involvement in other people's lives
  (v) An ability to 'lose' identity
  (vi) A romantic view coupled with a harsher realism
  (vii) A good memory for words
  (viii) A lack of self-consciousness or an ability to overcome it

MATHEMATICS

The particular context within which evidence regarding the recognition of mathematical talent may be discussed is best described by the Schools Council Mathematical Committee's comments below:

It was agreed to interpret 'gifted children' as comprising those pupils who are at the very top end of the full ability range for their age group; they are the best of the ablest pupils.
    Where one draws the line between the gifted and the very able is a moot point. Are the former a race apart, or is it a question of degree of ability only? Is there

a real qualitative difference between the able child, who may have developed a high degree of mathematical competence because of his high general intelligence, energy and ambition, and the gifted child who reveals an early flair and creativity in mathematics? Some suggest that approximately 2 per cent of the children could be designated gifted in this particular sense; others, 5 per cent. Whatever the percentage—probably higher than originally thought—it is an arbitrary one; we have to remind ourselves that the gifted child and the very able child have a moral right to the fulfilment of their latent abilities both for their own sake and that of society at large—the country can ill afford to lose exceptional quality of this kind.

There have always been a number of children in primary schools who, when given the opportunity, have developed mathematically very quickly and at an early age. In the past the needs of such pupils have not always been fully met; their work has been lacking in challenge and too limited in scope. To-day, with the liberalization of primary school mathematics, both in content and approach, and with the abolition of some of the traditional selection examinations, schools are in a better position to provide education suitable to the varied needs of their pupils. This unfortunately does not always obtain and the gifted child, who immediately concerns us here, may be an extremely vulnerable phenomenon. The statement that able children can take care of themselves is misleading: it may be true that mathematically able children can fend for themselves better than the less able but this does not mean they should be entirely responsible for their own programming; they are not sufficient unto themselves—they need guidance, encouragement and the right kind of opportunities and challenges to fulfil their promise. One suspects that exceptional mathematical flair is not always recognized and properly nourished in the primary school, and that it is stifled in its early years for lack of appropriate stimulation.

How does one recognize the gifted child in mathematics? Gauss revealed his genius at a very tender age through his gift for quick mental calculation. But not all mathematical geniuses have shown precocity; history does not tell us that Newton showed early manifestations of his mathematical talents—this, however, could be due to the fact that they passed unnoticed. Whether mathematical ability is correlated with precocity or not the important fact for schools is that high mathematical ability can, and often does show itself at a young age; it therefore behoves teachers to be careful, not to assume that no child should do any work other than what is normally done—they must not hold back able children because they have read a little Piaget!

Mathematical ability will show itself, when given opportunity, by its fruits. The gifted child learns quickly, understands easily, and will frequently reveal uncanny insight and intuition; he possesses a great deal of mental energy, persistence, stickability, and mathematical flair—he is often internally motivated to a high degree and is not so dependent on the spur of external reward as are some less able children. He shows flexibility in his thinking; originality and resource and develops reflective ways of thinking which in due course grow into powers of deep abstraction. He may not be orally very articulate but this should not be misconstrued; periods of silence are not necessarily periods of dumb mental inertia—they could well be reflective spells of mental incubation!

Facility in the use of the spoken word is not necessarily evidence of depth of thinking in mathematics!

The obvious importance of mathematics in the school curriculum, and the fact that certain young children reveal a very early facility with numbers, are factors making for the ready recognition of mathematical talent. Many case studies can be cited which note behaviours that are probably indicative of a potential mathematician; and it is economical therefore merely to list those descriptions which are most relevant from this point of view.

CASE STUDY EXTRACTS: THE BEHAVIOURAL CRITERIA OF
MATHEMATICAL TALENT

(i) His school work varies between good marks for subjects which he likes and appalling marks for those which do not interest him.

(ii) Rules regarding neatness and desk tidyness were a cause of friction between teachers and child.

(iii) Keen interest in a book of mathematical games.

(iv) An enthusiasm for electrical apparatus: no interest in ready made toys [but] is still (9 years) drawn to constructive toys (he preferred not to follow the illustrated assembly sketches but to make up his own models from the parts).

(v) (School report) 'generally acknowledged to have ability and one who is just as renowned for his lack of industry. He must snap out of his lack-a-daisical ways . . . has a temper and a sense of humour'.

(vi) Always enjoyed arithmetic; could count groupings at $3\frac{1}{2}$ years.

(vii) Scores well at card games even with adults ($9\frac{1}{2}$ years).

(viii) Went shopping for himself at 3 years of age.

(ix) Asked questions about how long division 'worked' at 4 years.

(x) Spontaneously sits down to calculate [e.g.] how many seconds he has to live until he is 20 years old.

(xi) Inclined to make arithmetical mistakes.

(xii) Sees what is required in a mathematical problem—at nine years he can tackle arithmetical problems which boggle a large proportion of adults.

(xiii) Early (6 years) awareness of approximations for 86×21 etc. Could work out answers mentally before he knew how to write them out.

(xiv) Sees relationships between mathematical patterns and geometrical shapes.

(xv) At 5 years attempted to count to a million by writing down the number he had reached every time he had to stop for a meal or bed. How he learnt to write such numbers is a mystery but he had counted for a week and was approaching the half a million mark when he lost the paper with the number on and decided not to continue in case he missed some out! Until 9 years his handwriting, writing of figures, ability to draw lines etc., was not very good . . . he made careless mistakes in calculations.

(xvi) Practised Bach Minuet in G . . . on spur of moment transposed into the key of F.

(xvii) Understood reversibility of addition and subtraction at $3\frac{1}{2}$ years.

(xviii) Revealed an understanding of cogwheel ratios at $6\frac{3}{4}$ years.
(xix) Preference for mental work; rarely seeks pencil and paper.
(xx) Quickly bored by easy and repetitive work.
(xxi) A relatively poor memory for rote type learning.
(xxii) A remarkable power of perseverance and concentration on (say) a jig-saw puzzle (100 pieces at $2\frac{1}{2}$ years).

Although it has perhaps now been implied that the recognition of mathematical talent is easy, even in the pre-school years, this would not be a correct inference. The home backgrounds of our case studies are invariably in some sense mathematical, and it may be that what was said about music has a greater application in mathematics than is generally suspected. How far potential mathematical talent is submerged in some homes is simply unknown, as was noted in more general terms earlier; but even disregarding this problem, there is no doubt that some children present behavioural patterns which are both intriguing and disconcerting. Consider the following comments which refer to a child with measured IQ about 170.

(*a*) Examples of work in number lessons:
(i) $3 \times 6 = 20 - 2$ (when teacher expects 18)
$$7 \times 7 = 94$$
$$£\frac{3}{4} = 57p$$
(ii) Lays out sums in a border round the page.
(iii) On occasions adds tens and units diagonally so that
$$31 + 46 = 95.$$
(*b*) Appears to reject all forms of formal teaching—he does not read for information—will not accept any given rule e.g. 'We start in the units row . . .' he will begin with the hundreds if it so pleases him. If asked for the rule in setting down subtraction, will reply 'put the smaller number at the bottom' if he thinks teacher intends, 'put larger number at the top'.
(*c*) Most of the time his 'original' thinking is hopelessly inadequate.

Has this child any real mathematical ability? Is the educational system geared to find out and advise the teachers involved, and of course the parents, on what should be done?

Finally it has to be remembered that the work of Professor Bowker was referred to earlier, and that his experience would seem to show somewhat unexpected individual differences in the way mathematical talent reveals itself. He writes:[7]

'There seems to be not just one way of being mathematically gifted. Some were specially gifted with numbers, others were good at logic, others still at geometry etc. Their attitudes to mathematics were also very different. About half of them enjoyed mathematics and sought to learn more. The other half were confused and could not understand the kind of mathematics they had been taught at school. Only by occasional insights were they distinguishable from the mathematically incapable.'

ENVIRONMENTAL STUDIES; PROJECTS; CENTRES OF INTEREST

Activities which occur under the various headings indicated above present a peculiar difficulty in any context of recognition. Unfortunately, it is a difficulty which cannot be ignored since these activities are tending to occupy a progressively increasing proportion of curriculum time. The difficulty, briefly, is that of establishing developmental standards in activities which appear to be valued for their 'process' rather than their 'product'. Proponents of such activities usually justify them on several grounds, the most important of which relates to the greater degree of individualization which is said to be possible. Thus, it is argued that gifted children benefit greatly from project work. They escape the 'lock step' curriculum; they pursue their own interests; they can study more widely and deeply than would otherwise be the case; there are no brakes on developmental rates, there are no barriers to maximum progress. They can even engage in them in spare time.

But we have to ask ourselves not merely whether there are no barriers in the most obvious sense, but also whether more subtle obstacles to maximum progress can arise. It has been shown that recognition of ability is essential if a child is to be encouraged to work in ways commensurate with his capabilities. It has been suggested that teacher expectation may be a powerful determinant of what a child, however gifted, will achieve. But both recognition and the construction of realistic expectations become formidable tasks in situations where different children are doing very different assignments in terms of content. The position is even more complex when the same child is doing work on widely dissimilar contents successively, as is of course usually the case.

It was put to us by one of the study groups that here we have one reason why recognition of the gifted is far more difficult in the modern classroom than has been the case in times past. Where different individuals spend much of their time doing different things, comparisons which are essential for the recognition of standards which are themselves the basis of expectation, recognition, and the construction of a developmental curriculum, are almost impossible.

And yet, the attempt has to be made unless there is a consensus of view that all children can and will progress at optimum rates, given only an opportunity to engage in project work. Even then, it seems likely that most teachers would prefer to base their learning situations on more than an act of faith; and, acting in accordance with this assumption, the problem will be raised again in Part II when the provisions made by teachers can be examined in terms of the ways standards are set for individual children (Ch. 7, p. 180 ff).

Conclusions to Part 1

In Part I the basic assumptions underlying the present enquiry have been stated; and the consequences in terms of recognizing gifted children and determining their fundamental needs have been outlined. An attempt has been made to provide case studies and describe certain views of teachers which taken together comprise basic data.

The findings of the study cited so far are seen to be of interest with regard to problems of both recognition and provision: recognition and provision have been shown to be merely different faces of one coin.

Our purpose has also been to suggest that only the complacent or biased can deny the existence of problems of giftedness; and that these problems are no more, and no less, than an important aspect of those teaching difficulties which are enshrined perhaps in the phrase 'the individualization of learning'. It thus becomes clear that the next stage in the inquiry must concern itself with two broad questions:

1   Under what conditions can the individualization of learning be said to be maximal?

2   How far do present circumstances approach the ideal and what would appear to constitute the major obstacles to further progress?

The goal of Part II is to provide some bases for the formulation of answers to these questions.

Notes

1   The information in this section was kindly provided in some instances by the Schools Council Music Committee.

2   Royal College of Music, Oct. 3, 1970.

3   We are grateful to Mr John Horton of the Schools Council Music Committee for drawing attention to this list and supplying his own comment on item 4.

4   *Daily Telegraph*, Feb. 23, 1971.

5   We are greatly indebted to HMI T. C. Keay and Mr K. Jameson for their constructions here.

6   We are indebted to Dr A. Little and his ILEA colleague for this description.

7   NAGC Newsletter, 1971.

Part II

Present policies,
provisions and practices

5 The individualization of learning

In the social sciences it is widely accepted that no understanding can be total, no theory all-embracing; and hence that all research even of the most modest factual kind must be biased. The questions to be asked, and the nature of the 'facts' to be uncovered, are to a great extent predetermined by the predilections of the researchers. They do not derive from some already existing body of objective data, they reflect a value judgement.

It is imperative therefore briefly to outline the concepts of individualization which guided the conduct of the present enquiry. As will become evident, not every element of provision has been treated in similar or sufficient detail, nor is any order of importance indicated or implied. It is possible, even probable, that the particular aspects of practice and provision which receive attention in the following chapters are not wholly those to which others would attribute great importance. Nevertheless, selection is an inescapable prerequisite of study inexorably thrust upon us by the exigencies of time as well as philosophy, and in the absence of further justification the principles upon which such selection is based require at least some explanation.

The concept of individualization

To some teachers the term individualization conjures up nothing more than the idea of a one-to-one pupil-teacher ratio. The problem of individualization is then reduced quite simply to one of impossible finance, and the degree of individualization inherent in the educational system can be quite precisely measured. All that is necessary is to divide the school day by the number of pupils, and lo! we discover that the primary school child on average is 'individualized' for a mere eight minutes per day.

This position cannot be dismissed as mere amusement. The project director personally experienced contact with some teachers who were prepared to state that all the ills of primary education are due wholly and solely to the very high pupil-teacher ratio, and that if only this were suitably reduced then every other problem would be solved.

The great majority of teachers, needless to say, adopt a more reasoned and balanced view; but it has to be stated, if it were not self-evident anyhow, that the individualization of learning does indeed depend upon the pupil-teacher ratio, and that all other advances would be greatly facilitated by an improvement at this crucial point. Items B.1 (iii) and B.1 (iv) findings imply that this is the case in the views of teachers, and the results of item B.2 (ix) confirm it, as shown in table 5.1.

B.1 (iii) As much attention should be given to 'gifted' children as is now given to those recognized as 'disadvantaged'

(iv) Many gifted children are disadvantaged by not being allowed to progress according to their ability

B.2 (ix) Failure to recognize potential giftedness [is a condition harmful to the development of giftedness]

Table 5.1 Individualization and the pupil-teacher ratio: items B.1 (iii), B.1 (iv) and B.2 (ix)

	No reply n %	Emphatically agree n %	n %	n %	n %	Emphatically disagree n %	Qualified reply n %
B.1 (iii)	5 1	229 62	89 24	23 6	16 4	6 2	2 1
B.1 (iv)	14 4	161 44	129 35	27 7	21 6	8 2	10 3
B.2 (ix)	8 2	279 75	60 16	12 3	6 2	2 1	3 1

The relevant contingency coefficients are given in table 5.2; in these and all the following tables a low contingency coefficient indicates a high correlation.

Table 5.2 Contingency coefficients related to table 5.1

Items	χ^2	C	(6 df)
B.1 (iii) + B.1 (iv)	30·07	0·198	(<0·001)
B.1 (iii) + B.2 (ix)	21·46	0·168	(<0·01)
B.2 (ix) + B.1 (iv)	79·94	0·312	(<0·001)

It appears from 5.2 that the association between B.1 (iii) and B.2 (ix) is stronger than that between B.1 (iv) and B.2 (ix). In no case of course is there anything approaching complete agreement, since all chi-squares are highly significant; nonetheless it is clear that almost the whole of the profession are deeply concerned about the pupil-teacher ratio and one reason is that under present conditions many gifted children are not being allowed to progress according to their ability.

There is some danger that since the profession's response to a question on pupil-teacher ratios is so highly predictable, there will be a strong tendency for the findings here to be discounted and dismissed. Just as some teachers protect themselves against any need even to re-examine their practices, much less change them, by saying nothing can be done unless the ratio is reduced; so others will point out that here we are merely discovering the obvious, and thereby hope to divert attention from the fundamental truth that whatever proposals may be put forward in the following sections, they must all in some significant way require change. We are concerned not to minimize and understress the fact that such change will be facilitated greatly by any reduction in pupil-teacher ratio, but it also has to be realized that this, of itself, will not guarantee an increased measure of individualization unless it is made clear what is meant by this educational goal.[1] Can it be true, for example, that the education of individuals is not education for individuality?

Individualized rates of learning: restrictive factors

The sphere of individual differences which has received most attention traditionally is probably that of learning rate: some children were expected to learn faster than others and arrangements were made for them to do so. It is these arrangements to which attention has been directed in our study of practices and provisions. In this preliminary section teachers' views in relation to aspects especially concerned with the encouragement of different rates of progress will be examined as an essential background to a review of present conditions.

It has already been shown that many teachers feel children tend not to have the opportunity to learn at optimal individual rates (p. 110). A number of items in the questionnaire were intended to elicit teachers' opinions as to why this might be so, and the findings are analysed for convenience in a single table, 5.3.

The responses to item B.2 (ii) are perhaps a little surprising since they would seem to imply that teachers feel under some degree of externally imposed inhibition in their attempts to facilitate the development of individual differences. But this is in fact the case; and, as may be seen from the responses to item B.2 (vii), there is by no means the same degree of support for the idea that schools themselves fail to encourage nonconformity. A measure of the difference is given by the values $\chi^2 = 36.80$, $C = 0.218$ (<0.001, 6df). Clearly teachers to some extent see themselves as being unable to individualize as much as they would wish, because of pressures from without the school rather than within.

It is interesting to record that as many as 60 per cent admit that there is an overemphasis on group and class work in the modern primary school. At the same time the logic of this finding is sound enough in that teachers have already criticized the present pupil-teacher ratio. But this is not to say that the degrees of approval for these two items are closely alike; on the contrary, the

Table 5.3 Some conditions inimical to the attainment of optimal learning rates

	No reply		Emphatically agree					Emphatically disagree		Qualified reply	
	n	%	n	%	n	%	n	%	n	%	n	%
B.2 (ii) Social pressures towards conformity	16	4	92	25	157	42	45	12	43	12	13 4	4 1
B.2 (iii) Over-emphasis in group or class work	17	5	98	26	126	34	72	19	44	12	9 2	4 1
B.2 (iv) Anti-intellectualism in the schools	52	14	95	26	100	27	64	17	35	9	14 4	10 3
B.2 (xii) Low expectations by parents and teachers	21	6	177	48	120	32	29	8	15	4	7 2	1 0
B.2 (vii) Failure of schools to encourage nonconformity	36	10	69	19	102	28	72	19	62	17	26 7	3 1

difference is shown by $\chi^2 = 189\cdot89$, $C = 0\cdot452$, and this may be a further indication that a number of teachers who require a lower pupil-teacher ratio have not yet made explicit, even to themselves, just what changes in practice would follow this move.

Item B.2 (iv) was included in the questionnaire in an effort to ascertain how far teachers might feel that recent emphasis particularly in primary schools on other than the traditional academic goals was reducing the urge to bring about maximum rates of achievement in young children. Attention could conceivably be concentrated on concepts like 'mental health', 'expression', 'enjoyment', 'precocity', and so on, at the expense of personal achievement and the attainment of outstanding capabilities. The notion that particular bodies of knowledge as such are of no importance might similarly influence learning rates adversely.

It cannot of course be construed that the line of reasoning above invariably reflects that of the 53 per cent of teachers who felt that some degree of 'anti-intellectualism' exists in our schools. The term itself is perhaps too imprecise for any sound conclusion to be drawn; indeed it may not be without significance that 17 per cent either ignored the item or qualified it. To say that teachers might pursue the matter further with profit is not however to stretch the evidence at all, since only 13 per cent actively deny the possibility.

The most intriguing results in the table are probably those from item B.2 (xii). It is by no means self-evident why 80 per cent of teachers should agree that low expectations are probably a powerful brake on the rate at which children progress. It can be argued with some cogency that all they mean is that low expectations *could be* rather than *are* a brake, but this interpretation probably ignores the general context of the item. Furthermore it fails to take account of the results of item B.1 (iv) (p. 110 above). The close correspondence between the two items is shown by the values $\chi^2 = 10.98$, $C = 0.121$ (ns), and it thus seems certain that teachers believe a good deal more might be demanded of very able children than is often now the case. This opinion, it has to be noted, is strongly held by teachers in infant schools where, it might perhaps have been thought, less dissatisfaction would have been expressed since the children are so young. A complete analysis of item B.2 (xii) is given in the appendix (table a.1) to show the nature of the consensus here apparent.

An examination of table a.1 suggests that:

1   Teachers with responsibility more frequently feel strongly that teachers' and parents' expectations are too low.

2   Teachers of younger children are possibly more self-critical than are others on this point.

3   Teachers in the private sector probably feel a little less vulnerable.

These findings show that teachers envisage a number of restrictive or possibly restrictive factors operating in the schools to retard individual progress. Certain other points must also be borne in mind as the evidence on present provisions is examined. They too can each be seen to influence the efficiency with which a teacher assesses a situation with regard to an individual's learning rate, and hence to govern the efficacy of his intervention. These points are conveniently listed as follows:

(*a*) The extent to which clear developmental patterns are related to age and ability levels.

(*b*) The degree to which such patterns are open-ended, in the sense that there are no artificial barriers to progress.

(*c*) The extent to which continuity is a reality, in that no unnecessary breaks and plateaux occur within the system itself.

(*d*) The accessibility of the required materials and equipment which are associated with different levels of work.

(*e*) The flexibility of work and time scheduling.

(*f*) The amount of class and group activity in relation to time spent on individual assignments.

(*g*) Readiness of access to teachers and other sources of 'expertise' at the appropriate level.

(*h*) The amount of positive encouragement possible within the system, including reinforcement by self evaluation and indirect reference to the teachers.

Facilitating factors

In addition to the pointers indicated in the preceding section, it is further apparent that some educational arrangements might be associated especially with an attempt to maximize individualization of learning rates and facilitate, in effect, the development of individual differences in achievement. Teachers' opinions with regard to these practices are clearly of importance and their responses to the relevant items are analysed in tables a.2 and a.3 in Appendix 5.

DAY RELEASE TO SPECIAL CLASSES

These tables reveal teachers' attitudes towards the idea of arranging for children of different ages to be released from school on a day basis in order to join special classes elsewhere in (say) a local college of education or teachers' centre. The first point which arises in the results is that an unusually large proportion of teachers (about 15 per cent) fail to indicate any views whatsoever with regard to the value of special classes. Why should this be so? It is apparent that many teachers of infants (41 per cent) are refusing to state an opinion about arrangements for 9–13 year olds and, conversely, that teachers of older children (15–22 per cent) are somewhat reluctant to say what conditions might be suited to 5–9 year olds.

The main reason for this action, as expressed verbally, is that 'I have no experience really of older/younger children', but whilst such a position may be accepted sympathetically and with some understanding, it can hardly be condoned. If children really are to be treated as individuals who differ very widely in learning rates, then all teachers must take steps to formulate views not merely about the education of the narrow age range they know well, but also about what should happen both before and after.

Present findings do not even suggest with any certainty that there is less reluctance to view the system *in toto* as teachers gain in experience and responsibility, although there is some indication that headteachers may be more willing to commit themselves. This interpretation may be confirmed by examining the patterns of responses for the other items in section B.3 of the questionnaire, and the zero columns in the tables referred to below will not be discussed further.

Considering now the opinions actually stated, there is a quite a strong consensus against the provision of special classes for 5–8 year olds, since 55 per cent disapprove, to a greater or lesser extent, whereas only 18 per cent approve. The fact that age is a quite crucial factor is shown by the results for 9–13 year olds which effectively reverse the proportions; thus, 58 per cent now approve and 18 per cent disapprove ($\chi^2 = 156 \cdot 05$, $C = 0 \cdot 417$).

With regard to the question as to which teachers disapprove, it would seem that headteachers form the important subgroup here. Certainly a much larger proportion of headteachers disapprove 'most strongly' than appears to be the case even with deputy headteachers; and this is still true with regard to the 9–13 year olds although the actual numbers who object are of course quite small in this case.

As might perhaps be expected, infant teachers approve of special classes for their children less frequently than do others, but it is more forcefully true that teachers in all types of school, with the possible exception of those in middle and preparatory types, disapprove, and this regardless of length of experience.

Almost the reverse is the case for 9–13 year olds; headteachers approve frequently, but do not feel especially strongly in many cases. Curiously enough, whereas many teachers in infant and junior schools would clearly approve the formation of special classes, the middle schools (in so far of course as our group is at all typical) do not hold similar views. Again, length of experience would seem not to have much influence on professional feelings regarding special classes actually held outside the school.

FULL-TIME SUPER-SELECTIVE CLASSES

Opinions regarding this practice were sought in item B.3 (ii) of the questionnaire and the findings are summarized in tables a.4 and a.5 of the appendix. Bearing in mind their opposition to special day release classes, it would be surprising probably if teachers failed to disapprove of full-time super-selective classes. Clearly the results of our investigations amply fulfil our expectations; opposition to these arrangements for 5–9 year olds is stronger than before (73 per cent instead of 55 per cent) and is maintained in some strength for 9–13 year olds as well (47 per cent). Only a mere 8 per cent approve for 5–8 year old children, and fewer than one in three are prepared to consider such permanent arrangements for 9–13 year olds. Nevertheless the trend is again clear. Teachers offer less opposition to segregation as children grow older, and the changing viewpoint is evidenced by $\chi^2 = 73.09$, $C = 0.300$ (<0.001).

Teaching experience as such appears to have no influence on opinions regarding young children. There is some indication that experienced teachers more frequently object most strongly in the case of older children, but this trend is more apparent if levels of responsibility are examined. It thus seems likely that a combination of experience and responsibility brings about an awareness of difficulties associated with the arrangements here being considered. Only infant teachers appear to diverge somewhat from this generalization; but this is likely to be a result of their tending to opt out from expressing a view. Had the questionnaire been a 'forced choice' exercise, it is hardly to be doubted that opposition to full time selective groups across the whole age range of 5–13 year olds would appear even stronger than it is.

In view of the close parallels that might occur between the findings above and those from item B.3 (xii), attention is turned at once to views on streaming.

STREAMING

Evidence regarding teachers' views on streaming is given in tables a.6 and a.7 (p. 231). Considering first the 5–8 year olds it is apparent that opposition to streaming matches that for day release and is weaker than that shown against full-time super-selection. Even though the numbers who disapprove are considerable (58 per cent) it is perhaps a little surprising that a larger proportion did not declare itself against streaming when 5–8 year old children are the only ones involved. It is unlikely to be without significance that headteachers and teachers in purely infant schools evince the strongest feelings on this issue, whereas teachers in preparatory schools are far less committed.

With older children the now familiar pattern is clearly repeated. Some 44 per cent actually approve of this arrangement (cf. 21 per cent, 5–8 years) and opposition falls from 58 per cent to 30 per cent.

Teaching experience has no effect on opinion, nor have the various levels of responsibility. It is noticeable however that nearly all the preparatory school teachers approve of the streaming arrangement, and that there may be some difference of view between teachers in combined infant-junior schools, and those acquainted with a narrower age range. Obviously one possible cause for this difference of opinion, if indeed it exists, might be an increased awareness of individual differences, which are greater perhaps where there is greater continuity of progress through the whole primary years. Little research on the effects of discontinuity appears to have occurred so speculation may be harmful at this time.[2]

In view of the fact that these findings show a greater degree of approval for streaming than might be foreseen, a further analysis of the results was carried out. It could reasonably be expected that the vast majority of teachers would not really approve of streaming, but that many feel the stress of a very large pupil-teacher ratio forces this system upon them. There is no information in the present study to check the effect of class size on opinion directly, and therefore table a.8 of the appendix is included as being of some interest. Teachers' views are there analysed by size of school on the assumption that the larger classes are found in larger schools.

It can be seen that the anticipated trend is discernible in neither of the tables. Indeed there is a suggestion of the reverse effect regarding teachers' views on older children, since some 35–40 per cent in large schools plainly disapprove; and it is interesting to notice that these would be the teachers with most experience of streaming probably.

It may of course be that the group of teachers here concerned are biased towards one type of school rather than another (cf. Barker Lunn 1970), but if this is so, the reasons are very obscure: only a small proportion of the schools visited by the project director were in fact streamed. It could alternatively be argued that the group is biased in that it has a stated interest in giftedness, and this is unquestionably true. Further comment on the point will be made in the discussion of items B.3 (vi) and B.3 (vii) below.

PERIODIC SPECIALIZATION

An examination of tables a.9 and a.10 of Appendix 5 shows that periodic specialization is clearly seen by teachers as an acceptable method for encouraging the development of giftedness which is, in contrast to the practices previously considered, relatively unencumbered by severe disadvantages. Even with regard to first-school children some 60 per cent of teachers are prepared to consider the possibility favourably, and this proportion increases to no less than 77 per cent for older children.

There would appear to be some rather interesting variations in views as between teachers in different types of school. Infant teachers favour some kind of specialization more frequently than do junior and middle school people apparently. Perhaps this finding reflects more a different interpretation of what 'periodic specialization' might mean than a real difference of opinion, but if this is true, then the fact that such a phrase receives a widely different reception implies a need to consider the matter further. At the same time, there is nothing to suggest that these differences of opinion are not based on genuine views about what young children need. There may be some tendency for teachers not in infant schools to underestimate the specific demands on expertise which even quite young children make. Certainly it would be untrue to think that junior teachers oppose some approach to specialization as a matter of principle, since it can be seen that 78 per cent approve it as applied to middle-school age ranges.

It is pertinent now to examine the degrees of correspondence which appear in relation to the preceding items which all have a bearing on selection and segregation. The relevant findings are presented in table a.11 of the appendix (p. 236) and the main points arising from the results are summarized briefly below.

POINTS FROM THE TABLES

First-school children

Of the four arrangements under discussion, only periodic specialized teaching meets general approval. The nearest approach to a similar set of views concerns streaming, but even here the degree of resemblance is not great. Full-time super-selection almost warrants the description of complete anathema.

Middle-school children

With all four items, significant changes of view occur, and they are all in the direction of increasing popularity. The largest move relates to day release and the smallest to streaming; but super-selection still finds favour with fewer than one in three, and the majority are very uncertain about streaming. Perhaps the most tendentious way of putting the findings with regard to super-selection is to point out that it meets, with regard to middle-school children, the same degree of approval or disapproval that streaming does in relation to first-school children.

Other interesting parallels in viewpoints occur in the tables but they do not further the analysis of present provisions and cannot therefore be discussed. Attention must now be focused on a second aspect of the concept of individualization.

Personal interests

Our discussion of the needs of gifted children drew attention to the fact that, on the one hand, some gifted children might often have wider and deeper interests than more average people; and on the other, that the development of a maximum number of gifted children required a 'cafeteria' curriculum within which the proffered pabulum contained a wide variety of choice. It is thus apparent that it is necessary to examine present practices and provisions particularly in regard to the number of distinguishably different activities in which children can become involved. But more than this: we also need to know how far these interests can be pursued.

Certain items in the questionnaire were constructed with these conditions in mind, and the required analyses are given in tables a.12 and a.13 of the appendix (pp. 237–9).

These tables make it immediately apparent that there is a massive consensus with regard to the values of enrichment, and that this is probably seen as even more suitable for younger children than for any others. It has also to be remarked that enrichment was here specifically linked to an unstreamed class, and we now have unquestionable refutation of any charge that our group is biased towards streaming as such (cf. p. 116 above). Teachers plainly see some organizational arrangements as generally preferable to others, but not in any exclusive sense. Their awareness of the variety of situations in which different schools find themselves is doubtless the reason for what could in the case of some individual teachers appear to be a conflict, or rather, contradiction of view.

It is noteworthy too that not only do teachers approve of enrichment in an unstreamed situation but they also very frequently approve emphatically. This implies that enrichment is seen as a most excellent way of providing for the individualization of learning, and particularly perhaps in the context of providing for wider and deeper personal interests. It will be necessary therefore to enquire how far enrichment is carried in present conditions, and if possible to discover what teachers intend by this term.[3] Meantime it is necessary to complete the background to the present section by restating the conditions which Kough (1960) listed as indispensable features of worthwhile enrichment programmes:

1   Has each classroom teacher identified and listed the students who are gifted? If teachers are unable to do this, a well planned classroom programme is not operating. If only some teachers have done it, the gifted child programme is not reaching all the gifted children in the school.

2   Can each teacher describe the specific curriculum modification being made for each bright youngster? Again, if each teacher cannot do this there is not a complete enrichment programme.

3   Does some person have supervisory responsibility for the entire programme? Such a person may help classroom teachers in the identification process and provide motivation, ideas and materials as the programme progresses.

Kough's third point has perhaps little relevance to British conditions, and in any event implies that enrichment concerns only the generally intellectually gifted. The first two however are very much a present concern and need to be accompanied by two cautions in American writings on the subject of enrichment:

1   Many times the good intentions of the instructor faded and became additional work assignments for the gifted but at a similar, if not lower, conceptual level. Many enrichment programmes have been found more on paper than in operation. (Gallagher, 1964, p. 80).

2   Too often enrichment has been nothing more than trivial or repetitive work . . . true enrichment requires released time for the teacher, curriculum consultants and semitutorial arrangements. The services of specialist teachers in certain areas is indispensable (Hildreth, 1966, p. 213).

Whilst accepting that 'enrichment' will mean different things to different people, and represents something of an amalgam in the minds of us all; the term probably implies certain features which include those indicated by the items from the questionnaire now to be reviewed.

WIDENING OF THE SCHOOL CURRICULUM

Item B.3 (xiii) afforded teachers an opportunity to consider this possibility and tables a.14 and a.15 summarize the findings (p. 239). They suggest that about 30 per cent of teachers are very undecided about issues taken under headings like 'curriculum widening'. A substantial number (50 per cent) approve such a trend for 5–8 year olds, and a majority (60 per cent) feel that it may be good for middle schools. The trend with age for this item is noticeably weak, however, compared with the previous items ($\chi^2 = 20{\cdot}03$, $C = 0{\cdot}162$) and it may be that the concept of curriculum width is too diffuse in the minds of teachers for any real trends to show through. The analysis in table 5.4 suggests that this interpretation is correct, and item B.3 (xv) so closely resembles B.3 (xiii) that no separate discussion is required.

Table 5.4   Degrees of correspondence among teachers' views on curriculum width and an extension of free choice opportunities

	Curriculum width (9–13)	Free choice opportunities 5–8	9–13
B.3 (xiii) (5–8 yrs)	20·03	14·48	51·03
	0·162	0·139	0·254
B.3 (xiii) (9–13 yrs)		18·70	20·19
		0·157	0·163
B.3 (v) (5–8 yrs)			20·57
			0·164

Note: Upper figures give χ^2, lower figures C.

PERIPATETIC SPECIALIST TEACHERS

It may be that more definite indications about views on the requirements for a really worthwhile programme of enrichment can be inferred from the findings of items B.3 (xi) and (xiv) which are given in tables a.16 to a.20 inclusive (pp. 241–4). Summarizing briefly, the following points are worth noting:

1   The use of more peripatetic help for 5–8 year old children is approved by 58 per cent of the group, whilst some 17 per cent actively disapprove. It is of no little interest that teachers in junior schools are those who seem to regard the suggestion least favourably, with some 32 per cent suspending judgement. There are indications too that young teachers express a need for this sort of help more frequently than do those with more experience.

2   There is a striking degree of approval for the 9–13 year olds, with a mere 5 per cent expressing disapproval. Nobody in fact in the middle school group indicates even a qualified reservation; and headteachers are especially keen on receiving extra peripatetic help. All teachers, experienced or otherwise, now feel that extra specialist help is urgently required.

3   With regard to the place of outside agencies, including parents with special expertise, the findings for the 5–8 year olds closely resemble those from the previous item (xi). If anything, there is even less opposition to this idea, although the relative preference previously expressed by more inexperienced teachers has now vanished.

4   The results for 9–13 year olds are not significantly different from those for 9–13 year olds in item (xi), so further discussion is unnecessary. Taking both items together, it can be seen that the main changes are due wholly to views on the different problems to be faced at the different ages. It is clear however that teachers in both first and middle schools would welcome both an extension of peripatetic help and the assistance of outside agencies including parents. The degree of individualization which characterizes the teaching of any school, particularly in relation to its most able pupils, is seen

to depend directly and in no small measure upon the amount of outside assistance it receives.

Summarizing now this section on individualization and personal interests, it appears that present provisions must be reviewed in terms of at least the following aspects:

1   The actual number of major activities recognized in the curriculum
2   The depth to which they can each be pursued
3   The degree of enrichment embodied in the system as indicated by trends towards:

(i) Widening the curriculum

(ii) Extending the free choice of activities

(iii) Increasing use of more peripatetic teachers representing a greater number of special interests

(iv) Accepting and actively encouraging a larger measure of help and co-operation from outside agencies.

These points need to be borne in mind when the schools case studies come under review in chapter 7.

Motivational differences

The concepts of 'interest' and 'motivation' are closely intertwined. The wider the opportunities open, the more likely it is that higher levels of general motivation are achieved since where children choose what they shall do, and when to engage in given activities, it can be expected that there they will experience continuous intrinsic motivation. It is important however for us to consider other motivational differences. Some of the case studies cited suggest that some children at least cannot sustain high levels of work under conditions where external motivations are steadfastly denied. Here must be included such elements as competition, awareness of peer group standards, and realistically expressed teacher expectations; and schools which generalize their approaches to any or all these factors, to that extent reduce the degree of individualization.

Extended work time

A further point arising in connexion with motivational differences is concerned with the actual amount of energy different children can expend, within a given time, and over different periods of time. Both are highly important; the first is of course connected with the previous discussion on learning rates and provisions related to them; the latter requires that we look at such arrangements as are made with a view to letting some children actually work longer than others. It is worth stressing that this element of time is likely to be of immense importance for the development of, and proper provision for, giftedness. Considering intellectual aspects alone it needs to be recalled that there are cogent reasons for proposing that the real factor under-lying overt differences in 'intelligence' derives from nothing more than differences in general levels of activity (Hayes, K. G., 1962). It is not, how-ever, necessary to subscribe to this interpretation, before the importance of an examination of ways whereby some children can spend more time than others on given activities is accepted. The extent to which this is at present possible requires review, and teachers' opinions on related organizational arrangements are analysed in the following paragraphs.

A firm possibility is presented by the practice of acceleration. This permits some children to work at a higher rate, and in effect 'concertinas' time. Teachers' opinions on the advisability of building acceleration into the system are indicated in tables a.21 and a.22 (pp. 246-7). There it can be seen that there is no consensus on this issue as far as 5-8 year olds are concerned. Almost exactly the same proportions (39-37 per cent) approve and disapprove, and it may be significant that most of these who approve do not do so emphati-cally. Why so relatively large a proportion of infant teachers should approve this measure is unclear.

A majority opinion (54 per cent) forms with regard to the 9-13 year old children ($\chi^2 = 38\cdot26$, $C = 0\cdot222$) and it thus seems likely that acceleration of some sort is acceptable to many teachers. It has to be noticed, of course, that the use of the term 'groups' was preferred to 'classes' for what seemed to be sound reasons; but it may be that, in the event, teachers' opinions have been obscured. Further light may be thrown on the problem by examin-ing the findings from item B.3 (v). These are given in table a.23 and are of the highest importance (p. 248).

Considering the potential difficulties inherent in the proposal to admit some children to school before others, it is surprising that almost two thirds of infant teachers appear to view the idea with some approval, and that taking the group as a whole there is a small majority in favour. Perhaps the reasons have to do with the suspicion that gifted children from poor home backgrounds may be lost to us if they are not brought early under the influence of profes-sional teachers. The Plowden Report stressed the need for nursery education in socially deprived areas, but our case studies suggest that very able children sometimes create serious problems for their parents regardless of their social environment or status. It would be strangely inimical to these particular individuals if they were to be denied an educational environment for which they were manifestly ready simply because their parents happened to be 'middle class'.

However that may be, the idea of acceleration is linked to the notion of vertical grouping in that proponents of the latter arrangement argue that the most able children are almost automatically accelerated since they gravitate naturally towards the work of the older children in the group. Opinions with regard to this particular problem were sought in item B.3 (vii), the findings from which are summarized in the tables a.24 and a.25 (p. 249–50). There it can be seen that even with regard to young children there is no majority in favour of vertical grouping. One third approve, and a quarter disapprove; the number disapproving strongly exactly matches the number approving to the same degree. Teaching experience has no influence on opinion nor does the level of responsibility; and the type of school affects mainly the teachers' willingness to respond at all. It is possible that views on vertical grouping differ depending upon how much experience a teacher has of this arrangement. The results are therefore additionally analysed by size of school in accordance with the thesis that small schools are vertically grouped whereas larger schools, in general, are not. It can be seen that there are no trends here either.

Much the same comments can be made with regard to vertical grouping and older children. The findings are almost exactly parallel to those for the 5–8 age group ($\chi^2 = 10.65$, $C = 0.119$), and it would appear that apart from noting the lack of consensus across the whole primary range, the most outstanding point is the large proportion of teachers who indicate, either by omission or replying in the centre of the scale, that they cannot formulate an opinion. Taking all the subsections of item B.3 together, the numbers opting out are greatest in connection with this question of vertical grouping.

It is perhaps appropriate at this stage to observe that the reluctance of teachers to comment on systems of which they have little experience is not due to any indecision on their part, and that however one views this tendency, one obvious implication of it is that if provisions for gifted children depend in any way upon the formulation of views by teachers, then such teachers will have either to be exposed to sound research findings and the views of other teachers who manifestly possess the required experience, or be given the relevant experience themselves. Perhaps far more strenuous efforts should be made to provide all three than is customary now.

Acceleration, however it is achieved, is aimed primarily at economizing time by concentrating more work into what is available. The alternative or supplementary way to cater for differences in activity levels and provide extended work time has been merely to permit some children to stay on at school longer and this, of course, is not a viable proposition during the primary years. It would, however, be possible to provide extra time for those children who need it by varying the length of the school day and the holidays. Teachers' views on these two possibilities for recognizing within the system what is clearly a most important manifestation of individual differences were therefore examined by items B.3 (ix) and B.3 (x). It is vital to notice as a preliminary to a review of the findings that the questions were prefaced by the proviso that no point should be taken to imply any change in teachers' conditions of service. The findings are presented in table 5.5 for the total groups only in each case.

Table 5.5 Extended time: lengthening the school day, B.3 (ix), and shortening the holidays, B.3 (x)

		No reply	Emphatically approve					Emphatically disapprove	Qualified reply
		n %	n %	n %	n %	n %	n %		n %
B.3 (ix)	(5–8)	36 10	4 1	7 2	25 7	62 17	235 64		1 0
B.3 (ix)	(9–13)	52 14	10 3	31 8	42 11	73 20	161 44		1 0
B.3 (x)	(5–8)	43 12	18 5	39 11	50 14	65 18	150 41		5 1
B.3 (x)	(9–13)	58 16	25 7	50 14	59 16	55 15	119 32		4 1

As the cynic might expect, there is a massive consensus against both measures, and particularly against a lengthening of the school day. Before these findings are summarily dismissed however, it needs to be noted that the reasons for these views may go beyond the obvious and are not necessarily confined to matters like conditions of service, which were in any event excluded from the question. Discussions with teachers reveal that they do not generally view 'school time' in isolation and straightforward observation shows how liberally large numbers of teachers interpret the phrase. Our response to the above findings must therefore wait upon the results of an examination as to how far teachers and children engage themselves in extra-mural activities. It was stressed earlier in Part I that the curriculum for gifted children must not be seen as merely what is provided, organized and directed by the school alone. It follows that what happens in 'school time' should bear a closer relationship than possibly now occurs with what goes on outside school hours.

Finally in this discussion of time and individualization, it is necessary to remember that homework was, and in secondary schools still is, a time honoured method of extending the school day for the child. The present trends regarding this sort of activity will clearly require attention, since it is perhaps the most able children who will wish to pursue their interests beyond the normal.

Styles of learning

Space does not permit a review of relevant literature and it thus has to be stated, somewhat dogmatically, that on the basis of recent research there is a growing body of opinion in favour of the view that different styles of learning and responding characterize different types of children who may be equally intelligent.[4] That different children thrive differentially in different environments is perhaps the most definitive conclusion to be drawn from much educational research. Some able children in the control group invariably contrive to outpace some of their peers in the experimental groups; and it is apparent therefore that we must examine schools not so much in terms of some concept of an 'ideal' structure (Haddon, 1968; Butcher, 1968; Torrance, 1962; Ogilvie, 1970) but rather in terms of the flexibility and variety of environments constructed.

Parental attitudes and home background

The requirement that different types of able children need different degrees of structure in their educational environment is clearly relevant to the problems of parental attitudes and home backgrounds. There is some evidence, for example, that certain immigrants demand a high element of sequential progression in the learning of their children, and take what some teachers informed the project director was 'almost too much interest' in what is happening in school. Others require nothing of their children, or the schools, and the only patterning of life might well come exclusively from that provided by teachers. The present study does no more than provide incidental comment on these problems, but their complexity cannot be allowed to deter us from mentioning them at all. It has already been shown that some study-group members were particularly concerned about provisions for the very able, but perhaps frequently submerged, lower class or immigrant child.

A further point here is that able children are more likely than others to be a source of differences of opinion between teachers and parents. As our case studies show, some parents come to school 'armed' with IQ test results. Others have, even in the absence of any objective evidence, what appears perhaps to be a massively inflated notion of their children's capabilities.

Whatever the truth in an individual case, it is obvious that the provisions for gifted children must involve a consideration of the counselling system for parents. If the view of either parents or teachers are to be realistic, they must be formulated together rather than separately; and if at this point particularly, the needs of the gifted overlap very greatly the needs of every child, then this is merely a further reason for drawing added attention to the necessity for taking a hard look at the educational information services generally. Television advertisements inform people about how to apply for social benefits. How many parents know the procedure for having their child's mental capabilities assessed?

Teacher personality

It is almost too self-evident to notice that children's learning must depend upon the interpersonal relationship between teacher and taught. It has however been made clear that recognition of giftedness is inefficient where only a very few teachers are involved. It should now be stressed that this is not a criticism of either teacher or child; it is simply a hard fact of life that different children respond differently to different adults. The important point here is that our case studies show able children as frequently being hypersensitive to the teaching environment, and sometimes (often?) engaging in behaviour which is likely to alienate some teachers more than others.

The conclusion to be drawn is simply that the above considerations reinforce the need to arrange deliberately for children to be exposed to a number of different teachers rather than just one. The extent to which this happens must be a crucial point of observation.

Group learning

The degree to which any system can be said to be individualized depends greatly upon the extent to which a child has to work within a group as distinct from being 'on his own'. Whilst it can be argued that the same stimulus imposed upon a whole class permits each child an individual response, and that group responses act to deepen individual depth of feeling, and so on, it nonetheless remains true that group activities in general must tend to produce 'normal' situations and 'normal' results.

One method of permitting a child to operate alone, or in at least a very small group, might be the much greater extension of teaching by machine. Teachers' views on the viability of this system were required by item B.3 (viii) analysed in tables a.27 and a.28 (pp. 252–3).

It is there made obvious that teachers' views on the use of teaching machines with young children range widely, and are almost randomly distributed across the whole approve/disapprove scale. There is some evidence that opposition strengthens as teachers gain experience, but to what extent 'experience' includes trials with machines is an open question.

There is, however, a strong degree of support for more exploration here, from teachers in all types of schools, as soon as consideration moves towards the older primary child ($\chi^2 = 61\cdot45$, $\theta = 0\cdot277$), and it will be important, therefore, to ask how far there is at present any trend towards increasing 'mechanization' and 'programming'.[5]

Summary

Table 5.6 is presented as a preliminary to the general summarizing comments which conclude the present chapter. It is considered helpful to list all the items in section B of the questionnaire in order of their 'popularity'. For this purpose it has been argued that we need to know not so much the order in terms of straightforward degrees of approval, but rather in terms both of the extent to which responsible teachers (i.e. for this purpose headteachers) support a proposal, and of the measure of active opposition which any attempt to instigate or extend the proposition might meet. When these two aspects are

Table 5.6 Conditions possibly conducive to the elicitation and development of giftedness: ease of introduction

		5–8 years	9–13 years
Easy to effect	1	Enrichment in unstreamed class	Greater involvement of outside agencies
" " "	2	Greater involvement of outside agencies	More peripatetic specialists
" " "	3	Extension of free choice opportunities	Periodic specialized teaching
" " "	4	Periodic specialized teaching	Enrichment in unstreamed class
" " "	5	More peripatetic specialists	Extension of free choice opportunities
" " "	6	Widening the curriculum	Widening the curriculum
" " "	7	Admittance to school early	Day release to special classes
" " "	8	Vertical groupings	Early promotion
" " "	9	Early promotion	Introduction of teaching machines
" " "	10	Introduction of teaching machines	Streaming
" " "	11	Day release to special classes	Full-time super-selection
" " "	12	Shortening of holidays	Vertical grouping
" " "	13	Streaming	Shortening of holidays
Difficult to	14	Full-time super-selection	Lengthening of school day
effect	15	Lengthening of school day	

taken into account simultaneously the order of 'ease of introduction' is in table 5.6.

The concept of 'individualization' has been seen to be fundamental to any attempt at surveying present provisions and practices. The preceding analysis has guided the investigation of teachers' views on a number of points closely related to the degree of individualization that characterizes an educational system. It will further become evident that observations to be described in the following chapters also show basic patterns similar to this analysis.

Notes

1   Recent ILEA research underlines this point. See the report in *The Teacher*, Oct. 29, 1971, p. 2.

2   What there is appears to be inconclusive; Joyce Morris (1958) suggests that as far as reading is concerned discontinuity improves standards. Pidgeon (1959) is of the opinion that in general terms the position is unknown and needs further research.

3   See below, p. 169 *et seq.*, esp. p. 180 ff.

4   See for example: Wallach and Kogan (1965), Wallach and Wing (1970), Hudson L. (1966 and 1969), Shouksmith G. (1970) and the previous discussion of thresholds.

5   A reading of the school case studies, chapter 7 below, will confirm the general impression conveyed by evidence presented throughout this paper that there is no discernible trend towards increasing 'mechanization' at present.

6 Provision by LEAs

Arrangements for ensuring effective recognition

In order to assess the extent of special provision designed to help teachers to recognize gifted pupils, LEAs were asked to indicate whether advisory staff gave any guidance in this area. The results are indicated in table 6.1, which also includes the findings from a second question, as to whether headteachers were encouraged to seek advice through an established referral system.

Table 6.1 The recognition of gifted children: training, guidance and established systems of referral

Item	Type of authority		No clear indication	Provision	No provision	Qualified reply
Guidance	County		3	12	26	2
to	County borough		8	9	48	1
teachers	London		1	1	14	0
	Wales		2	2	8	0
	Totals	n	14	24	96	3
		%	10·2	17·5	70·1	2·2
Established	County		2	14	25	2
referral	County borough		5	16	38	7
system	London		1	4	11	0
	Wales		2	2	8	0
	Totals	n	10	36	82	9
		%	7·3	26·3	59·9	6·5

These results suggest that much more could be done in many localities to direct the attention of teachers to the problems of recognizing gifted children. Even though it seems that established systems of referral exist in some 26 per cent of LEAs, there appears to be little doubt that they are used for 'problem' children generally, rather than for the examination of gifted children as such.

Although no questions were directly oriented towards arrangements for recognizing backward children, the project director's attention was drawn to the fact that many authorities screen pupils at about the age of eight with group IQ and reading tests. Two striking facts arose from one small investigation of this procedure:

1   The intelligence tests were never examined with a view to discovering the most able as well as the most backward.

2   The reading test in use had an age ceiling of 7·9 years. This has been changed, but the ceiling for the new test is only 11·8 years.

It may be of course that teachers unofficially and spontaneously use the findings from a 'slow learner survey' to spot the gifted, but this is unlikely to be common since the whole context in which such surveys are conducted is inimical to this response. When asked about this, headteachers sometimes averred that if the child was reading satisfactorily then all was well, and further commented on the errors of standardization in the test since some children scored 'too highly'. No action had however been taken to check this conclusion objectively; and it has now to be recalled that this tendency on the part of some teachers automatically to discount a high IQ score by a young child was commented upon quite independently by one of our study groups (see above, p. 42 ff).

One final point arises in connexion with surveys and referral systems. No mention was made during any of these conversations, or in the correspondence about the use of tests other than the traditional IQ type. How far educational priority areas experiment with different instruments, and the extent to which LEA psychologists are experimenting with so-called 'creativity' tests remain unknown. The evidence considered here cannot be viewed as especially encouraging. It is apparent that in a number of places the whole responsibility for recognizing gifted children is thrown entirely on the individual teacher, or, to put the matter in its best light, upon the individual school. The findings in this section have therefore to be related particularly to the discussions in chapter 3 and chapter 7.

Special Saturday morning classes and home tuition

Provisions of this nature are related directly to the breadth and depth of school curricula since, on the one hand, they may deal with activities not represented or present only on a minor scale in the school programme; and on the other, they expose children ideally to persons highly qualified and powerfully motivated towards a particular activity. Levels of empathized enthusiasm and intrinsic motivation borne of challenge are likely to be much higher here, in these circumstances, than under any conditions where the teacher, however good in wider terms, is limited to general encouragement.

It might thus be anticipated that such provisions would be an especially important feature of the educational system, and an analysis of the replies from LEAs to the relevant question is given in table 6.2, together with that for a second closely related item.

Table 6.2 Saturday morning classes and home tuition; registration with private organizations for training

	Type of local authority	No clear indication		Provision		No provision		Qualified reply	
Saturday	County	3	10	10	0	28	32	2	1
classes	County borough	13	19	14	3	37	43	2	1
(first figure);	London	2	6	6	1	7	9	1	0
Home tuition	Wales	2	4	2	1	8	7	0	0
(second figure)									
	Totals n	20	39	32	5	80	91	5	2
	%	14·4	28·5	23·4	3·7	58·4	66·4	3·7	1·5
Registration	County	8		10		24		1	
with private	County borough	18		26		18		4	
organizations	London	6		7		2		1	
	Wales	5		6		1		0	
	Totals: n	37		49		43		6	
	%	27·0		35·7		32·8		4·4	

With regard to support for Saturday morning classes, these findings can only be regarded as indicative of a situation in urgent need of serious review. Only about one quarter of all LEAs provide for such activities apparently, and judging from comments in correspondence, those Saturday morning centres which do operate are usually confined to musical activities. The director has been made aware of recent moves in some places to organize Saturday morning art centres, but attention can also be drawn to the failure of one LEA to support a privately run art centre, so there would appear to be no consistently progressive trend in the direction of extending these arrangements.

Why not? It is not for this report to comment on priorities, but it is to be recorded that any reply can have nothing to do with lack of demand. In the art centre recently started, only fifteen places were available for more than one hundred and fifty applications from children of primary age.

Finally, it must be noted that the enquiry has revealed not one single instance of the provision of a Saturday morning mathematics-science centre, or indeed of a language centre as such. Drama centres operate in some few places but much of what happens would appear to depend more upon the enthusiasm of individual advisers and teachers than upon any positive policy within LEAs as a whole. There would thus seem to be something of a traditional momentum about the place of music; and a failure perhaps by educationists to point out the implications of modern curriculum developments in (say) mathematics and creative writing, for the extension of support for extramural 'cultural' activities. This is not of course to imply that provisions for music are at all adequate. On the contrary, the contrast here between what is happening in schools and the essential supportive structure is quite plain. On the one hand we have musical development being stimulated on a scale wider than ever before, so much so that parliamentary questions refer to the 'great glockenspiel boom', and Mr John Osborne, M.P., is reported as saying that 'some primary schools have enough musical equipment to provide a band for each class'. At the same time, however, the further development of whatever incipient talent is being revealed in these more than ideal circumstances, is being inhibited by a failure to provide the essential concomitant expansion of specialist and professional external musical environment in the form of Saturday morning centres and increasing orchestral opportunities. With regard especially to the latter, it needs to be realized that where no 'junior' orchestra exists, an effective age barrier is very frequently in force such that primary children are barred from participation.

The provision of home tuition could not in any circumstances be seen as a substitute for Saturday morning centres, but it could be viewed in some situations as being an exceedingly useful complementary arrangement. The findings show that this method of providing for individual talent is seldom, if ever, used specifically for this purpose and it has at once to be admitted that expense alone must give it a very low priority everywhere.

Registration with private organizations

Particularly in the field of physical activities, semi-official and private organizations provide the avenues through which a child can pursue his specialized interests. Different localities naturally differ in the character of what is provided, but there is no reason to suppose that they need differ greatly in terms of extent. Clubs and associations both reflect and stimulate local demand, and it could thus be part of LEA policy to encourage such bodies to accept young children, and involve them in their training activities, competitions etc. Potential talent is obviously more likely to be evoked where these associations flourish.

With these circumstances in mind, LEAs were requested to indicate how far they positively encouraged youngsters to register with associations for training, and the results are given in table 6.2 above. There it can be seen that perhaps surprisingly few LEAs appear to take steps to facilitate the registration of young pupils with local associations, and probably even fewer positively promote it by say publishing a register sufficiently detailed to be of real help to primary teachers.

The award of scholarships or exhibitions to outside institutions

The forms of development considered this far need not, and should not presumably, fall into a category of provision for gifted children as such. Theoretically anyhow, all children, regardless of their particular prowess, might take advantage of the opportunities provided. Scholarships and exhibitions, however, by their very nature, are for the further development of already recognized talent, and it is clearly of interest to see how far these modes of encouragement are available. The relevant results are given in table 6.3.

Table 6.3 The award of scholarships and exhibitions; part-time and full-time

	Type of authority		No clear indication	Provision	No provision	Qualified reply
Part-time	County		7	17	14	5
	County borough		22	15	23	6
	London		2	14	0	0
	Wales		2	4	6	0
	Totals:	n	33	50	43	11
		%	24·1	36·5	31·4	8·0
Full-time	County		7	23	7	6
	County borough		11	31	19	5
	London		6	10	0	0
	Wales		1	5	6	0
	Totals:	n	25	69	32	11
		%	18·2	50·4	23·4	8·0

In general terms, only a minority of authorities provide for part-time tuition in colleges of music or other specialized institutions. There is an important contrast here, however, between the London authorities and those elsewhere. In the former, only two out of sixteen appear not to assist in the manner suggested, whereas fewer than 50 per cent of authorities outside London engage in the practice. It might be thought that the main reason for this imbalance is the availability of appropriate institutions, and this is no doubt a major factor. It would not appear to explain why county authorities should do more than county boroughs, however, and before discussing the matter further the figures for full-time scholarships require examination.

The numbers of authorities providing assistance for full-time tuition clearly improves from 36 per cent to 50 per cent, and it is apparent that there is some tendency for counties and county boroughs outside London to prefer this mode of help. The number of county boroughs in fact more than doubles. Nevertheless it has to be remarked that London again achieves a greater involvement here, and the inescapable conclusion would seem to be that as far as the development of talent and high ability is facilitated by provisions of the sort under discussion, just so far have children living in London better chances of achieving greatness.

Before it can be argued that such a situation is inevitable because London is the major centre for ballet, theatre, music and the like, and hence possesses something of an enviable monopoly on relevant teaching and professional personnel, it needs to be pointed out that this is a self-defeating situation based on an untenable logic. Relatively recently, major orchestras in the provinces have been disbanded for lack of support, and clearly because there has been a dramatic failure to appreciate the close connexion between the presence of an orchestra in a locality, and the supply of first class instrumental teachers.[1] It is surely something of a paradox that, at the very time when much is being done within the schools themselves to stimulate instrumental music of quality, further essential steps should fail to be taken to ensure continuity in the development thus begun. The need to look for artificial ceilings on advancement of talent has been stressed above. Such ceilings clearly appear in rather subtle fashion, and by no means as a consequence of conscious policy. It will, however, require a very deliberate policy indeed to reverse what can only be seen as a severely dysgenic spiral trend in musical education for the gifted, and more ultimately of course for every child.

Enrichment classes during normal school hours

It can be argued that some of the needs of gifted children in some localities can be more fully met by the organization of 'extended opportunity' or 'enrichment' classes. LEAs were, therefore, requested to supply information concerning provisions of this kind, and the responses are analysed in table 6.4.

Although the precise nature of these enrichment classes is not clear in every case, they appear generally to be linked to a local college, along the lines of the Brentwood experiment. At least one, however, is organized quite independently of any college, and brief details are given in chapter 7. There can be little doubt that the Liverpool University experiment is also unique, and this too is briefly discussed in the same chapter.

Table 6.4 Enrichment classes in school hours

Type of authority	No clear indication	Provision	No provision	Qualified reply
County	5	2	36	0
County borough	14	3	47	2
London	5	1	10	0
Wales	3	0	9	0
Totals: *n*	27	6	102	2
%	19·7	4·5	74·3	1·5

Special enrichment classes in school time can, however, clearly be said to remain very unpopular methods for providing special help to gifted children, except in the singular case of music tuition. Special classes here are of course exceedingly widespread, and are not therefore included in this present analysis. No precise estimate is available to us anyhow but one large authority has stated with some satisfaction that peripatetic music specialists are available in two-thirds of the authority's primary schools. Unless the other third has its own instrumental specialists, it is a moot point as to how satisfactory the situation really is, and it is to be regretted that we cannot say how representative this proportion might be.

Early admission to secondary schools

This arrangement is clearly linked to individualization by acceleration. In principle there is no difference between permitting a child to work with an older class within a school, or permanently with older children in a vertically grouped unit, and allowing him to proceed to another school earlier than usual. Unless this point is appreciated there may seem to be something contradictory in stating on the one hand that primary schools are already catering for children as individuals, and on the other, that early transfer is necessary and wise. It might even be thought that to arrange early transfers was to admit a failure to achieve the degree of individualization attained in schools elsewhere. The analysis in chapter 5 cautions against drawing such conclusions on the basis of an examination of one, or even a few dimensions of individualization; but it is nonetheless important to assess the extent of early age transfer arrangements and the findings are given in table 6.5.

Here it is apparent that at least a quarter of all LEAs have now dispensed with what was until fairly recently a universal practice. It can further be assumed that invariably LEAs exercise great caution here, even where early promotion is still theoretically possible. Social, emotional and physical developments, together with character traits, are invariably taken into account,

Table 6.5 Early admission to secondary schools

Type of authority	No clear indication	Provision	No provision	Qualified reply
County	5	31	5	2
County borough	8	32	26	0
London	3	9	2	2
Wales	3	5	4	0
Totals: n	19	77	37	4
%	13·9	56·2	27·0	2·9

and in any event many authorities limit advancement to periods less than one year above chronological age. On the whole it would appear that with increasing stress on individualization within the primary schools themselves, the felt need to 'promote' has decreased. It has also of course to be realized that any move to extend this particular procedure would require the implementation of some 8+/10+/13+ selection procedures, even where comprehensive schooling existed; and these considerations underline the need to consider most carefully how far individualization really has been carried within the primary schools themselves.

Summary

A number of possible arrangements for ensuring the maximum effectiveness in recognizing and developing talent have now been reviewed, and our evidence is that they each meet with varying degrees of approval. None are universal, and many are not included to any significant extent in the provisions of an appreciable number of authorities. The type of arrangement likely to be most favoured is that which whilst giving opportunity for the gifted child to excel can also be represented as part of 'proper' provision for every child who might wish to take part. This perhaps sufficiently explains why only one LEA, as far as we know, officially supports the activities of the NAGC by permitting the use of school premises on Saturday mornings, whereas a very large number support parental groups who wish to build swimming pools. The apparent exclusiveness of the one contrasts unfavourably with the openness of the other.

It must be added at once, however, that the preceding comment may be somewhat unfair to the extent that perhaps very few LEAs have in fact been approached for assistance of any kind specifically in relation to talented children. Unfortunately, the present study did not investigate this point directly but there is every indication that a very large number of chief officers would in fact treat any such approach sympathetically.

Notes

1   The reduction of BBC interests may also be a contributory factor and, if this is true, then there is here too a case for an educational grant of some kind for this specific purpose. Everything depends upon how far these professionals actually engage in the teaching of children.

7 Provision in schools

Brief studies of individual schools are presented below. It must be emphasized that these descriptions are partial surveys and make no attempt to review more than some aspects of a school from a particular point of view. It should be obvious, for example, that when one reports the statement, 'Notions of equality and fairness prevent some schools from giving anybody any special attention in anything', the comment is in the context of 'gifted' children and that had we been looking at remedial provision for other children then the statement would not have been made.

The general pattern for the summaries is given in Appendix 4, guidelines, section A (p. 220). Most of the comments are those given by teachers themselves and it has to be remembered that the sole purpose of these descriptions is to enable the interested reader to arrive at his own evaluation of the present position regarding the evocation and development of giftedness in all its forms as these occur within the schools he knows. Thus the examples are chosen to facilitate comparisons not amongst themselves so much as with similar situations elsewhere in the system. Rather than curtail individual descriptions the number of examples retained in the text has been reduced to a minimum and others may be found in Appendix 7.

Schools: summary descriptions and comments

SCHOOL A:

Location	City	*Socio-economic*	
		status	High
Roll	420 mixed	*Staff*	14 + 2 part-
			time (5/5)
Age range	5–11 years		(3 male)
School time	9–12, 1.45–4.00	*Peripatetics*	Nil

Grouping Systems
(i) Children are divided into 11 classes according to age as far as possible. In some instances, the brighter children are placed in the older group and the

duller children in a younger group. All classes are thus unstreamed: no vertical grouping occurs, even in the infant section. There are overlapping age-groups in some classes due to the rapid growth of the school from one-form entry to $1\frac{1}{2}$-form entry.

(ii, iii, iv) Within-class groupings are idiosyncratic and depend on the individual teacher. It is impossible to say how much 'class' work there is as compared with 'individual' work, as this varies according to the needs of the children: in classes of mixed ability the staff aim to give as much individual help as time will allow. All reading is individual and is achieved by the use of a basic reading scheme, several supplementary schemes, library books (both fiction and reference), the use of the borough travelling library, books from the 'Chip' club etc. In mathematics individualization is achieved by the use of text-books, individual assignment cards and apparatus. In language skills similar methods are used, including the use of the tape-recorder, BBC radio and television programmes, note-taking, creative writing, drama etc. Oral work and use of development of vocabulary is encouraged and is an integral part of the children's education.

Some other activities are class organized and some are group organized, either according to 'ability' or 'interest'.

Small groupings occur in connexion with remedial classes in English, reading and maths. The afternoon part-time teacher spends every afternoon teaching reading in small groups or taking children on a 'one to one' basis. In this connexion some of the brighter readers are also 'stretched' and encouraged. There are special groups of the very able children in mathematics, in the infant department and at the top of the junior department. The *En Avant* course is being followed in French and no special groupings have occurred as yet.

The ordinary classes usually recognize four or five ability groups within themselves, each of which would probably be working at a different point in the text-books and wordcards.

(v) The aims of the various groupings are to educate the children according to their ability, aptitude and interest. As far as the 'gifted' children are concerned, the aim of the groupings is to give these children the opportunity to be stimulated and stretched. The groups are flexible so that it is possible for children to move from one to another.

Staffing Patterns
(i) General communication is achieved by informal classroom and staffroom discussion. Staff meetings are also held as the need arises, when school events are planned and arranged and various educational topics are discussed and ideas exchanged. The heads of department call informal meetings from time to time to assess progress and discuss difficulties. An interesting innovation is the use of a 'day' book informing staff of daily events.

(ii) There is some team teaching in the organization although teachers operate within their own classrooms mainly. There is some specialization in music, art and craft and games/PE but even in the upper school no more than two periods per day on average are spent away from the class teacher. One part-time teacher often works with the class teachers but sometimes takes a group out. An experiment in taking groups of children who need 'stretching' has just begun. Considering relative isolation of the classes, the time devoted to inter-staff discussion is considerable. It is possible, however, that the special 'expertises' amongst the staff are not fully used. As yet, there are no peripatetic teachers, but opportunities for, say, instrumental music (e.g. violin, clarinet, flute) are available when needed.

Specialization is linked to posts of special responsibility for games, needle-work and music. The latter specialist is also deputy head and takes music throughout the school. Although he was a class teacher for a number of years, he is not now responsible for a class. The head feels that a reduction in class size offers fewer advantages to the school as a whole than the more specific support which 'accrues' from a deputy head who is not a full-time class teacher. He supports, guides and considers every member of staff, acts as liaison officer between the staff and the head, suggests new ideas, advises and supports the head and encourages first-appointment teachers and students. He uses his expertise in music for the benefit of every child and of the school as a whole. He has also been the leader in the teaching of swimming and in football and games training in the school. He is also responsible for aural and visual aids and timetabling all the BBC radio and BBC and ITV television programmes.

(iii) Advisers and inspectors afford general comments and support rather than give specific advice on how to deal with individual pupils, although this would be available if required. One PE adviser ran a gymnastics course in the school. This was very successful and in this way he was involved in teaching some of the infant and junior children. He 'highlighted' some potentially out-standing children in gymnastics who might not have been recognized so quickly. He also helped with the teaching of swimming in the school's teaching swimming bath one year.

(iv) Other agencies include museum and library services. The borough has a travelling library and books are exchanged regularly. Project boxes are also available. There is no music or picture-loan service but the LEA loan musical instruments of various kinds, including violins, when available.

There are football coaching courses run by teachers; the ladies' swimming club also runs coaching classes for children.

The school has its own teaching swimming pool and swimming has been taught successfully to all the children in the school for ten years. Members of staff have been on courses and have taught swimming under the leadership of the deputy, who is a qualified teacher of swimming. The older juniors who are swimmers attend the municipal baths for more advanced instruction in a large bath. The school takes part in the district swimming gala.

Timetable and curriculum content
(i) The school timetable merely lays down use of rooms and buildings etc. and offers no constraints outside these and the organization inherent in specialization for music etc. There are some 'extra-mural' or 'Club' activities which cut across the classes or age-groups, e.g.: recorder groups, choir, football and netball team practices.

(ii) Class timetables are idiosyncratic and depend upon individual teachers. The following activities are, however, generally recognized:

Music Singing, recorder and melodica playing, playing of percussion instruments. BBC *Time and Tune* and other musical programmes. Teaching of the language of music. Preparation for music festivals, concerts, *Noyes Fludde* performance in conjunction with a school for girls. Children's piano playing linked with home tuition.

PE Including swimming for all the infant and junior classes during the summer months. (Two lessons a week for all junior children in groups of 20.)

Games Football, cricket, netball, rounders, shinty, minor games. Coaching of football and netball teams. Athletics—preparation for Primary Schools' Sports Festival. Seven-a-side football. Netball rallies.

Art and craft Many types of craft work introduced, including weaving and clay modelling. (Hoping to purchase a kiln in the not too distant future.) Needlework with the girls.

Mathematics.

Languages (Including French for 3rd and 4th year juniors.) Nuffield *En Avant* course is being followed.

Reading First as a skill, then as the road to learning and the enjoyment of literature, poetry etc. The aim to encourage a love of books and learning.

Environmental studies Including geographical and historical topics, nature study, science topics etc. BBC radio and television programmes are followed in conjunction with topic work and some interesting work has been covered.

Drama Including dramatic presentations every Christmas.

Religious Education.

There is an extra-mural timetable for some activities such as recorder playing, choir practices and games. These groups meet several times a week either in lunch times or after school. There is a school orchestra which cuts across all age groups and is expanding and developing all the time. The orchestra plays every day in assembly.

There is no regular programme of homework but it is given when required and the children are encouraged to continue their topic work at home, to read and improve their vocabulary knowledge, to look up facts in reference books, to practise skills and on occasion to prepare stories or essays. Quite often the parents' co-operation is sought and gladly given.

The infant children take their reading books home and the teachers work in close co-operation with the parents, guiding them about the amount to be read, words to be learnt etc; the aim being to make certain the basic vocabulary is learnt and to encourage fluency in reading. In order to help with the individual teaching of reading and encourage speedy progress, members of staff teach individual children during the lunch hours. This is to some extent, therefore, a somewhat minimal 'extra-mural' activity.

(iii) Very detailed content of syllabuses is suggested in some areas but not so detailed in others.

The Reading Scheme is, at the moment, based on *Janet and John*, although a change to the *Rainbow Readers* is planned for September 1971. There are some supplementary schemes available at least in part, for example i.t.a., *Breakthrough to Literacy, Kathy and Mark, Pirate Books* etc. There is no SRA scheme available at present although this is under review as is the use of the 'talking book'.

A visit was made recently to the reading centre at Reading University and there is much discussion about the latest schemes and aids. The tape-recorder is also used in reading instruction.

Language skills
Sequential development is achieved here by the use of textbooks which children work with individually. Since much of the work is 'ungraded', expressive experience, a very careful record of the individual child's achievement is kept by each teacher. An important category not common now on record cards is that of 'general knowledge'. It is possible to gain a very good idea of the child's general knowledge through his general conversation, oral response, free writing and accounts of topics, use of vocabulary, use of reference books, hobbies etc.

The use of the dictionary is encouraged from the earliest stages—for spelling, finding the exact meaning of a word, word derivation, and as an aid to fostering the economical, precise and colourful use of words.

Good 'oral' expression is fostered and encouraged throughout every aspect of the child's education. In this respect one is 'teaching' all the time by example, correction and discussion.

As far as possible good spelling is encouraged and, from time to time, spelling and vocabulary exercises are given. Accuracy is still considered to be important.

The records do not include any 'objective' test scores and quotients. Objective tests are given but the results are recorded on separate lists.

Mathematics
The infant programme is given by means of a very detailed record sheet which indicates the stages of work to be covered. It is divided into two sections; one for number knowledge as such, the other for practical activities. It also enables the teacher to see how fast each child is progressing and is thus of great value in enabling her to recognize the most able children, given that there is a high proportion of individual work going on.

The upper school programme is also well detailed and at least five books suitable for the separate age ranges are recommended to the teachers. The fourth-year programme includes some geometry and simple algebra from *Exploring Mathematics.*

The usual pattern of teaching is for the class to be introduced to a topic and then individuals and small groups pursue the topic in the text-book at their own rates. New topics are taught to the class or groups or individuals when they are ready to learn another concept. Practical mathematics follows a similar pattern but is almost wholly group work.

The scheme does not indicate the numbers of children expected to complete it as this depends on the ability and aptitude of the children in the particular year group and will vary from year to year. The scheme as given is expected to 'stretch' the 'gifted' child mathematically. Children in mixed ability groups will reach varying stages in the scheme and it is hoped that they will progress from that point when they transfer to high schools. It is not intended that children shall be 'extended' in breadth rather than depth but it is felt that in mathematics particularly, it is important that each new concept shall be thoroughly understood and mastered before progressing to the next. However, the 'gifted' children can be stretched in both directions. There is liaison between our head of maths and the teachers in the high schools, as she is an active member of the mathematics group, and schemes of work and methods of teaching are frequently discussed and ideas are shared.

Centres of interest
In the class 'schemes of work', geographical, historical, nature study and science topics are suggested. There is, however, enough flexibility for topics to be chosen according to spontaneous interests and the value of this is revealed by the 'school design' topic and its results. As there is co-operation and frequent discussion between members of staff there is little danger of 'overlap'.

There is no formal method for checking the rates of individual progress achieved in and through topic work. This is a definite difficulty to which we all turn a 'blind eye' because there is no obvious solution.

It is not felt that there is much danger in the school of the children working at the same level of thought and knowledge over two or three years, but it is obviously something that we must be aware could happen. A related problem is the provision of books for such work which are suitable for the various levels of ability. It is by no means self-evident that even the most able children can pick out suitable texts for themselves and they must be guided in the use of suitable reference books by their teachers. It is often possible for a teacher to refer the children to a book about a special topic or to ask other members of staff if they have such a reference book in their class library. The greater the availability of books, the greater the probability of poor and inappropriate choices by children unless they are so guided.

Other curriculum areas

Detailed schemes of work are provided for the teaching of swimming, music, religious education, reading and needlework and the aim is for sequential development. The schemes indicate to the individual teachers the possibilities and, with experience, they will become fully aware of them. It may, of course, not be possible for the general teacher to be as skilled in the teaching of every subject as a 'specialist' teacher. The development of 'departmental' heads is probably essential if we are to improve standards 'across the board' since no teacher can pretend expertise in everything unfortunately.

Audio-visual technology

Some use is made of tape-recorders, film strips etc. for individualized learning. One class is running a weekly news item using the tape-recorder. The tape-recorder is also used in both departments for encouraging individual children in reading and language development. There is a lack of suitable programmes and 'learning unit' packs which teachers could use with children for experimental purposes. The school has a cassette tape recorder but no earphone sets.

As far as musical instruments are concerned, the school is constantly building up its supply and the parents are very interested, co-operative and generous in this respect.

There are no formal contacts with agencies, clubs and associations outside school but these were readily established in connexion with the swimming pool construction project. Although there is no formal PTA either, there is no doubt that there is an abundant reservoir of help of all kinds which the school can tap at any time. Parents have not been so involved in 'classroom' activities up to the present time, although they make costumes for plays, send materials of various kinds, and have given help with certain projects, including the school design competition. (The reasons for no further involvement were not made evident, presumably because we failed to put the question.)

There is a schools orchestra which able musicians can join. Good swimmers are well catered for by the local associations.

Recognition and treatment of gifted children

The psychologist will always help in the case of an individual difficulty. Objective VR tests are given and so there is some formal attempt to assess abilities before the allocation procedure takes place. It is possible to seek advice from the borough advisers about the treatment of 'gifted' children, and very able children can be considered for transfer to high school as 'under-age' candidates.

The school has not *formally* recognized its 'gifted' children. Individual differences in performances are noted in a number of cases and have led to the establishment recently of small groups, for instance in mathematics, where the aim is to 'stretch' the very able beyond what would occur if they were left in the ordinary group all the time. The limit to extensions of this kind is met by the need to maintain strong class-teacher relationships.

Musically, very able children have been recognized at an early stage and 'stretched', encouraged and fostered. Ten children in 1970 proved themselves to be very able musicians and are now progressing still further in their high schools.

Additional points

1   One teacher (LRAM) takes a few pupils during lunch times for pianoforte instruction. This is an experiment in group piano learning, and selection is determined by three main criteria: (i) piano at home, (ii) no other private tuition, (iii) general motivation. The 'extra' pianos have been secured as gifts.

2   It is not thought that children are 'put back' when they transfer to secondary education, but liaison is exceedingly close. Children from the primary school orchestra join in productions by the local high school on occasion and instrumental tuition begun in the primary school is continued in the secondary field. Headteachers are consulted as to which secondary school might be most suitable in terms of matching the child's special talents with what is offered in the secondary school.

3   From the school's point of view there seems to be a very rapid turnover of staff in the psychology department, and there is apparently a long waiting list. What effect this has on 'referral' rate is unassessable.

4   Secondary liaison was stimulated partly by an LEA one-day conference when all schools were closed. Permanent formal contacts were not established, however, as a result of this meeting.

5   Since 1970 two schools orchestras have been established within the borough. Admission standard approximately Grade IV. Meetings twice per term, 5.00–8.00 p.m. Friday evening and all day Saturday 10.00–5.00 p.m. for the 'general' orchestra; every Friday evening 6.00–7.00 p.m. for strings. Selection is generally in the hands of the music adviser.

6   The LEA encourages children who take part in recreational and sports activities of various kinds, for example, there are both boys' and girls' gym clubs held weekly throughout the year; FA coaching courses for selected players are held during two weeks in the summer holidays; fencing courses have been held on Saturday mornings; the School Sports' Association organ-

izes teams for outstanding players for a wide variety of games and other
activities and four places are taken annually for outstanding pupils at Outward
Bound centres. Schools are encouraged to liaise with local athletic clubs and
introduce young players to first-class coaching. The football coaching course
for schoolboys is held during the summer holiday, ten morning sessions 9.30
a.m. to 12.30 p.m., held Monday to Friday for two weeks for pupils aged 10
to 15 nominated by the School Football Association. The course is a selective
one financed by the Football Association under their coaching scheme for
schoolboys. This year's average attendance was approximately 100 pupils
daily. The course was staffed by six qualified football coaches supplied by
the Association of Football Coaches. Coaches are paid by the Football
Association.

SCHOOL B:

Location	Rural village	*SES*	Farmer and
Roll	30 mixed		labourer
Age range	5–11 years	*Staff*	2 (female)
School time	9–12, 1.30–3.30	*Peripatetics*	None

Grouping systems
(i) Two 'family' groups, 5–8 and 8–11. Maximum age in first set is 8 years.
Occasionally 6½ years able reader will be accelerated to second group.
   (ii, iii) Class 2 have TV lessons altogether, spelling, story-time and singing.
French is taken in two sections, 1st/2nd year and 3rd/4th year, but 3/4 join
1/2. Individualization is carried furthest in mathematics and languages by
means of textbooks and workbooks. The older children help the younger
ones, especially in reading or music. Other work is done in 'ability' groups—
often in pairs.
   (iv) About 5/6 of time will be spent in small group or individual work.
   (v) The main difficulty is the very wide age range, and even wider ability
range. All intellectual activities need to be grouped, and PE and games are
severely restricted. The advantages are social, and the bright child learns to
help others including the teacher.

Staffing pattern
With only two teachers no formal staff meetings are necessary. Both join for
assembly and occasionally for TV, singing etc. There is almost no external
help at all. Advisers and inspectors visit occasionally and offer general advice.

Timetable and curriculum content
(i, ii, iii) Heavily dependent upon teachers' own talents and interests in so
far as activities outside the 'basic skills' are concerned. The content of 'basic
skills' is derived from the usual textbooks and workbooks afore-mentioned.
The day is flexible in that no definite programme is laid down apart from TV

and radio broadcasts. The mornings are generally devoted to the 'basics' and the afternoons to music, art, French etc.

Extra-mural activities are limited to instrumental sessions with recorders and clarinet.

Homework is integral to school work for those who wish it—and all children do some. There is no problem of continuity since the schoolwork is taken home.

(iv) No individualized AV programmes are used. These were experimented with but children hadn't patience to work very long. Great need for 'kits' of the right kind and design. The usual scrambled texts are dull in the extreme.

Other linkages with outside agencies
There is no PTA though teacher knows all the parents well and has taught some of them herself. No other links occur even in terms of county orchestra and no games leagues are organized in the area. There are no Saturday morning classes.

Recognition and treatment of gifted children
Academically all children would seem to be well stretched. Almost all of them have been selected to attend grammar schools over the past ten years. Any limits on achievement here have to do with textbook content, and the school has no specific problem therefore.

Musically too the curriculum is 'open' as it is in French to a lesser degree. The latter subject is impossible to teach individually in the absence of more AVT.

The weakest activities are games, swimming, athletics, drama and movement, and possibly art and craft since the personal expertise of the two teachers cannot encompass every area, and facilities are not available. No long term handicaps apparent though.

Additional points
1   The wide age range is stated to be a major difficulty even with fewer than twenty in each class.

2   Secondary schools do not build on what has been done in some areas of the primary curriculum, notably in instrumental music and French reading. Neither are followed up with real continuity, despite the fact that some children start the clarinet.

3   The County Library service compares very unfavourably with what is done in some LEAs.

4   It is the teachers' view that AVT and types of programmed learning could be of immense value in extending individualization. An extensive mobile library of programmes and kits is necessary.

5   TV programmes geared to pairs of children of very similar ability as in

(say) *Mathematics Workshop* would be another method of individualizing. Too many programmes are 'general enrichment'.

SCHOOL C:

Location	City	SES	High
Roll	300	Staff	11 + 2 Part-
Age range	5–7 years		time ($\frac{4}{5}$)
School time	9–12, 1.30–4		Female
		Peripatetics	None

Grouping systems

(i) Children are grouped in ten classes with vertical grouping for the 5s and young 6s. Vertical grouping is not carried through to top infant classes because staff feel that for activities such as PE and story time, the ranges of ability become too wide. The building too is inconvenient, and does not provide a range of toilet sizes etc. at all points.

(ii, iii) Within-class groupings are based on an integrated day designed to cater for four types of activity through which the groups rotate generally each day. These are:

1   Reading and writing
2   Making things
3   Mathematics
4   Activities.

Additional periods include the class activities mentioned, and RE and music. Each group is based on reading ability mainly.

(iv) The time spent in each activity is the time for every child more or less and amounts to about $\frac{1}{5}$th of total time.

(v) The aims of the group system are:

1   To enable teacher to occupy children whilst she listens to children read.
2   To economize equipment.
3   To ensure all children have a turn at each major activity every day.
4   To organize smaller ability groups.
5   Vertical grouping eases children into groups easily. They settle in a new atmosphere very well. [This] avoids mid-year transfers etc.
6   To facilitate the use of part-timers and NAs who can be fitted into the system easily without changes of routine.

The groupings are not so rigid that every child must remain in one group all the time and move with it. Nevertheless children are expected to cover all four areas and the numbers in any 'corner' are equalized to some extent.

Staffing patterns

(i, ii) There is no specialization and no 'team' teaching. In one area two classes sometimes combine for music and story. The headteacher often helps with reading activities when there is time. Two NAs are usually attached to the school and these act as teachers' aides. The staff feel such assistance is of great value in helping them to give individual attention in reading especially.

No one teacher has responsibility for advising colleagues about curriculum development in any field (except a PSR for maths) and every member of staff is expected to keep up with all modern approaches.

Staff meetings occur only in connexion with special events. Informal discussion during lunch-time is found to be sufficient.

(iii, iv) There are no peripatetic specialists visiting the school for, say, violin teaching. The two part-timers are 'general' teachers who come for two mornings per week and help with reading mainly.

Advisers and Inspectors provide only general assistance and do not consider the needs of gifted children especially. No doubt advice would be forthcoming if asked for but no apparent need arises.

For AVT, the school is equipped better than most infant departments and possesses a tape-recorder and a cassette recorder. There is also a set of headphones so that groups of six children can sit and listen to stories, strip projections or commentaries etc. This use, however, is not yet attractive to staff who do not appear to be aware of the possibilities. Alternatively the reading of stories to groups of children of wide ability ranges may be now so well established in infant schools that we are no longer aware of the inadequacies. It may be too that only the most able infants can be left long listening to stories on tape and certainly one feels that a videotape would be vastly more effective. More research is needed here to establish just what the possibilities might be with infants who are well-trained and brought up to be accustomed to listening or watching with a minimum of supervision.

The production of story readings as part of 'activity' kits will need great care if the idea is not to be rejected out of hand on the grounds that such 'programmes' are impossible to produce.

No other equipment is used for individual or group activity. The school has no TV and the radio is used for class programmes. The strip projector is too hot to be used by infants on their own, and the risk of damage to equipment may be great.

Timetables and curriculum content
(i) The only areas where any kind of developmental sequences are laid down by the headteacher are in mathematics and reading.

Reading is organized through the *This is the Way I Go* (Longman) scheme. The degree to which this scheme is adhered to depends greatly on the individual teacher and some prefer a more haphazard approach. Others prefer to stick to the continuity of the scheme without asking every child to read every stage.

No records of objective reading test scores are kept. The teachers record every child's progress with considerable care, however, and in at least the most conscientious case every instance of teacher contact is recorded. These records show that teachers tend naturally to see more of the slow learners than of the most able readers; in fact the slow reader enjoys more than twice as many contacts with the teacher as the able child.

There is a mathematics scheme for the school which lays down lines of progress. No records exist, however, in the detail given for reading and one cannot say (a) whether reading skills and mathematical skills develop together or whether some children show an early bias one way or another; (b) whether the school has any potentially outstanding mathematicians who would benefit from further tuition beyond what the average child receives.

There would seem to be an over-reliance on recording what the young child *does* and not what he *understands*. The modern infant teacher might with some justice be said to be relying heavily on the maxim 'I do and I understand'. In so far as it is true, we need only record the 'doing' of course; and this enables us to avoid the problem of measuring levels of understanding.

Children who are 'gifted' in other activities will go unrecognized since no developmental sequences are laid down against which individual progress might be compared. Thus in the art and craft fields children are exposed to a variety of media, but are not taught any of the techniques relevant to the use of such media. This may be due to lack of expertise amongst staff or to the adoption of aims for these activities which do not require, or even eschew, the inculcation of skills, or to a sheer lack of time on the part of a teacher who with 35 children must spend nearly all her time on reading skills; or indeed to all three factors together.

No children have ever been seen to be so advanced as to go beyond the language and mathematics programmes as laid down. The books available go well into junior school age ranges as far as novels and information are concerned. No junior mathematics books are in use however.

There is no swimming and no French on the timetable at present.

(iv) As mentioned above no AVT is in widespread use. The usual equipment is of course available in mathematics etc., but individual programming is impossible in present circumstances and children must work in groups of about ten for most skills. Staff make their own workcards which are graded and cover the stated syllabus topics. Children can to some extent thus progress individually through these assignments. Textbooks are used as a basis for workcards but are not given to individual children to work through.

Links with outside agencies
There are none. The school is an island unto itself, although occasional visitors (policemen, postmen etc) talk to children now and then. No formal links with the junior school exist, though informally the two headteachers know one another well. The need for contacts would seem to be minimal.

There is no PTA and parents afford no continuous assistance to the school either outside the classroom or in it.

Recognition and treatment of gifted children
No attempt is made to recognize outstanding children as such and each child is carried along at his individual pace as far as one can tell. In general one can say probably:

(*a*) The most able readers get less individual attention, certainly in terms of actual teacher contact, than the least able.

(*b*) In mathematics there is less chance that the very able child progresses at his fullest rate since the programme is more 'general' than in the case with reading and various 'levels' of work are very ill-defined.

(*c*) In other areas the aims are to provide a wide variety of 'experiences' so that there are really no dimensions along which individual differences arise. Some children work faster and hence enjoy a greater range of experiences, and this is perhaps all that can be said. Musical activities are a good example possibly; children experience percussion instruments in great variety and experiment with sound. They do not learn any musical notation, however, and have no opportunity to develop any real skill on an instrument, say violin or recorder.

There is no extra-mural timetable, though teachers sometimes listen to the slow learners reading during lunch-time breaks. Able children are encouraged to read library books at home and school, but they are not given homework.

Staff views
The staff do not feel that even the most able infants are in any danger of not being 'stretched' in the infants school. They do not favour early entry to school, although there was some regret expressed at the loss of the nursery class. Outside the basic skills, where staff are confident that all is being done that can be done, there is seen to be a need at this stage for children merely to have opportunity to 'explore' a wide variety of activities, and to 'discover' their interests or gifts. It is the job of the later stages to develop such talents as the infant school may uncover, and children's interests at these ages are seen as being too ephemeral to require a prolonged period of attention.

There are no felt gaps in the curriculum at present. Neither swimming nor French are thought to be essential at this stage, although if facilities were available it might be possible to include them. French would be restricted to the most able in all probability. Only the headmistress feels that changes in methods and organization might be worth considering, and that the most able children are not in fact receiving suitable treatment at several points. Specific mention was made of the need to arrange things so that more use was made of the specific talents of the teachers themselves on behalf of all children but especially on behalf of the most able.

G.C.P.S.—6*

SCHOOL D:

Location	City	*SES*	High
Roll	506 (nearly all boys	*Staff*	42 + 12 part-time (music) (mostly male)
Age range	6–14 years	*Peripatetics*	None

School time 9–5.30 plus 'prep', with free time 12.00–1.00 (unless in games or 'activities'), 1.45–2.30; 4.30–5.30. Saturday mornings 8.00–11.50 (with 34 week year). Wednesdays, half-day holiday.

Grouping systems
After the first year setting for different subjects occurs in groups of twenty on average. There are five grades across each year group, and the amount of setting varies with age. Youngest children not setted at all, or streamed.

8 and 9 years setted only in mathematics; streamed in five groups

10 and 11 years setted in mathematics and French; streamed in five groups

12 and 13 years setted in all subjects, with English, history, geography in one 'block'

Acceleration occurs quite regularly as a matter of policy.

Staffing patterns
Every child has a form master and personal tutor who liaises with parents. Specialization expands parallel to the amount of setting which is organized. There is a very wide range of specialist help, especially in music which is paid for separately by parents.

Timetable and curriculum content
The timetable is rigid from 9 years on and relatively inflexible to meet specialist teaching requirements. The courses are largely planned to the requirements of the Public Schools scholarship and Common Entrance examinations. The mathematics syllabus is that drawn up by the Joint Committee of Preparatory and Public Schools. The main subjects and time distributions are as follows for the eleven-plus groups:

Mathematics and science	10 lessons + 3 preps
Classics	8 lessons + 3 preps
French	6 lessons + 2 preps
English, Divinity, history and geography	11 lessons + 5 preps
Art, handicraft and physical education	1 period each, i.e. 3 lessons in all.

A teaching period is 35 minutes and prep 30 minutes. The 'extra-mural' activities are very comprehensive, including judo and speech, bridge and chess clubs.

Links with outside agencies
Mainly IAPS committee links are used as advisory services for equipment and curriculum development. On the whole the school operates on its own resources. There are inter-school games leagues, however, including 7-a-side rugby. The school has three orchestras and one choir: it joins occasionally with other independent schools to produce concerts. The only link with the state system is through the local schools soccer league.

AVT
The school is equipped with two science laboratories and an 'audio active' language laboratory. There is a special mathematics room with standard equipment.

Teachers make use of modern visual aids and audio equipment including an overhead projector, two cine projectors and television sets. Several tape recorders and slide projectors are available together with radios and record players.

There is, however, little or no use of tapes and slides for individualized programming. Project 'kits' etc., are not in widespread use, and cassette recorders are not yet on the equipment list. Musical instruments are available for loan to beginners.

Recognition and treatment of gifted children
The grouping arrangements have already implied the steps which are taken to provide for individualization. The need to teach in groups is accepted without question, and the children generally operate at the average speed of their own particular sets, very much in the 'traditional' manner.

Staff views
(*a*) Good social training requires that the most able be subjected to some 'head shrinking' as well as some mixing of children of differing abilities.

(*b*) A child who has any bent at all practically can have a go at it here.

(*c*) Of course we believe in competition so long as it's not carried too far. We always praise the successful and those who make an effort. Only those who tend to 'look, listen and laze' need to be pushed, and these sometimes include very able boys in fact.

Supplementary information: headteachers' comments

In an attempt to amplify the descriptions above some headteachers were kind enough to offer comments on sets of statements deliberately couched in more provocative phraseology. Two examples are given below without detailed reference to the schools themselves.

SCHOOL E

Grouping systems : (i) initial comment

(i, ii, iii) The school is divided into 14 classes, all unstreamed year groups, with VRQ ranges from a few 150+ to 80+.

The class system is broken down for 'club' activities each Wednesday afternoon, and for groups of remedial readers and peripatetic instrumental teachers. Other less formal groupings occur, as when students from college take small groups of children for special learning sessions. These occasions do not lead to any permanent arrangements, however, and hence do not influence the patterns of learning established.

There are no longer 'team' teaching approaches which require classes to be combined. The average class size is 35.

The school thus has four classes in each year and some years ago the headteacher grouped children by ages in a 'stratified' arrangement whereby the age ranges were reduced to about 3 months in order to compensate to some extent for the wide ability ranges which appear when classes are unstreamed. This system had to be changed owing to the fact that the older children got far more than their 'fair share' of scholarship places, and this led to parental objections. In effect the oldest group formed what seemed to be the old A-stream in a new guise. Why the older groups should be more than normally successful is an unsolved problem. It could be simply that the standardized tests are improperly corrected for age differences when teaching is geared more closely to abilities; or the extra time older children spend in the infants school (this could be checked by seeing whether the differences increase or decrease with age, of course); or because teachers' expectations are higher for older children and actually result in a greater 'stretching' process than occurs with younger children in the same age group. (I would like to have your explanations for this phenomenon.) Of course if the number of scholarships is now equalled out across the age groups there would seem to be an *a priori* case for arguing that the older children are being held back assuming that the mean achievement for the whole year group is no better than it was, i.e. the average number of scholarships has remained the same.

The within-class groupings are idiosyncratic and depend upon the teacher's individual ideas as to what is appropriate. Since nearly all children read fairly well when they enter the school there is a fair amount of individual work based on workcards and textbooks, but more often classes work an integrated day based upon group activities. About 4 groups per class is the norm with the groups being based on language ability largely although 'interest' and 'friendship' groups are common in topic work and more specific abilities are recognized in PE and games.

(iv) Since groupings are so haphazard it is impossible to say just how long on average any child spends in any particular size or type of group. Possibly half time is spent in 'class' activities and the remainder in groups or individual activities. There would seem to be a lack of precision in what we intend by phrases like 'individual learning', 'working at his own level', 'group activities' etc. This leads to a lack of interest in the question as to just what kind of groups are required for what purposes, except when emotive factors are introduced into the discussion. Thus many teachers are certain that segregation to special schools inhibits a balanced social development, yet they have no idea of the length of time a child spends in a mixed social group within their own school.

Grouping systems: (ii) headteacher's observations
(i) The clubs and groupings, whilst not influencing the permanent 'class' pattern, *do* influence the patterns of learning, by, for example, starting activities and enthusiasms, which children continue in the class situation—in 'topic' work, or at home.

The *average* class size is now 40.

(ii) The 4 month age-groupings were merely a follow-on from the Infants, when children were put into these groups as they entered school. The 'random mixture' substitute did not come about through any parental objections, but because we felt that we were not fulfilling our non-stream philosophy, which our parents were told by me we followed, and that the 'O' group *did* seem to operate as an 'A' group, towards 11.

I had always assumed that the older children were more successful because of the almost-a-year's longer schooling than the young ones.

The unstreamed arrangement has evened out the passes, class by class.

(iv) Yes, I must acknowledge that we have not 'gone into' grouping systems for specific purposes. We feel that 'setting' would be against our individual philosophy. The groups are not on 'language ability', and may be of any number or for any length of time, by no means arbitrarily 4.

Staffing patterns: (i) initial comment
(i) PSRs exist for deputy head, music, mathematics, science, art, PE (gymnastics) and library. The emphasis on gymnastics grew out of an awareness that overstress on movement had led to a serious deterioration in the capabilities of those children able to perform gymnastics extremely well.

(ii, iii) As noted, there is no 'team' teaching. Specialists teach music (throughout the school), PE and games (upper school) and art and craft (upper school), otherwise individual teachers use their special expertise in the 'club' periods. Two classes are shared between four part-time teachers in order to permit two 'floaters' to specialize most of the time.

Staff meetings do not occur regularly, and are organized around special events. One occasion was used for the head of the infants school to outline her mathematics scheme. There is considerable informal discussion in the staff room at lunch times.

Advisers and Inspectors do not help specifically with advice on how to 'stretch' gifted children. Nevertheless general assistance has important side effects exemplified here by the provision of Olympic gymnastic apparatus which has resulted in some children being able to show outstanding potential.

The art adviser runs an art centre in the City. Again this is not specifically for gifted children but the associated exhibitions can set standards of achievement if properly organized. Children of primary ages do not attend this centre.

Other centres—maths and science—do not run any courses for children, but concentrate on in-service training. One course of relevance to teaching gifted children was arranged to include a series of talks by outstanding people in various fields—poetry, art, architecture etc.

There is a nature club run by the museum which meets weekly, and summer holiday courses are organized by museum staff too where youngsters are encouraged to attend.

There is, of course, the library service which can be used, but the school has an excellent library of its own. Objets d'art can also be borrowed.

Staffing patterns: (ii) headteacher's observations
(i) Substitute 'educational gymnastics' for 'movement'.

(ii) Staff meetings, whilst not occurring regularly, average about once-a-week. For instance, we met 3 times last week to decide 'capitation' spending for the year (£500 on metric equipment; £300 on library, £100 on visual and aural aids etc.). This week we have had 3 meetings—very lively—on 'gifted'.

The local Inspectors, through teachers' centres and visits, do help in keeping up standards. Much advice and equipment was given on use of our spinney. The local Inspectors also organized a symposium on giftedness, when speakers were Geo. Robb and J. McNally. Many in-service courses are run to raise teachers' own performance-levels.

Children can and do attend the art centre, both for exhibiting and appreciation.

There is no library service. A local branch library operates in basement, which children use. We used to use it in school time, until our own library was built up. But we feel we can select books better for ourselves. We have well over 10,000 library books, carefully selected.

Timetables and curriculum content: (i) initial comment
(i) The School Programme recognizes the following activities:

Language (English—but not French since LEA started a pilot project elsewhere and prevented other schools from continuing their own programmes)

Mathematics—practical and number

Science (Environmental Studies? Engaged in Schools Council Science Project)

PE and games (including gymnastics, swimming for 3rd/4th years plus very able 1st/2nd years)

Art and craft (including needlework)
Religious education
Music (instruments include recorder, clarinet, violin, viola, cello and brass)
'Clubs' (see later)
Movement and drama.

There are no detailed syllabuses, and programmes in various fields derive from:

1   Textbooks—mathematics and language skills especially
2   Teachers' handbooks—PE and games, art and craft
3   Reading schemes (lower school only). There is no SRA type reading scheme for upper school
4   Individual teachers—PSRs are expected to keep up with curriculum developments in their fields.

There are no secondary school texts available and secondary school teachers have not been consulted as to curriculum content in any field. There is a strong tendency to aim at 'breadth' rather than 'depth' studies in, say, mathematics.

Progress in the basic skills is based on records of children's work kept in the individual child's own 'work book' and comprehensive records of individual performances are not thought to be worthwhile. They 'tend to drift'. Achievement tests are arranged, however, avoiding 'examination' atmospheres and children look forward to these—occur mainly in connexion with mathematical operations (the Four Rules etc.) and language skills (reading, spelling and comprehension).

Standardized objective tests are used only in connexion with $11+$ selection procedures, and with allocations to remedial reading groups. For the latter, IQ tests are administered at 8 years of age, but these tests are not used to identify 'gifted' as well as retarded pupils.

Homework as such is not encouraged. Children often do project work at home as a 'carry over' from school and if any child specifically asked for homework in formal skills no doubt this would be suggested. In practice little of the more formal work is done.

The 'club' activities include a wide variety of interests, e.g., football, art, paper sculpture, drama, gymnastics, nature study, instrumental music (orchestra), German and needlework.

A noteworthy omission would appear to be girls' games, but altogether these activities represent a very considerable extension of the curriculum in 'depth' rather than 'breadth' in some sense. The fact that children can only pursue their 'interest' for one term, however, is a weakness, and possibly an important one, since several of the activities are in fact already represented in the ordinary timetable and cannot thus be justified as an extension to it. The purpose in these areas must be to enable children to pursue a 'study' in greater depth; and a term seems likely to be too short a time for much to happen. One term of German for example, would seem to be of little use really.

The extra-mural activities are not timetabled officially, but generally recorder groups, the orchestra and gymnastic clubs meet once per week during lunch times. There are no other regular meetings apart from team games practices, and a visit to the Swimming Baths after school once per week. Only 3rd/4th year children enjoy this facility, but a few exceptional 1st/2nd years are included.

(iv) *Use of AVT:* The school possesses all the usual gear—16 mm projector, strip projector, 1 tape recorder, 2 record players, 2 radios, 3 TVs, and a pottery kiln.

The tape recorder is used to individualize activities to some extent by having children read into it their stories or from books and then listen to play-backs as part of a self-correcting exercise. Children even in first year successfully operate this themselves and there is room for a great extension of this sort of 'self-directed' exercise. The use of projects and TVs by children themselves may be retarded by danger of damage to equipment rather than inability of children to operate the mechanisms.

There are no teaching machines partly because suitable 'learning kits' are not available.

The Museum and Art Loan Service help to provide contact with reputable works of art, and should stimulate able children to emulate the 'great'.

Timetables and curriculum content: (ii) headteacher's observations
(i) The LEA did *not* prevent. They followed the Schools Council's advice on French, at the time, which, I believe, expressed concern at continuity and suggested 'pilot' trial areas!

(ii) Syllabuses (item 3): SRA was considered, but thought much too rigid. Breadth and depth in reading for our kind of pupil thought best served by our library of almost 10,000 books, supplied from capitation and by Parents Association.

'Breadth.' Yes, we have a general concern, we hope, for *all* our children, not just gifted, and only 'breadth' enables as many as possible to find their individual 'gifts'.

But 'depth' also is considered as, for example, we have many other 'maths' texts, as well as our main series, on to which we put gifted individuals. Indeed some *are* 'secondary' texts.

(iii) Comprehensive records are kept on all children, in addition to their own 'workbook' ones, by giving achievement tests, and obtaining standardized scores in (*a*) composition, (*b*) comprehension, (*c*) use of English, (*d*) maths problem solving, (*e*) maths concept understanding, (*f*) general knowledge.

In addition at least two verbal quotients are obtained through NFER and Moray House tests. All this goes on cumulative record cards. Reports go out to parents once a year and these are compiled on Plowden Letter Grade lines, with the letters based on yearly tests. These reports are immediately followed by a 'personal appointment' for parents with each child's class teacher. (A long and arduous business which will take most members of staff 3 or 4 evenings next week until up to 10 o'clock.) We also have 'Getting to know teacher' personal interviews each October. 'Reading age' tests have also been used. We certainly take note of our IQ tests to identify 'gifted', but not to make detailed individual 'stretching' syllabuses. There is good liaison between staff on records.

The older girls (ages 9–10–11) have specific 'games' periods weekly. Although I said many children changed clubs termly, some clubs are continuous; e.g. art and music. There are keen musicians and artists who have been in these clubs for 2 years and pursue their own choice activities either in 'depth' or 'breadth'.

I believe the activities of the clubs can certainly be justified as extension of ordinary timetable, as there is the essential 'seen' element of individual choice, which, though it may also be apparent in class, is not always 'seen' to be so to the children. It is the 'choice' element which is special about the clubs.

The German Club continues and will continue.

Some clubs—music, gym, movement—meet at dinner time several times a week, and also after school.

Recorder groups, orchestra, gym club also meet *after* school, as well as games teams. Various concerts, festivals, displays, drama performances for parents, are prepared for. (Example—the recorder club from the city is coming tonight, to play, with children for the parents.) A Red Cross Link meets every Tuesday after school for girls and boys interested in nursing. A youth centre meets every Thursday evening, 7–9, run by local Church and by a youth leader, at which many of our children attend.

(iv) *Use of AVT :* further tape recorders/cassette recorders, transistor radios are being bought this year.

Children operating equipment—the comment on damage only applied to one class. The majority are capable of operating and careful.

There are various programmed texts in school for extending individuals; not many, I admit.

Links with extra-mural agencies : (i) initial comment
Apart from those mentioned incidentally above, the school maintains positive links (in the sense that children will be deliberately guided there) with the local ASA and schools orchestra, with the local polytechnic PE department and with the local teachers' college.

Special mention should be made of the place of competitions in other fields. These arise in some sense incidentally but not haphazardly and by mere accident. The headteacher and staff deliberately encourage children to enter a variety of competitions including those for children of secondary age where no minimum age limit is laid down. Thus the competition has produced several bronze and silver medallists, and the Times Educational Supplement Poetry Competition has given rise to high standards of work. The vital point is that this attitude to competitions enables children of widely different types of talent to attempt a challenge which will 'stretch' them beyond the normal in a field where they have already discovered their ability to some extent. In some sense, moreover, it enables the school itself to check on its own achievements in various fields.

There are no evening or Saturday morning classes for children under twelve/thirteen in any fields beyond those mentioned above.

In the past 'experts' of various kinds have been invited to join in the teaching associated with 'club activities', and university people have on occasion joined in these opportunities. This system does not, however, appear to work at all well and the whole thing has fallen through despite the headteacher's efforts to keep it alive. The reasons why such an arrangement fails to work are of interest and not self-evident.

The PTA provides considerable sums of money but no parents help in the classroom.

The psychological services take no positive interest in 'gifted' children as such, and the school has not found it necessary to approach them for advice on the treatment of any gifted individual.

There are no formal links with local soccer clubs and amateur associations of any kind.

Links with extra-mural agencies: (ii) headteacher's observations
The Times Educational Supplement Poetry Competition: actually for secondary pupils, but some of our children's poems were quoted from.

'Experts'. Wrong choice. Six came from University selected by Dr K from those willing and able. (Some, I gathered, were a little superior, others even apprehensive about talking to 'mites'.) Two went well; the astronomer who started a club which continued after school, with fathers involved, for about a year, until the teacher left. Also a local history expert was successful. The others were too much up in the clouds and the children found them difficult to understand and became bored. 'Ordinary' visitors: police/fire/blind/local ornithologist/gamekeeper. Parental help, football coaching—swimming (Parent ASA coach). Red Cross, group of mothers act as telephonist and help with expeditions.

Re: Psychological Service. It is quite possible the local service is interested in 'gifted'. But we have not approached them. The waiting list for under-achievers is far too long!

Recognition and treatment of gifted children : general views of staff
(i) initial comment
As noted incidentally above, 'gifted' children are recognized only in connexion
with specific activities or needs. Thus the 11+ selection procedure reveals
pupils who are outstandingly able in the general intellectual sense, the
teachers select games players for school teams, instrumental players for town
and school orchestras, and swimmers for school and town galas. Apart from
these selection processes which are without doubt immensely valuable in
stimulating teachers to recognize very able pupils the school tries to treat all
children in accordance with their individual needs and capacities. The plain
fact is, however, that effective recognition only derives from a knowledge of
what educational treatment might be effective; and where we do not know
how to lead the child further along his chosen path, there is no point in doing
more than remark the fact that he could probably go further if only we had
the resources, the 'know-how' etc.

Staff do not find that the most able children are already sufficiently advantaged not to require very careful treatment. Special mention is made of certain
needs which, though not specific to 'gifted' children, are associated with them
in a more extreme form. Thus:

1   Emotional and social development may be out of step with intellect.

2   Parents frequently fail to treat the child as a child and he acts like a
'little adult'. This can be irritating in itself since child will join in discussions
on topics which he knows almost nothing about.

3   Teachers find precocity disturbing, and may be made to feel insecure
themselves either by parents or by child or both.

4   Child must be stretched if he is not to be bored and frustrated.

5   Counselling of parents—there is often a 'pressurized' environment at
home based on the best of motives perhaps but not in the best interests of the
child necessarily. Some certainly minimize in the eyes of the child the importance of, say, artistic activities or sport or indeed straightforward play
activities.

6   Tolerance of imbalance—teachers stress balanced development and
good social/emotional growth to a much greater degree than may be justifiable
by the facts. Some certainly fail to differentiate 'balance' as this applied to
personality traits from 'integration'. The former, within very wide limits, is
not essential to the latter since most of us are 'unbalanced' intellectually or
otherwise but we cannot be sensibly termed 'disintegrated' in the same
degree.

7   Gifted children also need identifying, and the most important dimensions as the primary age would seem to derive from the curriculum of the
school as given. A widening of the curriculum ought to occur in terms of
more variety in ball games and the inclusion of a second language.

8   More opportunity to be 'unbalanced' was suggested by some teachers

in that they felt that for some children there could be too much stress on mathematics for too long. The conditions under which individual children should be permitted to drop maths were specified only in terms of having attained a reasonable grasp of 'basic knowledge'.

Staff views on recognition : (ii) headteacher's observations
(ii) [alter wording] after Thus: The staff expressed concern over the following:

1

2

3   I would not say 'disturbing', rather the occasional irritant as in para. 2. Occasionally 'inadequate', never insecure. (Staff felt strongly on this.)

5   (This may be due to continuance of 11+ here.)

7   We play 'shinty', rounders, cricket, netball, football, already. Second language: again, refer to Schools Council's findings. Resources are limited and priorities need to be watched.

Other points : (i) initial comment
We need somehow to increase the place of specialist teaching whilst at the same time maintaining something of the traditional 'class teacher' relationship. There is a place for 'specialist' rooms for some activities—art/craft, science, music, and for quiet individual study, practising, 'machine' programmes etc.

Individualized learning is talked about *ad nauseam* but is not carried far enough even in the best schools. Circumstances inimical to extension include:

1   Too large a pupil/teacher ratio

2   Insufficient space

3   Insufficient equipment, especially 'learning kits' and 'programmes'

4   Too little opportunity for staff to use individual talents, and in some areas (e.g. maths) too few knowledgeable teachers anyhow

5   Inability of headteachers to play a more positive part in selecting their 'team'.

There is some evidence that advice against buying sets of textbooks has been interpreted by teachers as advice against textbooks as such. Hence vast amounts of time that could be used in other ways is consumed in making up individual cards which are no more than textbook extracts.

The interference of an LEA in the curriculum provision on grounds of lack of 'continuity' in the secondary schools is dangerous in terms of provision for 'gifted' children particularly since they include 'gifted' linguists whose potential in French remains undeveloped during a crucial period of life as a result.

Other points : (ii) headteacher's observations
4   Individual talents. I do not honestly see how we could do more to foster use of individual teacher's talents.

5   Selecting 'team'. Initially staff are appointed. There is consultation with our staffing officer, but heads are not concerned in interview. Beyond this, all SR posts are influenced by head (i.e. he is involved in interview), and he is consulted on deputy head's appointment.

Textbook provision: children work individually at own pace through:

Beta Mathematics series plus lateral additions of various kinds, *Alpha*, OUP, Flavell and Wakelam, some Sealey, some Fletcher and various sets of individual cards and topic books, using variety of apparatus. Much decimal material and metric.

English in Action series

Reading to Some Purpose series (lower school)

Dictionaries—progressive. Each child has dictionary.

(i) *2000 words for Reading and Writing* (picture)

(ii) *A First Dictionary*

(iii) *Kingsway Dictionary*

(iv) *Collins Etymological**

Nelson's Handwriting Workbooks (15 mins per day in lower school)

Wide Range Readers or *Ladybird* or *Data*, according to child, with questions, in lower school, for most children.

These are the basic texts, and at the upper end of the school, the children plan their own weekly assignments with their teacher's advice. The teacher helps on request, and checks regularly on achievement with each child.

I thought our textbooks were amply in evidence and casual card material really quite small.

Final para: It was the Schools Council's 'interference' (according to our local inspector), in the language field, and *their* recommendation which influenced the policy.*

SCHOOL F

Grouping systems: (i) initial comment

(i, ii, iii) Nine classes grouped in years. First and second years are unstreamed; third and fourth years are streamed as A and B. A streams are bigger in size to facilitate remedial work and smaller groupings in B streams. Within class, groupings are not left wholly in the hands of individual teachers. The unstreamed lower school must group for mathematics and language skills—usually four groups for each class. In the upper school, the B stream classes

---

* This work is linked with training in using reference books. The dictionaries overlap, as, of course, many children in Is are capable of using *A First Dictionary*.

There are 16 sets of encyclopaedias in the school, both in library and for each year group (quickly get-attable). We try to train children early to use alphabetical order to look up word meanings, to look up references, so that they can find their own information in 'discovery' or other work.

tend to group as in lower school, whereas A streams tend to be taught as a class. Ability is the basis of grouping in language, mathematics and games; mixed abilities in project work, drama, handwork, music etc.

Remedial groups occur for reading, 6 children per group, each group receiving daily practice where necessary, others only twice per week. No remedial work needed in fourth year.

Other groups are associated with two visiting string teachers (cello, violin and viola).

(iv, v) It is impossible to say how much time any child spends working in groups or as an individual or in personal contact with the teacher. The probability is that the amount is less than one third of the time in other than class groupings, for all but remedial teaching; and that the amount of personal individual contact with the teacher is almost nil. Certainly there is a tendency to overlook how little individual work is in fact achieved, even in, say, mathematics.

Grouping systems: (ii) headteacher's observations
(i, ii, iii) There is a good deal more individual work than your comment suggests. The usual four groups in unstreamed classes (for language and mathematics) are not equal in size. In a second year class, by Christmas, in formal English say, I would expect more than half the class to be using the second year book, but the children would be well spaced out through it. A few children would have begun the third year book, perhaps some still using the first year book, and a fourth group working through special books supplied by the remedial teacher.

Groupings *are* left to individual class teachers apart from remedial groups. I would expect the composition of groups to vary from subject to subject.

(iv, v) I cannot agree that individual contact with teacher is nil, e.g. I expect each teacher to go round the class examining work being done at least once each maths and English lesson.

Staffing patterns: (i) initial comment
(i, ii, iii) *Areas of co-operation:* general co-operation and intercommunication is achieved by informal discussion. No regular staff meetings are held, and formal meetings occur on an *ad hoc* basis to deal with particular events. Individuals are brought up for discussion only if they are a nuisance in some way.

Specialization occurs in needlework, art and craft, physical education, and music (upper school). French is developing this way. Team teaching occurs in relation to recorder groups, and the school orchestra is run by two teachers co-operatively. Responsibility allowances bear no relation to 'specialist' responsibility. Note that these allowances have increased the mobility of teachers— from smaller schools to larger ones. Thus the smaller tend to have more rapid turnovers and less experienced people than bigger schools.

Visiting teachers assist as follows:
1 Remedial reading every morning
2 Instrumental music—viola, violin and cello (3 hours per week)
3 PE specialist teachers for one whole day per week
4 Drama—one morning per week (class teacher takes remedial group)
5 Science—Nuffield teacher for 2 mornings per week

The aim behind visiting teachers, music apart, is to help the retarded or is a form of in-service training for teachers. There has so far been no evidence that very able children as such have benefited from the presence of a 'subject expert'. The reasons for this are obscure.

Little use is made of unpaid visiting experts other than, say, policemen. Parents are not involved in school work in any capacity whatsoever. An interesting exchange of staff in connexion with a visit to the Field Study Centre is noteworthy though.

Advisers play only a general role. Occasionally will take class of children but have not helped to plan special programmes for the very able. Most teachers don't ask for guidance directly.

Music organizer runs three orchestras in the town, especially for primary children. *But for strings only.*

Inspectors show no interest in the very able child as such. Keen on un-streaming and the creation of mixed ability groups.

There are local museum and library services, but neither run special classes in the evenings or on Saturday mornings.

Staffing patterns: (ii) headteacher's observations
(i, ii, iii) In a school of this size, a great deal can be achieved by informal discussion. The atmosphere in this staff-room is such that I can introduce a subject and obtain teachers' views more freely indeed than if I announced that I was holding a 'staff meeting'.

Usually individuals are brought up for discussion etc., but there is discussion of gifted children and work is shown to other members of staff. Each class displays work in turn on large display panel in corridor.

There is only one Scale One graded post in the school between nine teachers. (Compare with a school of twelve and/or sixteen teachers.) Your point about turnover is very important and might well be emphasized more.

Primary orchestra for strings only because only stringed instruments are supplied to primary schools under committee scheme, though I have arranged tuition for two girls who have bought own clarinets.

'Most teachers don't ask for guidance directly' you might add 'but the head-teacher has called in organizers to help individual teachers' and in-service courses are held continually at teachers' centre.

Timetable and curriculum content : (i) initial comment

(i) The school timetable provides constraints only through use of special rooms—hall etc. and specialist teacher commitments. The total time involved in these 'rigid' elements approximates 5 hours per week in lower school and 7 hours per week in upper school. No 'club' activities cut across classes other than recorder groups.

There is no timetable of extra-mural activities which are in any case confined to recorder groups and games. The choir meets occasionally, as does the country dancing group.

(ii) The class timetable is determined by the individual teacher and no generalizations are possible beyond the point that the mornings generally are occupied with 'basic skills' work. A detailed analysis is thus required to allocate time to particular activities. The activities generally recognized are:

1 Music—singing and instrumental opportunities
2 PE—including swimming for 2nd/3rd/4th years
3 Games
4 Art and craft—excluding pottery
5 Mathematics
6 Language—including French for 2nd/3rd/4th years
7 RE (West Riding syllabus)
8 Environmental studies.

(iii) The school syllabuses are not detailed and comprise a set of schemes of work. The amount of progress expected is left for individual teachers to decide.

Reading progress is guided by the usual schemes. Each member of staff keeps own records in own way. No centralized records of reading ages are kept. Older children simply read library books. See notes.

Mathematics is more closely controlled by means of a carefully constructed sequential scheme. Individualization of progress is achieved by use of textbooks which accord fairly well with scheme.

Environmental studies schemes indicate broad topics to avoid overlap from year to year, and a balance of coverage. No particular body of knowledge is aimed for. The assessment of individual progress is not attempted.

Language, comprising speaking, creative writing and language skills. Only the latter are individualized in terms of progressive development and are based on textbooks as in mathematics.

Clear patterns of developmental sequences are not laid down in other aspects of the curriculum. In art and craft there is a gradually widening range of materials which children experience.

Homework is encouraged and the following work is available:

(i) *Assessment Papers in English*, J. M. Bond (Nelson)
(ii) *New Assessment Papers in Mathematics*, J. M. Bond (Nelson)

(iii) *6 A Day (Metric Edition)*, A. L. Griffiths (Oliver and Boyd)
(iv) *Graded Arithmetic Practice Book*, K. A. Hess (Longman)

Parents buy these but poorer children can borrow them from school.

(iv) *Use of AVT :* The usual film and slide projectors are available with 3 tape recorders used mainly for French and broadcasts. Two microscopes are used, but no cameras.

ATV is not used by individuals or small groups, and there are no tape or slide programmes which could be made available to enable very intelligent children to go forward at a faster pace than the rest.

BBC broadcasts tend to become class lessons, and are aimed at wide ability ranges in general. They are thus not a means of stretching the able apparently.

Timetable and curriculum content : (ii) headteacher's observations
(i) Recorder groups cut across classes.

(iii) 'Keeps records in own way' applies in this case to reading, but all teachers have the same type of record book in which they record work done week by week, including reading. 'Simply read library books?' A good deal of reading is involved in project work. In third and fourth year a child will produce, perhaps eight projects a year. In some cases a project will be over forty double sided pages of writing and illustrations.

I'm not sure what is meant by 'no particular body of knowledge is aimed for'. If we want all children to develop fully we cannot lay down exactly what each child will learn especially in a school like this where the range of ability is so huge. I aim to make a scheme which only the most brilliant child could complete. The others must progress as far as they can. It is the teacher's job to see that they do so. Individual work is marked A–E scale.

(iv) I agree with this, but until we have more equipment, e.g., video tape recorder, we must either ignore the BBC or accept the class lesson criticism.

Linking structures : (i) initial comment
(i) PTA becoming more active recently. Two meetings per term—1 business and 1 social. There is no counselling at an individual level as yet; nor have parents been used as 'aides' or sources of a variety of expertises.

Educational psychologists would be helpful in confirming teachers' recognition no doubt, but are unhelpful when it comes to offering advice on the kinds of work the 'gifted' children ought to be doing.

Apart from an isolated instance of sending a child to a gymnastics class, there are no other links. Saturday morning groups (except for string music and games) do not exist.

Linking structures : (ii) headteacher's observations
(i) PTA was started by me one year ago. It is now becoming *very* active.
'No counselling?' We have one open afternoon and one open evening (6.00–

8.30 p.m.) when all parents are invited (and come) to meet teachers and discuss work.

Parents are encouraged to see me at any time without ceremony and *do*.

Recognition and treatment of gifted children : (i) initial comment
There is a first year IQ test in order to select those in need of remedial treatment which reveals some children with IQs of 140+ including an odd one or two who cannot read. This apart there is no special treatment of those who display exceptional potential at this point, or indeed at any point. Advancement in one year possible.

Instrumental groups are selected by the peripatetic teacher who also chooses those who are to go to Saturday string orchestra. The demand for violins is always greater than the supply.

The school recorder groups are graded and the difficulty here is that there are no external orchestras or other means for allowing the very best to extend themselves to, say, flute or clarinet.

School examinations in the 3 Rs are conducted each summer and are the basis of a report, and classes run their own examinations each term.

There are also examinations in connexion with the direct grant grammar school. Children can be entered for these at any age from 8 years onwards, and one or two children change schools each year. It can be said, therefore, that the intellectually able are recognized in many cases, though not necessarily all of course. How far able children get more appropriate treatment at the grammar school than if they remain [here] is an open question it seems. The fact that these examinations exist tends to strengthen the concentration on reading ability at the earliest ages and there is very close liaison with the infant school about this aspect of work. The recognition of other kinds of gifts is far less efficient, as noted, and this probably has to do with our inability to be clear about what we should do with, say, the outstanding artist, even when we see him. This is a bigger problem than that of 'recognition' itself in all probability.

Recognition and treatment of gifted children : (ii) headteacher's observations
'No special treatment' etc. Children may be advanced one year if they display exceptional potential and sent on to comprehensive school a year early. In practice this rarely happens.

May progress to woodwind after eleven years.

Apart from grammar school for boys there is a direct grant school—high school for girls, and others of similar character. So far this year we have been offered 21 places in these schools on roll of 266 children with more places still to come. The majority of these are young children. Parents in the main do not regard education in these junior departments as in any way superior; but they want to get their children in when they can. They do not want them to go to a comprehensive, and think the competition for places fiercer at eleven years, as indeed it is.

Staff views, case studies and general points
Needs of gifted:
(i) To be extended, to experience friendly competition
(ii) To have contacts with others equally gifted
(iii) To have parents who understand their capabilities—counselling by close contact with teachers and school
(iv) All round social development—despite the presence of the grammar school, the staff are not in favour of segregation. The provision of a network of 'supportive' agencies of various kinds is widely advocated here instead.

The removal of the 11+ could lead to declining standards in basic skills which is not compensated for by a 'broadening' of the curriculum.

Use of specialist visitors divorces 'lesson' content from rest of curriculum and minimizes individual treatment anyway.

Establishment of a central teacher pool? Prefers a school based team—an extra teacher permanently rather than a group of visiting specialists.

The preservation of the 'general teacher' role for social reasons has dangers for the development of special gifts. We have to compromise and extend the possibilities for getting children exposed to more teachers more often. AVT might be of great help here. The presence of a science specialist with the children on a school visit brought about rising standards of work which were most noticeably achieved by the very able children. This came about mainly as a result of her ability to direct them more effectively. She 'gave them so many things to do'.

'Club' activities are in urgent need of extension—chess, mathematics, art, all should be included in, say, a 'Saturday morning centre'.

The preceding descriptions of schools together with the related dialogues demonstrates the difficulties involved in assessing the degree of individualization inherent in the practice and provision of any particular school. The first step in any attempt at such an evaluation is clearly to relate the school description to our analysis of the concept of individualization provided above and seek clear answers to questions implied by points such as those listed on pages 113, 119 and 121. A second essential step would be to apply the checklist criteria provided in Part III below and thus arrive at a summary description which would at one and the same time evaluate the situation and indicate methods of improvement.

To some extent these tasks must be left to the individual reader, but certain conclusions are inescapable and must be stated, however unpalatable they may be:

1   The degree of real individualization which occurs in primary schools is far from sufficient.

2   Some groups of children experience a much greater degree of individual treatment than others, and very able children are seldom the focus of efforts to individualize.

3   Where there is any concentration on talented children as such this is confined almost always to music and sport, and even here provision is exceedingly patchy.

4   Schools which attempt to extend their personalized approach to cover wide ability ranges and multifarious interests are, in present circumstances, labouring under very great difficulties and constraints, many of which are by no means of their own making.

Special groups of gifted children

The schools described above have not in the main provided for special groupings and programmes for the gifted as such. A small number of special experimental groups do, however, exist and it is to this element of present provisions, therefore, that attention may now be directed.

THE TEMPEST GROUP (LIVERPOOL UNIVERSITY)

One of the aims of this experiment, which began in 1967, was to teach a group of 15 gifted children (IQ 130 upwards, WISC) over the four junior school years (age 7–11) in order to develop curriculum materials which might be of use to a teacher with one or two such children in a normal primary class. The teaching has been under the control of a single teacher during that time, and the class has been attached to an ordinary primary school in much the same way as special classes for slow learners are organized in some places. The teacher has received assistance from a university psychologist, a grammar school teacher of German, a music tutor from a college of education, and a scientist from the University School of Education. The project has been financed by the Leverhulme Trust.

It is not the function of the present investigator to anticipate Professor Tempest's own report on his study. Only one or two points of immediate importance are, therefore, listed here.

1   In spite of the careful selection process, not all the children appeared to be exceptionally able.

2   Many of the group present very uneven profiles of attainment.

3   There is a very high level of conceptualization within the group but the average social and emotional development does not differ markedly from that of children of the same age. One or two children, however, show responsibility beyond their years.

4   Highly structured 'kits' of materials, reference books etc., have been developed to enable children to work by themselves at their own speeds.

5   The teacher involved has found the task of providing for a mere fifteen able children immensely onerous and time consuming. They have shown a powerful need to know precise detail and fact with regard to historical incidents etc., which goes beyond anything one individual can provide. This teacher finds that he cannot always keep up with merely suggesting useful sources of the required information: so much so, that on occasion he has not been sure whether in fact the required information was available at all anywhere.

6   In mathematics, provision for the wide range of achievement was made by specially constructed assignment cards designed to supplement the normal work books.

7   In general, the use of expensive equipment was avoided in order to keep conditions of the experiment as close as possible to those normally obtaining in primary schools.

AN 'EXTENDED ACTIVITIES' GROUP IN WEST SUSSEX

This type of group is exemplified most obviously by the 'Brentwood experiment' which has been fully described in the book by Dr Bridges. No additional information is required here therefore, and the only worthwhile comment arising from a visit to one of the schools involved was that there was far too little liaison with the schools. The work in which the children engaged showed little carry-over into the life of the school itself, and the teachers remained largely in ignorance of what was being attempted. It has to be remembered, of course, as Dr Bridges himself points out, that the main aim of the experiment was to increase student awareness of child capability rather than to cater specially for the particular needs of a group of children or schools.

Not that the children were mere 'guinea pigs'. The briefest glance at Bridges' book shows what valuable work was done; and it transpired in any event that had one girl not been involved at Brentwood, she might have been with her class doing a French course which she had in fact already completed a year earlier.

At the same time, it is obvious that 'extended activity' classes in which there is a very great degree of co-operation between all the teachers to whom any child is exposed are maximally advantageous, and it is important therefore, to review the work of such a group. The major aim behind the creation of the teaching arrangements to be described is stated by the organizers as follows:

[We] hope that this will help us to work out means by which the children can best be taught; our aim here is to develop ways in which these children, in general, can be helped in normal schools rather than to provide them with some segregated form of education.

The general philosophy behind the project is perhaps best summarized by noticing that

It was agreed to designate the group as 'The Extended Activities Group' rather than as a 'Part time class for gifted children'. The chosen title indicates the desirability for the children involved to pursue their Group activities in their own schools should the opportunities arise.

The children involved number fourteen, 3 girls and 11 boys aged between 8 years and 10 years. They were chosen from nine schools in one locality, first on the basis of teaching recommendation and later on the advice of the county psychologist. The exact procedure is a model of its kind, but at this point it is sufficient to quote only that portion of the procedure which focuses with perhaps surprising fidelity on much of what has been discussed in the present study regarding definitions and recognitions:

The children whom we wish to consider are those whose skills in some areas of functioning are so far above those of the average children in the class that their teachers feel unable to do full justice to helping them develop their exceptional skills within the framework of 'normal' everyday teaching.

The staff were selected in order to provide coverage in terms of the four main areas of 'expertise' in the primary school curriculum, although this was not the only factor taken into account, and comprise two headteachers, one deputy head and one assistant teacher, from four different schools, some of which are involved through the children as well. There is thus the possibility of having the same people observe children's behaviour both in school and in the Extended Activities Group, and the several advantages of this cross-fertilization arrangement are probably self-evident. The two sexes are equally represented amongst the staff involved.

Extra equipment has been provided for this group, and includes such items as prismatic compasses, microscopes, Instamatic and movie cameras, a 35 mm single reflex automatic exposure camera, dissecting kits, tape recorders etc. The group, which meets for one full day per week, is located within a large school so that this equipment is fully utilized by far more than the small number of children actually in the experiment.

This particular 'extended activities' arrangement has not been continued long enough for any definite conclusions to be drawn, and clearly anything which can be said at this very early stage must be highly tentative and may well perhaps miss what will later turn out to be the most important issues and discoveries. The following somewhat disconnected observations are, therefore, to be regarded with the preceding caution very much in mind:

1   When the group first started, evidence of the 'stint' syndrome remarked by Bridges, and seen by Tempest as something of a continuing phenomenon, was immediately noticed.

2   Standards of accuracy, neatness, consistency have already risen visibly. Task completion which previously was not regarded by some as at all essential is now accepted as a usual goal.

3   The average length of a project study is far greater than it was. The level of associated discussion is noticeably higher than that which is common in the normal class.

4   The children try to avoid failure 'like the plague', and will use their depth of comprehension to create all kinds of reasons either for not even tackling a job or for explaining away what they conceive to be their own ineffectiveness.

5   They seem deliberately to avoid achieving beyond what their nearest 'friends' can do, and have no idea of their own capabilities really. It is possible that very bright pupils who are not quite so good at something apply a 'group brake' more than those who are manifestly weaker.

6   With one child seen in school as 'eccentric, demanding, vocal, questioning, adult in conversation to the point sometimes of rudeness, impulsive', there has been no visible change so far as a result of involvement in the class. The child's actual work however exemplifies all the improvements noted in previous paragraphs.

7   The type of work being given is almost wholly that which might be called 'enrichment', as may be seen from the sample programme given below.

The extended activities group: outline of weekly activities
This outline indicates the main areas of study undertaken by the children. During these activities opportunities are taken to deepen and order each child's thought processes to initiate discussion and to raise fresh problems which demand further creative thinking.

17.9.70 *Free choice*   Work areas in maths, English, science, art/craft, social studies.

24.9.70 *Trip to woodland*   To survive, man needs food, shelter and protection from extremes of temperature.

1.10.70 *Aspects of survival*   Flora, communication, early man.

8.10.70 *Haslemere Museum Visit*—Morning. Afternoon—aspects of visit linked to theme of survival.

4.3.71 *Visit to Easebourne Church*   Architecture and history arising from the church and its development.

11.3.71 *Devising games*   Children invented new games, devised rules and discussed improvements.

18.3.71 *Follow up to church visit and individual study*

8   Finally a list of questions, together with the replies of the staff involved, are appended below. These questions were put reluctantly in that the whole arrangement is at too early a stage for proper enquiry to occur. In fairness therefore it has to be restressed that this information is solely for interest, and cannot be used either to congratulate or criticize. We are only grateful that busy teachers should have been kind enough to make some helpful response, knowing full well that their experience at present is so inadequate. The questioner's

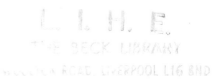

experience of course is perhaps even more inadequate, and no pretence at appropriateness of question is implied by the mere putting of it:

(a) *Is it your view that some, perhaps all, of the children were under-achieving in their own schools, and/or learning work habits which would not really be desirable?*

Some bright children (not all) are under-achieving in their own schools and adopting work habits which are not really desirable. (This is a comparative answer since it can be said that *every* child underachieves and learns some undesirable work habits at school.)

(b) *Is it true that peer group pressures alone can create deliberate under-achievement in bright children?*

Peer group pressures alone can create deliberate underachievement with some children. So much depends on the child and the circumstances.

(c) *Are teachers probably over-confident about their capacity to recognize a very able child?*

Some teachers are over-confident but others lack confidence to recognize very able children at all. 'Confident' teachers frequently know little about 'gifted' children.

(d) *Has experience with this group enabled you to recognize more efficiently the gifted children remaining in your own school?*

Yes. All experience and knowledge helps.

(e) *Has there been any 'spin-off' in terms of method and materials for the benefit of your own schools which would not occur without exposure to the activities of the able children?*

Again, all experience helps. The interaction of four experienced staff is bound to bring benefits. However, no important specific extra 'spin-off' can be accredited to exposure to this particular group.

(f) *Is the wide age range of the group something of a nuisance?*

A wide age range is not a nuisance but some difficulties are apparent with the younger members of the group.

(g) *Why has the curriculum chosen tended strongly towards 'enrichment' rather than towards, say, rapid sequential progress through a series of mathematics tests?*

The curriculum of the group was not predetermined except in its broadest sense but has evolved by experiment and care for the needs and interests of the children. Some of the reasons that we have concentrated upon 'enrichment' might be (i) one of the basic functions of the group is to bring together bright children isolated in small schools for social interaction. Rapid sequential progress through testing would require individual patterns of study at a variety of levels. Such study would isolate rather than integrate the children. (ii) The staff are experienced in providing a broad-based pattern of study which involves enrichment. (iii) The children's interests are so diverse that an enrichment emphasis seems best to cater for their needs. It must be stressed that, within our programme, patterns of rapid sequential development have taken place in groups and by individuals.

(h) *In the group of four teachers is it your view that there is sufficient 'expertise' to cover the broad range of interests displayed by the children?*

So far, with this particular group of children, the four staff have had sufficient expertise between them to cover the broad range of interests required.

(*j*) *Has there been any negative/positive feedback from the schools involved apart from Mr —'s case?*

Yes in varied amounts.

(*k*) *Has any definite attempt been made to compare the levels of work which the children turn out in the extended activities period with what they do in their own schools the rest of the time?*

Not specifically, except where the staff have children from the group in their own schools.

(*l*) *Have you formulated any tentative ideas as to the implications for practice in ordinary schools assuming that segregation even of this temporary kind is rejected as undesirable on general social grounds.*

We are in the process of discussing implications for practice in ordinary schools. At this stage ideas have not been sufficiently consolidated to formulate a list of suggestions.

SPECIAL CLASSES FOR GIFTED CHILDREN IN ESSEX

The decision to establish the classes

In 1970 the decision was taken to set up, on an experimental basis, in the North East Division of Essex, four special classes for intellectually gifted children. Children were to be withdrawn from their normal schools to attend these classes. Thus each group met twice weekly for one session. The group size was provisionally set at 4–8 children, dependent on available facilities.

There were a number of reasons for this decision being taken; as follows:

(*a*) Where only one or two such intellectually gifted children exist within a class or school, it was felt that they suffer from a lack of competition, and their level of achievement, whilst higher than that of their class-mates, is often well below their potential.

(*b*) Such children need opportunities to learn the techniques of acquiring knowledge that they are especially capable of using.

(*c*) Such children should have made available to them the opportunities to foster interests in depth and pursue lines of enquiry at length.

(*d*) For all these children, and in particular those suffering from any personality or emotional disturbances as a direct or indirect result of their level of intelligence, an opportunity to meet their intellectual peers is invaluable in order to counteract any feeling of being isolated or different from others.

Thus, in general, it was felt that the classes were necessary to fulfil those needs of these children that the ordinary school was unable to meet.

In order to select children for the classes, head teachers were asked to submit the names of likely children to the N.E. Divisional Office. These were then individually tested and those achieving the highest scores selected. However, some children with scores less than 140 were selected for social or therapeutic reasons. Thus, generally, no less than two children were selected from each school, and some children whose progress was declining, or who seemed to be suffering from emotional disturbance, were selected; in these latter cases the test results were, in any event, likely to be underestimates.

The intention was that classes should meet in secondary schools so that greater facilities and the advice of specialist staff should be available. Another essential requirement was that the head and staff of the host school should be friendly and sympathetic to the aims and needs of the class. These conditions have, for the most part, been met.

The aims of the classes

As a general principle, the aims of the classes are apparent in the reasons for which they were established. However, the individual day-to-day practical aims of the classes and their teachers merit attention: They are as follows:

(*a*) To make the acquisition of knowledge interesting and enjoyable.

(*b*) To build the children's confidence to inquire and research for themselves: to teach them the skills that will enable them to study independently or to know where and how to get help.

(*c*) To develop the children's skills of concentration, exploration in depth, observation and classification.

(*d*) To stimulate new interests and keep them alert to current events and developments in all fields.

(*e*) To counteract the children's reticence to commit themselves in fields where they are less proficient.

(*f*) To complement the school curriculum rather than cover it.

(*g*) To satisfy the children's need to talk and be listened to, and develop skill in discussion.

(*h*) To foster awareness of their surroundings, and enhance their verbal and creative abilities.

Activities in the classes

In general, the project or topic method of study has been adopted by the teachers as this has proven the most profitable in terms of fulfilling the aims outlined above. However, the following activities have been incorporated within this framework.

(*a*) Discussions of interests and activities. Use of a tape-recorder in this and recording talks to others on individual subjects.

(*b*) Use of the tape-recorder to learn how to make précis and abstracts, or make notes preliminary to written work. Use of tape-recorder to record ideas quickly preliminary to writing.

(*c*) Extension of vocabulary and use of English.

(*d*) Oral and written work mixed with expeditions and practical work. Projects and work requiring division of labour and co-operation by the whole group.

(*e*) Use of television and reference books to research subjects in depth.

(*f*) Exploration of facilities of the secondary school.

(*g*) Use of current events to stimulate interests and encourage the desire to find out.

Attitudes of the parents

The majority of the children come from stable homes where the parents are both interested and helpful. However, despite their appreciation and interest, they may not always provide a sufficiently stimulating background for the children. In most cases, the parents are vocal, care about education, are well-educated themselves, and delighted that their children have this opportunity, give the classes their full support and co-operation.

However, in one or two cases, the parents have seemed over-concerned, indeed, obsessed with their child's progress, producing academic interests in the child at the expense of practical, creative, or social interests. However, cases such as this, where the home background has an adverse effect on the child, have proved rare.

Attitudes of the teachers

The classes were greeted at first with cautious optimism. Some teachers expressed concern that the children might become arrogant, cause jealousy or feel conspicuous or even more isolated. Some teachers feel the intelligence level of the children does not merit this special treatment, or that they can provide the extra help within the school, and that the disadvantages—missing lessons, disruption of routine, and travelling—outweigh the benefits to the child. In one case there is indeed a small group where such children's needs could be met, but generally the nature of the school organization and the type of school population mean that this is impossible.

Generally, teachers report no social difficulties, although at first one or two children began to get rather conceited. The resultant school attitude, after one year of the classes being held is one of co-operation, interest and satisfaction.

Attitudes of the children

At first, some of the children had an inflated sense of their own importance; this was not apparent within the group, but in the school some boasting occurred about being 'special'; this is, however, often seen in children who attend special classes, of whatever nature, and soon dies down.

Within the group the children's attitudes to work are very different. Not all are academic or eager to learn.

Results and implications

Both the teachers of the special classes and the children's teachers at their normal schools have seen a great improvement in the children since attending the classes. They seem happier, more mature, more aware and interested, more responsive and responsible. They are less precocious, less bored, and their concentration has more depth and duration. In addition, their school

work has improved, and many are only now starting to realize their true potential.

Naturally, the results of this sort of experiment are hard to evaluate. However, it is apparent that the children have benefited from the stimulus of their intellectual peers, both socially and academically. The chance to really talk and express their own views has provided invaluable. In fact, despite some initial reticence, the scheme has gained the support of the vast majority of parents and teachers, and has, therefore, been extended this year (1971).

In concluding this section describing special classes for gifted children attention is drawn to the relevant comments in the more general context of Part III, especially on curriculum development, p. 192.

More specific observations regarding present practices

Since it is impossible in the confines of the present report fully to describe every context, additional very brief pointers to aspects of provision for individualization are now summarized below:

1   Some teachers do not appear to know the bases of selection with respect to children in their own class; others do not know them for the school as a whole.

2   In an area where heretofore 8+ children in 'infant' schools were retained in school half an hour longer than those 5–7 year designated 'infants', the practice since they became 'first' schools has been for all children to leave school at the same time, i.e. half an hour earlier than formerly for the eldest.

3   There may be some failure by some teachers to appreciate the massive differences in mental ages, linguistic code levels etc., that exist amongst children even at the age of 7 or 8 in 'normal' schools. Thus classes in junior schools vertically grouped over two or three years regularly have the same stories read to the whole group. One such class was divided into only two groups for an appreciable amount of language work, and in so far as general discussion was concerned, the whole group often acted as one according to the teacher.

4   In a school where a form of team teaching has been instigated the following comments were made:

(a) Need for 'team' meetings is very great; at least one per week.

(b) Boxes of 'structured' equipment and associated assignments are absolutely essential.

(c) Taped assignments with earphones for small groups were immensely valuable but time consuming to make. Plenty available for remedial work but none for the most able.

(d) Individual children had to be responsible very largely for recording own progress on wall charts.

(e) All books were colour coded according to reading levels—required to facilitate children's unaided choice.

(f) The extension of 'general project' work frees teachers for more small group discussion *but* 'complete individualization involves the teacher in too much replication, time wastage in queues . . . we were killing ourselves trying to provide individual assignment cards in mathematics. Now the fifteen slow learners are withdrawn, and the rest are in four groups. (There are three teachers to eighty children in a team group so two extra teachers are needed for this to happen—one is the head, the other a remedial peripatetic.) Each ability group meets the mathematics specialist in the team for one afternoon per week, and work for the next fortnight is planned.

5   By January of the school year in one class a girl, one year younger than the rest, had already completed twice the number of mathematics assignment cards done by the next best child, and from the wall record clearly had only a few more to do. When asked what she would do next, the teacher replied to the effect that the thought horrified him since he just couldn't keep up with the girl. He was thinking of persuading her to do 'project' work instead!

6   One class maths scheme consisted of 100 cards, and no textbooks were in use at all. Every child worked through the cards in order, apart from a remedial group who had their own cards until they could begin the main course.

7   The record below is from one class within a school where exceptional efforts are made to 'individualize' work. The subject is mathematics, but much the same situation would describe more formal aspects of language work. The time at which this situation was arising is April.

Class: second-year juniors, unstreamed

Book 1	No. of children	1	1	2	1	1	1	1	1	1	1	1						
	Page of work	18	29	49	50	61	63	65	67	68	69	76						
Book 2	No. of children	2	2	1	1	1	1	2	1	1	1	1	1	4	1	1	1
	Page of work	12	15	16	17	18	19	24	25	26	27	29	31	33	39	50	58

8   Class teaching is commonplace in French teaching, and individual differences are often being very largely ignored. Visiting peripatetic secondary teachers appear to be less perturbed by this situation than are primary teachers, but neither consider it as other than poor practice forced upon them by lack of equipment and classes of forty.

9   No evidence of an awareness that some very able children do not read at all well at first is apparent in book provision. Much is made of the need for topics in readers to be suited to the needs and interests of the less intelligent, but nothing of the need to relate the content of primers to the 'adult' interests of able boys and girls.

10   A secondary headteacher argues that when children come up to the secondary school he wants them all to feel able to make a fresh start. They all therefore start on the same work together.

11   A number of constraints exist even in schools which start schemes of work with such phrases as 'our concern is the individual child'. Thus:
(*a*) The most advanced texts available are all Book IVs. There is in effect a

'Book Four Barrier' in many schools, and the use of workcards merely hides its presence.

(*b*) Teachers are advised that history lessons can be regarded as 'story' periods—for everybody? That quotation marks and the possessive apostrophe should be left until the fourth year: and that the use of set plays should be avoided.

(*c*) Many clubs and associations and LEA grant systems appear to treat the age of eleven as a mystical threshold before which nothing is possible, but after which all is simple.

(*d*) Recent changes in methodology emphasize the value of discussion. No significant comment appears to be made about the value of discussion as it relates to the ability and attainment ranges represented in these discussion groups, and yet the average 'code' must set a 'ceiling' on every discourse.

12   The complexity of the issues involved in assessing the real extent of individualization which characterizes a system can perhaps be sensed through a consideration of the following statement which is provided as a conclusion to the present section:

About fifteen years ago . . . I had a variety of mechanical/mental/problem books in arithmetic but the main book was B and A arithmetic. . . . Each page had two sets of about 40 sums, 80 to a page. No one would dare use it now. There were always at least 40–48 children in the class.

We had a fixed system with this book. They did the first ten examples and marked them themselves. If they had them all right and only one wrong they did the last five then started the next set. If they had 7 or 8 right they did the next ten and if 6 or less correct they came to me. I spent part of the lesson attending to these few and the rest of the time going round and round the class.

Now you can regard this as hopelessly old fashioned and find it incredible that this situation should exist only 15 years ago or you can regard it as an early form of programmed learning which puts me in with the 'moderns'. [Now] if you were to visit some school you would find each child busy with his individual card obviously doing work different from his neighbour whilst in my old class were 48 children working from the same book. Yet if at the end of the year you were to list the work done in the 'modern' class by each child you would find that everybody had followed the same course. Some would have progressed further certainly but what they had done would be exactly the same (sequence) in every case. In my old class every single child had followed a different path through the book. Some would have progressed further but their paths would be quite individual dictated solely by their needs throughout the year.

Which is the greater degree of individualization?

The richness of enrichment

PROJECT WORK

It is already apparent that in practice 'enrichment' refers to the kind of work undertaken as a 'project' or 'centre of interest', school journey and the like. Observation in schools reveals what must be considered as a serious and most difficult situation. On the one hand there is a progressive extension of such work, often exaggerated by the tendency to provide 'stints' or fixed assignments in 'basic' work and then encourage children to use their spare time on 'topics', and, on the other, a concomitant failure to evaluate the child's products in any but the most general manner. The reality of the latter problem can readily be illustrated as under:

1   A headteacher writes, 'I was sorting out examples of environmental studies work (for a course lecture) and I was amazed when I compared 1970 work with the earlier stuff (1966) which I had thought was good'.

2   If an index of 'thought level' which is relatively independent of the content of written work is applied to project products previously graded by teachers, typical findings are as follows:

Teacher's expectations and their reality basis

Teacher's grading of child (project work)		Child's output level (think index)		Type of school and grouping
1	A	A	1·60	Town: traditional (i.t.a.)
2	A	A	1·29	Town: traditional
3	A+	B	1·12	Town: traditional (i.t.a.)
4	A	A	1·42	Town: traditional (i.t.a.)
5	A+	B	1·08	Town: traditional
6	A+	B	0·83	Village: vertical
7	A+	B	0·87	Village: vertical
8	A	A	1·30	Town: traditional
9	A++	C	0·69	Town: vertical
10	B	B	0·87	Village: vertical
11	B+++	E	0·00	Village: vertical
12	B	B	1·01	Town: traditional
13	B	B	1·00	Village: vertical
14	B	B	0·85	Town: traditional (i.t.a.)
15	B	B	0·86	Town: traditional (i.t.a.)
16	B	B	0·84	Town: traditional (i.t.a.)
17	B−	A	1·26	Town: traditional (i.t.a.)
18	B+	C	0·76	Town: vertical
19	B+	C	0·70	Town: vertical
20	C−	B	0·82	Village: vertical
21	C−	B	0·95	Village: vertical
22	C−	B	0·81	Village: vertical
23	C	C	0·77	Village: vertical
24	C−	B	1·19	Town: traditional (i.t.a.)
25	C−	B	1·03	Town: traditional (i.t.a.)
26	C	C	0·71	Town: vertical
27	D−−	B	0·84	Town: traditional (i.t.a.)

+ = too high a grading or too low an output to match expectation
− = too low a grading or an output higher than expectation

Note: If this index is applied to the children's writings given earlier (p. 60) the results are: Case study 5 = 3·5; Case study 6 = 3·5; Case study 7 = 4·0. The zero figure for no. 11 above represents no words of more than one syllable used.

We are not concerned here to suggest more than that there is an urgent need to institute a variety of measures for increasing the individual teacher's ability to compare what different children achieve in project work with reference both to their own previous work and to the work of others. A multi-modal attack is required on this evaluation problem, and one or two points will be mentioned in this connexion later. Meantime it has to be further pointed out that the problem is not confined merely to the individual child's output. It is essentially a problem of input in relation to output such that the books in use for an individual project match the child's capability and raise the quality of his output. It is abysmally inadequate simply to assert for instance that the school library is 'excellent'; every school library almost invariably is, but how many can boast the 10,000 volumes possessed by one of the schools visited? Whatever the size of the school library, unless there is some relation between its contents and the topics studied the probability is that the project 'input' is so parsimonious as to be restrictive to able children.

It is furthermore important to stress that both 'input' and 'output' need evaluating in terms of both factual extent, or content, and levels of thought. Many of the booklets examined have been of a purely descriptive character, others contain some simple relational thinking, and a very few have a scientific character.

The main reason may well be of course that 'discovery' learning of any worthwhile kind presupposes the teaching of some elements of scientific method, and such teaching is conspicuous by its absence in many project sequences without a doubt. This may be due in some cases to an over-reliance on so-called 'discovery' and 'autonomous' learning, but it is also due to the difficulty of assessing progress in 'environmental studies'. Another major factor of course concerns the 'expertise' of the teacher involved, and although difficult to prove, the assertion is here made that exceedingly wide differences between teachers as to what they find acceptable from children of very similar ages and abilities are readily observable even within the same school. Between schools matters may be far more serious: how, for example, ought we to view the fact that in one class a study of ducks involves a child in the techniques of imprinting whereas, in another, a child does little more than copy snippets of information from an observer's book of birds? One thing is certain; in the first case 'enrichment' is real, but in the second it is mere mockery. And the relation between what occurs and what ought to occur has far more to do in present circumstances with the particular interests of the teacher, than with the particular interests and abilities of the child.

In conclusion it is helpful perhaps to note that the general problems outlined here have greatly concerned the directors of Schools Council Curriculum Projects, and the Science Project has, of course, endeavoured to lay down in no little detail some developmental criteria. What we are concerned to stress is that such efforts should be unrelentingly pursued and that additional methods of injecting far greater degrees of exactitude into teachers expectations must be invoked at once. The problems involved are continuous and cyclical: they will not permit of a once-and-for-all solution since our goal must be to achieve ever-rising standards. The solution, therefore, must be thought of in terms of building into the system self-checking and continuously correcting procedures which enforce and enable teachers to become ever more precise in their judgements as to the real consequences for able children of whatever is currently regarded as enrichment. The emphasis now being put on the dangers, for very able children especially, of failing to approach the problem of evaluating 'enrichment' is such as to be a divergence of significance from the views of the Plowden Committee (551). It cannot be the function of H.M. Inspectors to do more than examine the methods of evaluation in use. The time involved and the knowledge of an individual child that would be necessary to enable a person to advise a teacher on what to expect from that child just is not available to inspectors: in many authorities it is not available even to the advisory and psychological services. Moreover it has to be observed that we are concerned to see that teachers know what to expect from children not so much 'in the circumstances of their neighbourhood', but rather regardless of such circumstances. Teachers themselves must have opportunities to compare what is achieved by their children with those elsewhere, and these opportunities must be quite frequent.

STAFF EXPERTISE

As noted, the degree of enrichment in any curriculum depends directly on the character of the interests represented amongst the staff. It is necessary, therefore, to enquire into the present position, accepting of course that very small schools must be relatively inadequate at this particular point. One finding only is reported below since it alone is sufficient to show that among primary teachers there is in fact a surprising range of expertise much of which remains almost wholly untapped in present conditions.

Range of interests and talents among staff in one primary school
The headteacher listed no fewer than 133 activities, some divided into quite specific forms. Art for example is analysed as Modern, Impressionist, Oils, Water Colours, Landscapes, Portraits, Animals and Abstract.

Of the 133 items, thirty-four were marked as being covered by at least one member of staff who could be properly described as possessing 'considerable expertise', and a further thirty-eight were, or rather could be, catered for at the level of 'some expertise'. These terms derive from a five point scale from 'mildly interested' upwards, and it is obvious, therefore, that this team presents considerable strength across a remarkably broad field. The list does, however, present certain disquieting features:

G.C.P.S.—7*

1 Nobody claimed 'considerable expertise' in English literature or music, or mathematics.

2 A group comprising archaeology, astronomy, biology, chemistry and physics had nobody in either of the top two levels of expertise.

3 The same is true of medicine, astrology, architecture, card games, swimming, educational dance, ballet, 'do-it-yourself' and gardening.

Opinions doubtless differ as to the value of astrology, and since one member of staff has considerable expertise in Urdu no doubt the lack of astrology will not be serious. But it is important to observe that a major group of sciences very closely associated with the major areas subsumed under 'enrichment' programmes are not strongly represented amongst this staff at all. This dangerous imbalance becomes especially remarkable when set against the known interests of a considerable number of the very able pupils, including—as our case studies show—not a few girls.

One factor involved here no doubt is the predominance of women in primary schools, but this is not the only reason for what must be seen as a major constraint. The situation requires a much closer examination than is possible here.

EXTRA-MURAL ACTIVITIES: SCHOOL CLUBS

It has already been made apparent that notable differences exist between schools as to what happens with regard to extra-mural activities. The situation can be underlined most effectively by setting the following statements against the evidence from school studies above:

1 There is no extra-mural timetable since this depends on the voluntary actions of staff. A recorder group meets regularly at lunchtime, and the boys play soccer with a member of staff fairly frequently.

2 All (46) children aged 7–11 in groups of 6–8 are responsible for producing two assemblies per week. They arrange and rehearse during playtimes and lunch hours without staff involvement A senior recorder group (12 children) meets on Tuesdays 3.45–4.30 p.m. Rehearsals for school presentations often occupy half-an-hour of lunch break for 4–5 weeks before Christmas. Swimming on a voluntary basis occurs for 1 hour daily before general swimming starts in the summer, and thereafter for one hour on Fridays. In the summer vacation the pool is available for one daily session supervised by a rota of parents.

Other activities—occasional football team practices and cycling proficiency training, and the headteacher here continues:

It may be argued that our children are very well provided with stimulating activities outside their normal school time because a large percentage of them belong to Brownies, Guides, Cubs and Scouts. However I would like to see more done under the auspices of the school. There is talent available on the staff to form such groups as art clubs, puppet clubs, science, gardening and mathematics clubs.

Observation in schools reveals not only the wide differences here, but also the different character of 'club' activities in school time which might be considered a substitute for extra-mural work. In some schools there are virtually none; in others the range reflects the kinds of expertise to which we have already drawn attention. One feature stands out, however, in almost every case, and this is that these club sessions are ephemeral. They last for a term, or even half a term, and the child must then change. The aim is thus to introduce an interest, and not to both introduce and develop. These arrangements contrast therefore significantly with extra-mural clubs and can never be a substitute for the latter. Indeed it is plain that without supportive continuity much of their value must be lost.

COMPENSATORY PROGRAMMES OF ENRICHMENT

There is a dearth of enrichment programmes which use the method of direct teaching according to a relatively narrow developmental programme. The only instance in fact would seem to occur in connexion with the extra assistance given to certain children who happen to live in EP Areas. Thus it appears that language programmes are arranged in some places for immigrants and others with linguistic problems. The common procedure in these programmes, however, is for a child to be returned to his normal class as soon as he attains a sufficient level of skill to 'get by' with the average group. There is a very grave danger here. The most able children clearly return to their ordinary classes much sooner than do the slow learners. Effectively this must be to impoverish the linguistic environment of a child just because he is able, and this will be especially true in areas where average levels of linguistic skill are low in any case. The answers to this problem are not self-evident, but the practice of automatically returning a 'deprived' child to a 'normal' routine at the earliest practicable moment needs review, especially as it affects outstandingly able immigrants and others. Their performance in selection tests for example, must to some extent depend upon exposure to compensatory teaching.

The main point remains, however, that no instance of enrichment by direct teaching of an advanced syllabus has been brought to our attention. Even in schools where small 'sets' have been established for, say, mathematics, there is a very strong tendency to provide work according to the 'mushroom' model. The group proceeds rapidly through Book IV and then effectively bumps up against a 'tropopause' and has to engage in 'width' studies. The value of 'width' studies is not the issue here; what is important is the reason most frequently given for not proceeding with both broadening and deepening, and that is the stated need to avoid trespassing on secondary school work. Space permits us to do no more than add that this view depends in no way upon close liaison with, and a careful assessment of the views of secondary teachers. On the contrary, there is a failure to bring primary and secondary teachers together, and the 'mushroom' programme is a direct consequence of it. Even the composition of Schools Council Subject Committees appears to reflect this 'great divide'.

Conclusion

The preceding survey is and must remain incomplete. It is consistent with the modest goals of the present enquiry, and it is only necessary now to suggest that there are good reasons for anticipating that teachers are not at all satisfied with the progress made this far in our attempts to increase the measure of individualization which characterizes the school and its supportive environment. A stage has thus been reached when it is necessary and appropriate for us to consider what steps might be taken to bring about improvements. A number of suggestions have already been made and implied, but more specific discussions of views are required, and these are contained in Part III below.

Notes

1   The author is indebted to Mr G. Robb, County Psychologist, for this account.

Part III

The future

8 Implications and wider issues

The preceding description of present practices and provisions when viewed in relation to Part I above contains a number of important implications for improvement which can only be assessed and given an order of priority in relation to the particular circumstances of each teacher, school and LEA. Provided that it is not seen as a substitute for reading the paper as a whole it may be helpful now to present what would seem to be the major points in a convenient summary form as a series of question-statements. Adopting this mode of exposition will enable us to construct in essence a checklist which will be of use to those who wish to evaluate their own individual situation in relation to what can be found in whole or in part somewhere in present LEA provision. For convenience the statements are divided into two sections as they refer to the internal or external environments of a school but it has repeatedly been stressed here that the two aspects must more than ever before be seen as one totality.

A third and final section briefly discusses one or two wider issues arising from the main study.

The external environment of the school

ATTITUDES WITHIN ADMINISTRATION

The adoption, consciously or unconsciously, of certain attitudes predisposes a system towards inactivity, and apart from that most dangerous state of general complacency which is apparent in perhaps only a very few places, the following positions clearly tend to inertia, apathy and a deadening indifference:

1 A failure to associate problems of giftedness with the problem of individualization of learning which is central to all educational advance.

2 An assumption that to make provision for pupils to become outstanding is to deny provision to others apparently less fortunate, or that because some cannot have it, nobody must.

3 The view that gifted children cannot be retarded by environmental circumstance or that, if they are, then such retardation is of a temporary inconsequential nature.

4 A presumption that some single organizational structure such as

'vertical grouping' or 'streaming', of itself, goes a long way to solve all the problems. This is particularly pernicious where the organizational arrangements eulogized are precisely those which already characterize an area for reasons which have little to do with individualization as such.

5   The opinion that degrees of individualization depend only upon the skill of the individual teacher, and that nothing therefore can be done in the short term.

An essential first question then is: Do these attitudes exist?

PROVISION OF AVT

Teachers in some areas believe that talk of the use in schools of video tapes and individualized learning situations based on technology is 'pie in the sky'. Either confirmation of this view should be unequivocally stated, or some of the following possibilities translated at once into action:

1   Establish research groups to create learning kits, series of developmental workbooks, cards, study packages, story reading tapes and slides in more than one language. These groups to include primary and secondary teachers, tutors etc.

2   Create a local resources centre of these materials together with technology and technicians, and linked to Saturday centres.

3   Liaise with local radio and TV with regard to programmes for small groups and individuals aimed at enrichment in depth as well as in breadth.

STANDING COMMITTEES AND WORKING PARTIES

Liaison between primary and secondary schools is inadequate wherever it depends upon sporadic one-day mass meetings, or a one-way traffic of secondary teachers making very occasional voluntary visits to local primary schools. Permanent committees with power to recommend and arrange inter-staff communication could create a continuous monitoring of the position.

Similarly liaison between teachers and local clubs and associations need not be haphazard. A booklet of information for both teachers and parents is essential. Clubs which provide tuition to youngsters should be supported, provided that teachers sit on their committees and that age 'floors' are not enforced, e.g. 'over 11 years only'.

Advisory, psychological and child guidance sectors need to be very closely associated, and not in situations of rivalry. The provision of peripatetic help is a single system concerning which schools themselves might usefully be consulted regularly.

SUPPORT TEAMS AND INTERACTION OF STAFF

Inspector/adviser groups need the assistance of teacher-teams whose function it is to provide support for schools requiring specialist help, or general help in order to make use of their own specialist.

Schools might be zoned under a rotating group of headteachers whose function would include recognition of able pupils, evaluation of enrichment programmes etc.

A number of very small schools might be joined under one headteacher so that staff and children become mobile and able to work as occasion required in more than one place. Small schools might be linked with a larger one even more beneficially.

Support teams might spend a period (1 month?) in any school receiving and giving help and advice. Members of such support teams might be seconded from their schools for such periods.

In-service training and college of education links might strengthen support teams by involving tutors and students.

INFORMATION SERVICES: A HANDBOOK

Contents might include details concerned with the following:

1   Organized testing services should be available and parents and teachers should know procedures for obtaining objective individual test results. Every headteacher ought to be permitted to administer his own testing service, assuming necessary training, so that psychological services are not the front line of action. A booklet on 'recognition' is essential.

2   A register of experts willing to be consulted should be compiled and kept up-to-date; this register to include any secondary teachers who are prepared to be involved. Parents who are mobile and willing to help in any local area school might also be listed here to avoid possible problems arising from parental presence in 'own' schools. The term 'expert' needs liberal interpretation.

3   If zoning of schools has to be very rigid, then every parent should have the choice of two. Details of such choice obviously needs publicizing. Reasons for rigidity need re-examination regularly.

4   Details of extra-mural activities in schools will require wider publicity than within the school itself if the next section leads to action.

5   Other information implied herein (e.g. catalogue of learning kits).

EXTENDED ACTIVITY CENTRES, SUMMER SCHOOLS AND RESIDENTIAL WEEK-ENDS

The location of these centres would not seem to be a difficult issue since primary schools are little used in many places outside school hours. The variety of activities is the major feature requiring attention, and both language and mathematics/science studies should receive support. Ideally these centres should mirror parental demand (see final section), and not be confined only to school terms. Week-end residential meetings could be considered occasionally perhaps in connexion with in-service courses in some specific field.

AGE LIMITS

Age limits, where they exist, in whatever area—not excluding release of children from school without supervision, 'adult' library membership and the like—should be ruthlessly examined, and removed, unless present conditions still justify their retention.

COURSES FOR PARENTS, INCLUDING COUNSELLING SERVICES

These should be available in colleges of education and elsewhere. They should be linked to home economics courses in secondary schools so that potential parents learn how great is their power for good, and how important it is for them to know and actively engage in the educational processes to which their children will be exposed.

CURRICULUM DEVELOPMENT

Booklets of suggestions should not be for (say) 'Primary Mathematics'. They should cover the whole school age range and be constructed by teams covering the required range, and beyond.

Research organizations should be involved at all stages and inbuilt evaluation should occur on the basis of expert advice.

If 'extended activity' groups are to be encouraged then they should each be viewed as curriculum development experiments, and experiments in child observation. They should very frequently be associated with specific talents, and they should all be subjected to scientific scrutiny. An arrangement which is so loosely controlled that no definite findings can arise is likely to become little more than a new form of 'segregation', 'streaming', or whatever other description individuals decide the situation warrants. Links with Saturday centres would help.

INTERRELATIONSHIPS WITH THE PRIVATE SECTOR

It needs to be considered how far links with private schools should be deliberately strengthened. There is, apart from the scholarship systems noticed, an almost complete absence of articulation between the public and private sectors; and a massive ignorance among teachers as to the real characteristics of either the one or the other which is to the detriment of both. There is some truth in the contention that the private sector must be criticized for its exclusiveness, and yet its critics take every possible step to increase the degree of exclusiveness by insisting on exclusion. Are LEA teachers' centres really intended to be for one set of teachers only? Is one child to be denied access to an extended activity centre on Saturdays simply because he attends a private school, and another access to membership of an outstanding musical ensemble because the latter is associated with a special music school which he does not attend? Is a school which is small in order to provide for the needs of talented (say) musicians to be denied the manifold and manifest benefits of interaction to which attention has already been drawn, for no reason other than that fees are charged?

The close connexion between this section and the one following needs no demonstration.

LEVELS OF EXPECTATION

1   The use of objective tests is essential.

2   Learner Surveys should be extended to cover the whole spectrum and not just the lower end.

3   Private exhibitions of work in given fields accompanied by case study details and teachers' evaluations should be mounted regularly.

4   All arrangements for staff interaction should be strengthened as a matter of utmost importance.

SUPPORT FOR REGIONAL ORGANIZATIONS

Support for 'teaching' associations has been noted. The relevance of this to teacher supply necessary for high level specialist activities is in need of vital consideration, especially with regard to regional orchestras and music associations, drama societies etc. The case would appear to be very strong wherever a close link between teacher supply and membership of the organization can be shown to exist.

LOAN SCHEMES

Loan of instruments including scientific instruments is an essential part of provision for the talented and might well be linked to attendance at activity centres, extra-mural groups and summer schools.

Finally in this section might be included those questions which were asked of LEAs with regard to their present provisions. Negative responses may in at least some cases require review, see page 201.

The internal environment of the school

1   Internal groupings of children should be in accordance with a perceivable and detailed pattern. Flexibility can only be said to exist if the framework within which it occurs is specifiable. To what extent do able children assist less able peers? How do groupings relate to the concept of individualization?

2   Staff expertise in special areas may remain unused, with a consequent narrowing of the curriculum. How often do children, able in a particular field, meet with an appropriately interested teacher?

3   Formal discussions are as necessary as informal discussions.

4   Forms of co-operative teaching which permit more teachers to have

close contact with more children will improve recognition of children's talents and facilitate their development.

5   'Club' activities relate to extra-mural activities in a very direct way if their full value is to be realized.

6   What is the scope of the extra-mural programme? Is there a school(s) orchestra, soccer team, chess league? Are sports for girls as well organized and integrated as those for boys?

7   To what extent are special responsibility posts linked to specialist expertise as well as to first class general teaching capability?

8   In what areas can 'Book IV barriers' be seen to operate? Can secondary colleagues suggest ways to break them?

9   Are there other barriers notably in adhering to aural/oral class methods for second language teaching? Can individual children press ahead with writing and reading in a second language just as they commonly do in English? Are taped stories of literary quality available?

10   Does 'enrichment' include visits to France?

11   Are advisers/inspectors/psychologists/child guidance personnel invited to staff meetings where individual pupils will be discussed?

12   Have university/college tutors been approached with a view to helping in 'club' activities? Are sources of 'expertise' used only for 'class' discussion?

13   What place can parents play in extending individualization? Small group supervision in games, music, chess, drama? Visits to museums may only be possible now for some children if they go in official parties; and large parties minimize individual learning. Can parents assist in the setting up and use of AVT?

14   In what ways can the presence of students, aides and helpers be seen to increase the degree of personalized learning which occurs?

15   How often are TV/radio programmes used for viewing by whole groups compared with periods of partially or wholly unsupervised viewing by smaller sets?

16   Is homework confined to 'project' enrichment activities? Positively encouraged? Or based upon a proper assessment of individual interest? Are parents' views taken into account?

17   Is there a formal detection and referral system within the school whereby somebody becomes responsible for arranging comparisons of outstanding pupils with experience elsewhere? Several teachers might be involved depending on the nature of the suspected talent of course in a particular case.

18   Can different styles of learning be recognized and matched to different styles of teaching? How firmly does any teacher cling only to one role, say that of guide-consultant, and never change to diagnostician-director, or vice versa, rather than respond in accordance with the individual child's proclivities one way or the other? This is connected of course to the question as to how far we force divergent questions on convergent children and vice versa;

or the extent to which a child can choose a quiet environment rather than a noisy one, an individual activity rather than be in a group (see 19) and so on.

19   Is there a balance between individual sports and team games? What is the element of choice here?

20   Does the school handbook of information for parents contain advice on how to obtain professional views on the aptitudes and abilities of children? Are there suggestions as to the value of a second opinion? Do parents receive encouragement to inform the school of their children's outside-school interests, personality traits, school reactions etc., at frequent intervals?

21   In addition to the usual school records, are arrangements made to retain certain 'work samples' which indicate an individual's best work and keenest interest at given ages?

22   Examine the contents of the school magazine: is there evidence of an unwarrantable degree of bias towards the literary and to the aspects of school work which may be difficult to compare and contrast with work elsewhere? Are samples of work in mathematics and science included? To what extent?

Wider issues

Space does not permit of a summary of all the proposals for action that might be formulated from a study of earlier chapters. Indeed it should now be apparent that we are far from being in a position where safe generalizations about the inadequacy of provision for talented children are possible. The foregoing is however a working paper rather than a report and it is permissible, therefore, now briefly to attend to one or two wider issues in an attempt to provoke further discussion and practical experiment.

PERSONALIZED EDUCATION

It is probably inevitable that during ordinary day school time most attention will always be given to a 'general' education; opportunities to pursue a particular bent will be restricted. The time has come, therefore, to consider carefully such elements of the system as the length of a 'school' day, vacation periods, extended activities classes, part-time centres which provide for 'academic' as well as other 'hobbies'; and the availability of specialist teaching for young children.

There can moreover be little doubt that it is becoming imperative to seek out ways of injecting a much greater degree of personal choice into the state system, especially with regard to which educational opportunities should be available in any particular region. An adherence merely to traditional cultural activities, themselves often determined in the end by the predilections of a chief education officer, is not in tune with modern democratic attitudes to choice. It cannot be right that some children effectively receive subsidies in order to pursue their chosen hobbies whereas other children, through no fault of their own, do not; or that some talents are favoured, whilst others are not.

Clearly a radical change in the system is required if the present pattern in relation to the foregoing is to be broken. The problem is simply expressed as follows: How can individual children be presented with a greater proportion of 'choice' time together with the means—teaching resources etc.—to make effective use of it?'

One answer would seem to lie in the use of vouchers. By issuing parents with educational purchasing power, a demand would be created which would quite soon be reflected in the tuition provided. Extra-mural activities would come to be serviced by those teachers who wished to take part in them and be rewarded for doing so. Teachers with other commitments would simply refrain from volunteering their services and the whole scheme would thus be staffed entirely by 'specialist' teachers who were self-involved.

Nobody would deny the difficulties, both seen and unseen, which are being glossed over here. Nobody would advocate a nationwide experiment at this time. Would it not be equally rash to dismiss the idea out of hand as being entirely impracticable? A straightforward voucher notion is by no means new, and what is being suggested for consideration here is a very much more restricted use of such a system since it would be confined to extra-mural activities alone. We are in any event merely asking whether a scheme ought not to be drawn up and tried out, with proper government backing and supervision, in one small area of the country. Features associated with the scheme are in Appendix 5.

This brief discussion may perhaps best be terminated by suggesting that another method of taking at least a small step along the road indicated might be to permit and encourage children of any age to attend 'twilight' classes in local further education colleges. It is surely difficult to find acceptable reasons why a nine-year-old who clearly excels in (say) French, should not attend classes where the level of teaching matches his extraordinary capabilities.

INCREASING RANGE OF ABILITIES AND INTERESTS

If many of the proposals adumbrated in this paper were to be taken up, at least one major consequence can safely be predicted. There would be a very rapid widening of interests among children together with a concomitant increase in ranges of abilities. This would pose a situation in primary schools somewhat similar to that which now prevails in secondary schools at (say) age fifteen. The cyclical changes in organization, management and equipment which can be foreseen as becoming necessary would create formidable problems: problems only exceeded by those which would face our secondary teachers when considerable numbers of very advanced children appeared in their first year classes. Perhaps it is an intuitive fear of these events that lies at the back of our apparent reluctance seriously to attempt to bring them about on a large scale.

COMPLEXITY AND COMPLACENCY

Certain conditions in the educational world can be seen to be particularly conducive to complacency. When preliminary consideration of a set of problems brings about a realization that they involve study of highly complex factors, there is a tendency to turn attention away from such difficulties towards matters more amenable, congenial and capable of evoking ready public approbation. This tendency is exaggerated where the preliminary examination suggests that to activate the problem may involve a threat to some firmly held sentiment, or call into question some neoteric practice which we have just adopted.

The relation of the foregoing propositions to the concept of 'giftedness' should be clear enough. It is easy to convince oneself that talent can look after itself: that giftedness will out. Such thoughts are immensely comforting; by adopting them we need not involve ourselves in awkward questions as to whether equality of opportunity is compatible with equality; or how far it may be desirable to seek out the potentially very able children now submerged in an educational priority area. It is certainly a bit futile to wonder whether some adult books ought to be available with infant-size print.

It is unnecessary to labour these matters further. Complexity characterizes problems associated with giftedness, however defined, and we are concerned only to prevent complacency towards them becoming equally evident. Fortunately there is available a measure of such complacency: it relates simply to the extent that experimentation and research which is oriented towards talented children is a feature of our educational scene.

Within the obvious limits of its scope the present study has provided information which will enable others to survey their own particular scene and consider what actions might be taken to improve provisions for the recognition and development of talent. It is hoped that what has been said reflects with no little fidelity many of the views of those teachers who helped the enquiry, the parents who so willingly gave information, the administrators and Schools Council committees who supplied so much encouragement, as well as those of the working party itself.

Appendices

Appendix I

Letter to chief education officers

SCHOOLS COUNCIL

160 Great Portland Street, London W1

20th August 1970

TEACHING OF GIFTED CHILDREN IN PRIMARY SCHOOLS

I have been commissioned by the Schools Council to make a twelve months' study of the teaching of gifted children in primary schools. At the end of it I hope to produce an account which will contain suggestions and case studies of practical use to teachers and LEAs.

There are three ways in which I hope it will be possible for you to help me. But first of all I should like to make it clear how the word 'gifted' is being used. I am not attempting a precise definition. I am using the word as teachers would use it in ordinary conversation to indicate any child who is outstanding in either a general or specific ability, in a relatively broad or narrow field of endeavour. Where generally recognized tests exist as (say) in the case of 'intelligence' then giftedness would be defined by test scores. Where no recognized tests exist, the subjective opinions of 'experts' in the various fields would be the criteria in mind. I am not assuming, however, that gifted children are a separate species or that a line can always be drawn at certain fixed points to distinguish them from the non-gifted.

The LEA's provision

The first way in which I hope you will help me is by answering the following questions about the facilities provided by your authority. I should be glad to have details in those cases where your answer is 'yes'.

1   Does your advisory staff give any special guidance or training to teachers to help them recognize and provide for the needs of gifted children?

2   Are heads encouraged to seek professional advice from (say) an adviser or educational psychologist if they know or suspect that a child is gifted in

one or more areas of activity—i.e. is there an established system of 'referral' as perhaps with backward children?

3 Does the LEA help gifted children:

(*a*) by running special Saturday morning classes or by providing home tuition by peripatetic teachers?

(*b*) by awarding scholarships or exhibitions to outside institutions (e.g. Colleges of Music, Royal Ballet School etc.) for Saturday morning or full-time instruction?

(*c*) by supporting or organizing enrichment classes during normal school hours (e.g. at a College of Education)?

(*d*) by encouraging children to register with private organizations for training—e.g. sports clubs etc.?

(*e*) by arranging admission to secondary education before the normal age of transfer?

(*f*) by the provision or loan of special materials or an increase in capitation allowances?

(*g*) by any other means?

4 Are there any other ways in which you would like to make better provision for gifted children—supply of teachers, building programmes etc., permitting?

Nomination of schools

I hope to make a fairly detailed study of about twenty primary schools which, by their organization, provision of equipment and facilities, or by the way they use specialists within or without the school, provide outstanding help and opportunities for gifted children. I should be grateful if you could suggest the names of two or three such schools in your area which I could visit. May I add these guidelines to assist your selection:

(*a*) provision for the gifted should be within the context of 'a good primary school' which meets the needs of children of all abilities.

(*b*) provision should be made for children with various gifts—academic, aesthetic, athletic etc.

(*c*) it would be helpful to include examples of schools working along 'traditional' as well as along 'progressive' lines and of schools not in predominantly middle-class areas.

Teacher study groups

The provision of facilities for gifted children bristles with difficulties. It would therefore be of enormous help to me if a study group of interested teachers could be formed to discuss and comment on some of the issues which I shall be dealing with. If your authority would be willing to sponsor the formation of such a group I should be glad to know the name of the adviser, teachers' centre leader etc., who would act as convenor.

I have asked a lot of questions and I appreciate that it may take some little time for you to send a reply. I am anxious to make contacts with schools as quickly as possible, however, and I should be glad if you would therefore not delay your nomination of schools if you are ready with them before the other information has been got together.

Would you please send your reply to me at:

38 Charlbury Close
Preston
Weymouth
Dorset

Yours sincerely,
E. Ogilvie, B.Sc., M.Ed., Ph.D.

A second letter was sent on 9th June 1971 to those authorities who did not reply. This repeated the questions about the LEA's provision, without asking for the nomination of schools or the formation of study groups.

Appendix 2

Locations of LEA study groups

Bristol	London (ILEA)	Southport
Canterbury	Manchester	Sutton
Devon	Northumberland	Tynemouth
Doncaster	Plymouth	Yeovil
Croydon	Rugby	Wakefield
Enfield	Sheffield	Worcestershire

Appendix 3

Questionnaire, and notes for study groups

SCHOOLS COUNCIL ENQUIRY INTO THE TEACHING OF GIFTED
CHILDREN IN PRIMARY SCHOOLS: TEACHERS' VIEWS

The following questionnaire is intended to elicit teachers' views about some
of the problems of 'giftedness'. The term 'gifted' is used to indicate any child
who is outstanding in either a general or specific ability, in a relatively broad
or narrow field of endeavour. Definitions in this complex field present a
particularly difficult problem, but most terms can be understood as carrying
the meaning given to them by teachers in their ordinary conversation. Where
generally recognized tests exist, as (say) in the case of 'intelligence', then
'giftedness' would be defined by test scores. Where no recognized tests exist,
it can be assumed that the subjective opinions of 'experts' in the various fields
on the creative qualities of originality and imagination displayed would be the
criteria we have in mind.

Dr. E. Ogilvie

YOUR NAME_____ MR/MRS/MISS
POSITION IN SCHOOL—HEAD   DEPUTY HEAD   ASSISTANT
NAME OF SCHOOL_____
NO. ON ROLL_____NO. OF FULL TIME STAFF_____
NO. OF PART-TIME AND PERIPATETIC STAFF_____
IS THE SCHOOL IN AN URBAN OR A RURAL SETTING? URBAN/RURAL

NOTES ON COMPLETING THE QUESTIONNAIRE

It is hoped that you will be able to answer most of these questions without too
much labour. You may wish to add a comment or qualification to some of
your answers and a space is therefore provided below each item to enable you
to do so. You will probably find it helpful to read through the questionnaire
before attempting to complete it since it presents in toto the general setting
for a consideration of the problems with which we are all concerned.

The questionnaire includes a number of statements which you may agree or disagree with, approve or disapprove of, more or less strongly. In order that you can express the strength of your opinions, each statement is accompanied by a rating scale upon which your views can be indicated by placing a tick at the appropriate point on the continuum. Thus

(a)

would indicate practically complete agreement or approval;

(b)

would imply no strong views at all, and

(c)

would indicate disagreement or disapproval of fair but not extreme proportions.

The questionnaire is divided into two sections: the first is concerned with the recognition and nature of giftedness; the second focuses on questions of policy and provision.

A. RECOGNITION AND NATURE OF GIFTEDNESS

1 Please tick those characteristics which you have found to be the most reliable indicators of giftedness.

(i) Display of extraordinary initiative
(ii) Intense curiosity
(iii) Daydreaming
(iv) Delinquent behaviour
(v) Divergent behaviour, i.e. unusual and original but not delinquent
(vi) Memorizing reams of poetry etc.
(vii) Inability to understand aggression in others
(viii) Imaginative writing
(ix) Rapid reading
(x) Wide vocabulary
(xi) Extraordinary perseverance
(xii) Extreme independence
(xiii) Extreme unpopularity
(xiv) High achievement test scores
(xv) High intelligence test scores
(xvi) High creativity test scores
(xvii) Rejection of school work

(xviii) Exasperation in the face of constraint

(xix) Exceptional physical characteristics

(xx) Any others

2   Children can be gifted with a high general intelligence or in specific areas of activity—music, history, sport, mathematics etc. Which is more common—the general or the specific ability?

3   The following are some specific areas of activity where children may display high gifts: music, mathematics, painting, craft and constructional work, games and athletics, movement, drama, science, spoken or written language. (Think of other areas if you wish.)

In which of these areas have you found giftedness most common?

4   Is it your experience that children gifted in any or all of these specific areas are also of high general intelligence?

5   Is it your experience that children of average or below average intelligence can be gifted in any of these areas?

If so, which?

6   Giftedness in any of these areas below might show itself when properly supported and developed in a number of ways—e.g. as quickness of apprehension, skill and facility in execution, originality or imaginativeness in thought or production etc., etc.

What form does giftedness most commonly take in:

Music	Movement
Mathematics	Drama
Painting	Science
Craft and Constructional Work	Spoken or Written Language
Games and athletics	

7   The following statements express points of view about the need to recognize giftedness in primary school children. Please indicate your attitude in the scale provided. [A scale, as described earlier, was appended to each part of the question.]

(i) It is important to recognize the highly intelligent child

(ii) It is important to recognize the highly creative child

(iii) The early detection of exceptional talent is vitally important

(iv) Many gifted children probably go unrecognized in school

(v) Early specialization is unimportant for the development of exceptional talent. (If you disagree please indicate which areas, in your view, require early specialization.)

B. POLICIES, PROVISIONS AND PROCEDURES

1   The following statements provide opportunities for an expression of your views regarding aspects of educational policy towards, and provision for, the gifted. Please complete the scales as necessary. [A scale was given for each statement.]

(i) Gifted children present special problems to teachers

(ii) Gifted children need contacts with teachers who are similarly gifted

(iii) As much attention should be given to 'gifted' children as is now given to those recognized as 'disadvantaged'

(iv) Many gifted children are disadvantaged by not being allowed to progress according to their ability

(v) The needs of gifted children can be adequately met in the unstreamed class

(vi) Special attention to the needs of the gifted can be expected to have beneficial spin-off effects for the teaching of other children

(vii) In-service training courses on helping gifted children would be a waste of teachers' time in present circumstances

2   If a school is to make proper provision for gifted children, it must take account of conditions that are thought to be harmful to the development of giftedness. Some of these conditions are listed below, and you are asked to indicate the degree of importance you would attach to each in the context of planning your school provision. [A scale was appended to each.]

Conditions possibly harmful to the development of giftedness

(i) Unstimulating home background

(ii) Social pressures towards conformity

(iii) Over-emphasis on group or class work

(iv) Anti-intellectualism in schools

(v) Over-emphasis on 'disadvantaged' children

(vi) Lack of opportunities to exercise specific talents

(vii) Failure of schools to encourage nonconformity

(viii) Insufficient range of talents amongst the staff

(ix) An overlarge pupil/teacher ratio

(x) Failure to recognize potential giftedness

(xi) Failure to provide supporting provision outside school

(xii) Low expectations by parents and teachers

(xiii) Too few men teachers for encouragement of boys' sports

(xiv) Too much direction of children's activities by teachers

(xv) The change from 'informal' primary to 'formal' secondary schools

(xvi) Too many inexperienced teachers

(xvii) Too rapid turnover of teachers

(xviii) Conformist parents

(xix) Any others?

3   Certain conditions may be thought to be especially conducive to the development of giftedness and some possibilities are listed below. Please indicate your views with regard to each of the following. (None should be taken to imply a change in teachers' conditions of service.) [Two scales were given for each condition listed, one for 5–8 years and one for 9–13 years.]

(i) Day release to 'special-class classes' in (say) local colleges, teachers' centres etc.

(ii) Full-time 'super selective' classes

(iii) Periodic specialized teaching within the school

(iv) Early promotion to more advanced groups

(v) Admittance to nursery school or to infant school before normal age

(vi) Enrichment within the normal unstreamed class

(vii) Vertical groupings

(viii) Introduction of teaching machines

(ix) A lengthening of the school day

(x) A shortening of the holidays

(xi) Use of a larger number and variety of peripatetic specialist teachers

(xii) Streaming

(xiii) Widening of the school curriculum

(xiv) Greater involvement of outside agencies. (Local football club, museum curator, parent with special knowledge.)

(xv) An extension of opportunities for a free choice of activities

(xvi) Any other major possibility you suggest:

4   Please indicate below those activities in which you feel your school is either highly successful or unsuccessful in providing for its gifted children, and suggest what you consider to be the major factors in your relative success or failure. [Each of the items below allowed space for the answers.]

(i) Relatively successful areas;   main reasons for success

(ii) Relatively unsuccessful areas;   main reasons for failure

(iii) Areas which go unexplored which probably ought to be included in the curriculum.

(iv) Please suggest briefly below any items of equipment and materials which you feel are, or might be, of special help in making better provision for gifted children.

5   Please suggest in the space below what appear in your view to be the main changes facing gifted children in primary schools and which can be overcome by changes in organization methods and resources backed by skilful teachers. Include also any comment on problems related to giftedness which have been omitted from this questionnaire but which you feel are of major importance.

Notes for the consideration of teachers' study groups

1.0. INTRODUCTION: GENERAL CONTEXT FOR THE SUGGESTIONS

1.1.   The present investigation is of a fact-finding nature and is not a programme of experimental research. The kind of work envisaged for a study group at this stage thus comprises, in the main, a series of straightforward discussions of various possibilities and, if time permits, the undertaking of assignments by individual teachers within their own schools.

1.2.   It is hoped that the findings of the study groups and brief reports of their discussions will form the basis of papers which, taken together, will provide a valuable assessment of the present educational provision for gifted children in primary schools and a summary of teachers' views on what future trends and policies should be.

1.3.   Three main themes would seem to dominate:
(a) Recognition and Selection
(b) Current Practices in Schools in Relation to Outstanding Pupils
(c) Future Possibilities

The following notes and study suggestions are classified under the three headings, and it is hoped that study groups will find it convenient to provide reports of their various discussions under these same headings. It may frequently be the case that a study group will have insufficient time to discuss every topic in every section. Fortunately there are varying degrees (sometimes substantial), of overlapping amongst the various points, and a judicious choice will guarantee that each main theme receives attention at some stage in the sequence of work.

2.0. SECTION A. RECOGNITION AND SELECTION

2.1.   It seems generally to be accepted that all children should be educated according to age, aptitude and ability. This cannot be taken, presumably, to imply that teachers must try to develop any and every type of talent or achievement, otherwise the production of a highly creative telephone kiosk thief would be a laudable gaol. Can the study group formulate a short list of the kinds of talent and achievement which it thinks ought to be provided for within the educational system somewhere during the primary years?

2.11.   In formulating its list of activities can it be taken as axiomatic that the group intends such activities to be organized in such a manner as to ensure that any child possessing exceptional gifts would have the opportunity to develop them to the utmost?

2.12.   Where the group finds itself including in its proposals certain kinds of activity which it believes cannot, or should not be included in the curriculum of the ordinary school as part of a 'general' education, but which nevertheless ought to be available within the child's educational environment, broadly defined; an indication to this effect, together with, if possible, an outline of the principle underlying these decisions would provide important data.

2.2.   In its response to the preceding questions the study group has presumably implied that certain kinds of talent and achievement are usefully recognizable. It does not necessarily follow that recognition of an activity or type of achievement as being of particular educational value further implies special treatment of some sort for those children who appear to be especially good at it.

2.21.   Two issues arise in this general context:

(i) How far ought problems of recognition and segregation to be kept separate in discussions about gifted children? Some teachers argue that if there is to be no special segregation of any kind there is no point in worrying about recognition.

(ii) Some people, perhaps a great many, believe that gifted children are already sufficiently advantaged not to need any special attention of any kind either in the ordinary primary school or elsewhere. Not infrequently there is coupled with this attitude the view that 'giftedness' will emerge regardless of environmental conditions, and an implicit definition of 'giftedness' which is somewhat circular in that it is taken to indicate a level of talent so high as to ensure that nothing but death can prevent its emergence.

2.22.   Is there any consensus of view in the study group on these matters? In more concrete terms, would the group support a proposal to assist a potential football 'star' or 'Olympic' swimmer in some way over and above the provision made for average children? Would it support a talented musician but not a footballer? Can it suggest where a line should be drawn between those gifts which should receive special support and those which should not? Or should no talent be specially supported during the primary years?

2.3.   To what extent does the group feel that the interests of an apparently talented youngster will best be served by some degree of concentration on his particular gift? Some teachers argue that such concentration removes the child's freedom to decide his own future; others argue that refusal to develop such potential similarly restricts the child's freedom of choice.

2.31.   What is the group's view regarding special schools which, whilst providing exceptional opportunities and tuition in one particular area, also provide, or purport to provide, a good general education? How do the group members relate their attitudes towards 'special' schools to the suggestion that provision for gifted children can and should be made in the ordinary school by means of special programmes of tuition? In regard to either system is it important whether the apparently talented youngster maintains his outstanding position in later life or not?

2.4. What are the main needs of gifted children in so far as they differ significantly from those of average children? Which needs might be said to be inadequately met very often in schools now? The group might feel it necessary to discuss small rural schools and large urban schools separately. We would especially like the study group's comments on the need for gifted children to be 'stretched' or 'challenged', the need to achieve emotional stability, and the need to secure good social development without sacrificing, for example, intellectual growth. How far is it thought that gifted children need contact with other similarly gifted children as well as with more ordinary peers?

2.5.   There is evidence to suggest that when teachers are asked to nominate intellectually gifted children from amongst those in their charge, they omit, perhaps, fifty per cent of those who are, by other criteria, undoubtedly gifted and usually they include a few who are not. Thus, in response to a request to indicate intellectually gifted children, a group of teachers omitted nearly a half of those with measured IQs of 130+ and included several below 110. One nominee had an IQ of only 84.

2.51.   Can the group comment on this situation? If it is true that a sizeable number of very able children are not recognized as possessing very high potential it seems likely that such children are not sufficiently encouraged to move forward at rates commensurate with their capacities. (The children involved above were 7 years old.)

2.52.   If it is not as easy to recognize an intellectually gifted child as many seem to believe, can the same thing be said about the recognition of other talents; e.g. in music, soccer, or swimming?

2.53.   The study group is asked to list briefly the kinds of behavioural criteria by which, it believes, the talented or potentially talented youngsters might be recognized. Various types of talent might usefully be considered separately; and, for the purposes of this problem, individual members of the study group might like to describe a case study with which they are especially familiar and which reveals various cues and pointers that were instrumental in bringing about recognition of that particular child. These case studies taken together would enable the group to formulate sets of behavioural criteria related to major curriculum activities which might be of great assistance to any, but especially one feels to the inexperienced, teacher.

2.6.   *Individual assignments*

2.61.   In addition to contributing to general discussions some members of the group might like to pursue the general topic of 'recognition' in relation to their own school situation. The following brief paragraphs therefore propose possible lines of approach.

2.62. Investigate the incidence of various types of giftedness by consulting colleagues and checking with regard to given classes the opinions of the staff against one another. Do different teachers recognize different children? Do they differ in readiness to look for different kinds of talent?

2.63. Consider the various grouping systems regularly in use in the school and list the selection processes involved in the formation of each type of group. How efficient in terms of recognizing talent are these processes in your view?

2.64 Experiment with (say) a creativity test, or other relatively objective measure and discover the extent to which some children reveal unexpectedly high scores. Explain the discrepancies.

2.65. It would clearly be of great interest for members of the group undertaking any of these, or similar, activities to have the opportunity to report back to the full study group.

3.0. STUDY SUGGESTIONS, SECTION B: CURRENT PRACTICES IN SCHOOLS

3.1. In considering the following set of problems the study group may on occasion wish to differentiate children of infant or first school ages from those of middle or junior school ages. Where this is the case, members are requested to conduct the discussions separately so that their conclusions are clearly linked to the age range concerned.

3.20. *Organization and methods*

3.21. What ways and means of giving children special individual attention suggest themselves to the group as likely to offer most return in terms of the evocation and development of various types of giftedness?

3.22. In discussing 3.21. the following points might usefully be raised:
(i) Have we reached a stage where the concept of a 'general' teacher who tries to be all things to all children has become something of a 'sacred cow'. What is the study group's view of the proposal that if we wish to preserve the essentials of the primary teacher's 'general' role, there are two major difficulties which must be resolved and which have not been sufficiently faced in the past; namely, the impossibility of providing a sufficient measure of individual attention in classes of forty, or even thirty; and the probable fact that few

teachers would pretend sufficient expertise and/or interest in every curriculum area to be in a position properly to guide and challenge every kind of talent which appears.

(ii) Is it true that even young children reach such levels of skill and/or depth of knowledge, albeit possibly in a fairly circumscribed area of the curriculum, that the individual teacher may frequently be limited to general encouragement only. Is it the view of the study group (for example), that young boys ought to have contact with a man of some demonstrable skill in the art and science of soccer during the primary years? By what age should we ensure that this happens, if in fact it is an essential requirement for the proper elicitation of potential talent?

(iii) Is the problem of 'special expertise', adumbrated above, confined only to areas of the primary curriculum outside the fields of mathematics and English language?

(iv) What kinds of special expertise ought the primary teacher to be able to draw upon, if and when the performance of a child begins to make him sensitive to new needs? If the study group feels that some form of 'team' or 'cooperative' teaching supplies an answer, can the group describe such an organization in terms of the 'expertises' required, the size of school implied by the argument, and the internal structure necessary in the school to ensure the essential measure of cooperation and flexibility amongst staff and children.

(v) Does the group feel that a gifted child is in a particularly unfavourable position in a small rural school? To what extent does a low pupil/teacher ratio compensate for the relatively narrow range of talent amongst the staff?

(vi) Is there any value in providing 'support' teams with a more direct teaching function than is usually expected from advisers and inspectors?

(vii) Is there a case for more flexibility in the provision of 'supportive' assistance than is now generally the case? Ought schools to have a more positive role in stating their 'supportive' needs?

(viii) Can the study group draw up a 'blue print' for the kind of 'supportive' system necessary to ensure that any gifted child receives the proper level of instruction in the area of his talent regardless of the particular interests and gifts of his immediate class teacher?

3.3. *Individual assignments*

3.31. List the special expertises available amongst the staff at your school. List areas of inadequacy in relation to:

(a) Other LEA supportive provision—advisers etc.

(b) Other possible sources of help if financial backing were available.

Is there any consensus on your staff in terms of what is required to 'close the gaps'?

3.32.   Select:

(i) A child in your school who seems to be able, yet never seems to achieve the level that people feel represents his 'true' potential. In the light of a close study of his personality and circumstances outline what additional attention you would recommend and indicate the elements in the school situation which are missing or unused.

(ii) An able child whose parents are either disinterested or less able than the child so that they cannot, or will not, help him at home. Engage your colleagues in a discussion of this situation and elicit views on (i) homework for gifted children and (ii) a counselling service for parents of exceptional children.

3.33.   Describe elements in your school provision which are, or were, oriented towards getting good 11+ results. Consider which, in the eyes of you and your school colleagues, remain desirable elements of content, organization and method whether there is a selection process in your area or not. Indicate also those features which are inimical to the gifted in your view.

3.34.   Describe your school structure in terms of special responsibility allowances. Analyse the implications of this arrangement in relation to the problem of the adequacy of the 'general' teacher, and the postulated need for a 'support' system. How does the special responsibility policy relate to improving provision for the gifted children specifically?

3.40.   *Materials and equipment*

3.41.   The study group's previous discussions may have emphasized that problems of teaching gifted children are frequently concerned with the wider problem of the individualization of instruction. In so far as this is true, two main areas of difficulty arise:

(i) The needs for teachers to have sufficient time to organize and provide for widely differing levels of skill in a large variety of areas.

(ii) The need to engage a child in activities at a level which may be beyond what the teacher herself can achieve in that particular field.

These areas overlap. Solutions for one may partly solve the other since some items of equipment and materials may, at one and the same time, free the teacher and enable her to give more individual help; and expose children to learning sequences which have been devised for advanced children by experts in particular fields. At some points clearly, the teacher herself may be the expert concerned.

34.11.   The study group is asked to consider how far it agrees with 3.41 as a general statement, and to make clear any important qualifications which it feels are necessary.

G.C.P.S.—8*

34.2. Members of the group are each requested to suggest and describe, for comment and criticism by the group as a whole, any materials or items of equipment which they have found to be especially useful in providing individual children with a learning programme or self-instruction unit.

34.21. Can the group formulate specific views on present availability of materials, equipment and programmes suitable for gifted pupils of all types? If possible, members are asked to provide examples from their own experience of how such provision has enabled some children to proceed at a pace far beyond that of average pupils in the class. Can the group comment on the case of two eleven year old girls who read a college level unit from a programmed reading scheme? Are such 'high grade' activities commonplace? Are they facilitated by the deliberate provision of special materials? Is it the view of the group that children's reading is frequently very haphazard once they have left the school reading scheme as such behind and attained a reading age of about nine?

34.22. It is the experience of some primary teachers, especially those in infant schools who have experimented with 'scrambled' texts and very simple teaching machines, that young children become bored once the initial novelty has worn off? Is this the general view of the study group?

Some would argue that, on the basis of the experiences outlined, teachers have too readily rejected programmed learning out of hand. And yet some teachers are using tape recorders to tell stories to slow learners! The children of these teachers contrive to handle cassette machines to record their own responses to a variety of assignments, and the teacher thus frees himself sufficiently to be able to give individual children more of his time.

34.23. Does the study group feel that modern technology provides a superb opportunity to gear all kinds of electronic equipment to the task of freeing a child from having to make continuous contact with his teachers?

As an example of what might be looked at as a concrete and specific possibility in the context of this item, the group might like to consider what use a skilful teacher could make (in terms of individualizing instruction) of a television camera, a video tape and receiver. These items can now be produced surprisingly cheaply on a 'do-it-yourself' basis, and one can envisage a 'bank' of taped activities to which children might have access under guidance, and which were a straightforward extension of the teacher herself. Clearly teachers would need time to create their video tape learning situations, but this merely strengthens any arguments the group may have already put forward regarding the need for a 'teaching support' team.

34.24. Following the above discussions, the study group will presumably be in a position both to recommend various materials and equipment, and to formulate an experimental programme of use. It may be that members will feel able to outline, at least tentatively, a policy concerning the availability of materials, equipment, and programmes suited to the needs of gifted children in the various fields. There would seem to be a dearth of such provision, partly because capital expenditure is involved, but partly because some teachers fear they will be somehow replaced. It may also be that teachers are not yet turning their energies to the creative use of even the unsophisticated 'aids', and it would be greatly helpful for the study group to state blunt evaluations of the present position as they see it. If, in addition, they can exemplify, either from their own experience or simply as a matter of theory, the use of (say) a cassette tape recorder to individualize some given learning situation, then this would be extremely valuable.

34.3.   Many teachers argue that 'projects' enable every child to work to the level of his capabilities, and that therefore there is no need to worry about whether the gifted child is being sufficiently extended or not. Other teachers, however, suggest that this is a sort of 'clots always find their slots' mythology, and that the quality and general level of achievement in 'open ended' situations depends upon many factors beyond mere capability. For example, the books available in schools are mostly suited to the 'average' children, and library services are not run in consultation with teachers. In any event, these teachers argue, gifted children are sometimes, perhaps often, quite lazy and feel no need to extend themselves. Can the study group formulate any views here? Though most teachers probably regard their book provision as inevitably inadequate, can it be truthfully suggested that the intellectually gifted child probably suffers most?

34.4.   *Individual Assignments*

34.41.   What text books are in common use in your school? Consider their distribution and use in relation to extending the most able pupils and formulate answers to the following questions:
(i) Are any pupils working with texts intended for older children?
(ii) Are any secondary school texts available? Why? Why not?
(iii) What use is made of graded 'workbooks'?

34.42.   Gather from colleagues an inventory of audio-visual aids which are or might be of use with able pupils.

34.43.   Vertical grouping is said to help gifted pupils because they witness older and more skilful children at work, and thus are encouraged to achieve more advanced performances themselves. Discover the views of your colleagues on this issue.

4.0. FUTURE TRENDS AND POLICIES

4.1. The Plowden Committee felt that, in general, gifted children could be amply provided for in the 'good' primary school. In so far as the study group has in previous discussions decided against complete segregation for gifted individuals regardless of their particular talents can it now draw up a 'grand design' for the 'good' school? The headings in the School Visit booklet might be useful here.

4.2. If during the primary years all children were extended to their utmost it seems likely that very wide differences in interests and achievements would result. Obviously this situation is to some extent with us already but it is possible that, as a greater degree of individualization occurs in methods of teaching, so will individual differences become exaggerated beyond what we now find.

Can the study group comment on this proposition? To what extent will such a situation require a more flexible approach in secondary schools? Are gifted children retarded in their early secondary years by having to repeat work done already in primary schools?

4.3. *Individual Assignments*

4.31. Consider your own school 'set up' in relation to the study group's 'grand design'. List its major inadequacies and make recommendations for improvement starting with those changes which can more easily be carried out.

4.32. Suggest means whereby the relatively high academic standards which some believe were (or are) associated with the need to coach for 11+ examinations can be improved upon when the stimulus of external competition is removed.

4.33. Select a curriculum activity in which you consider yourself relatively ill-equipped. Discover the most able child in the school in that area. Draw up a programme of work for this child which will enable him to advance rapidly and without hindrance.

Now select an area wherein you are relatively expert and perform the same exercise.

Draw conclusions from this experience relating provision for able children to team and cooperative teaching, 'supportive' agencies and the availability of self instructional equipment.

Suggestions for contents headings which might be found useful by the editing committee for a study group paper

1   The particular needs of gifted children: A definition of 'giftedness' which highlights problems presented to teachers by the presence of one or more pupils who are outstanding.

2   Problems of recognition: behaviours characteristic of gifted children. Selected case studies.

Present provisions and practices: conditions helpful/inimical to the development of potential talent.

3   Observations and suggestions related to future trends and policies.

Appendix 4

General procedure to be followed at schools visited

1 Complete section A of the enclosed paper by means of interview with the headteacher.
2 Meet all the staff and
(i) Request completion of questionnaire.
(ii) Arrange for the staff to consider sections B and C of the enclosed paper.
3 Request written case studies of one or two gifted children recently, or at present, in the school, on the basis of the headings appended to the following paper.
4 Request samples of writings by gifted children about themselves and their work.

Schools as case studies: procedural guidelines

This paper provides guidelines for the study of selected schools. It is divided into three sections each of which either requires a different method of approach or focuses on a different field of information.

GUIDELINES SECTION A
The purpose of the interview at this point is to construct a general picture of present school organization under the following headings and sub-headings.

1 Grouping systems in common use
(i) Criteria of selection—age, vertical, horizontal, ability etc.
(ii) Within school—within class.
(iii) Types of activity associated with each type and size of group.
(iv) Time spent by children in each type on average.
(v) Main aims behind each grouping system—its advantages and disadvantages especially in terms of gifted children.

2 Staffing patterns
(i) Areas of cooperation amongst staff.

(ii) Methods of cooperation—team teaching, formal discussions etc.

(iii) Use of specialist interests of teachers, and peripatetic and part-time teachers. The role of advisers and inspectors.

(iv) Use of other agencies and experts for specialist help.

3   Timetables and curriculum content
(i) The school programme.

(ii) The class programme.

(iii) Extent to which detailed content is suggested.

(iv) Use of materials, equipment and audio visual techniques (for individual needs especially).

4   Established structures linking school to other elements in
child's educational environment
(i) PTA, psychological service etc.

5   General questions on organization as it relates to gifted children particularly
(i) Have you any children who might be described as gifted now in school?

(ii) Who recognized them first? At what age? How?

(iii) What adjustments have been made to the normal programme as a result of recognition? Why? or Why not?

GUIDELINES SECTION B

Teachers' views on the needs and achievements of the gifted,
and the extent to which the school provides optimally
It is hoped that the staff will meet me and discuss some or all of the questions listed below. If these questions arouse sufficient interest the staff may wish to continue the discussion among themselves at a later date and to send me a brief report of their conclusions.

1   What are the main needs of gifted children in so far as they differ significantly from those of average children? Which group of needs can be said to be met inadequately in school now?

2   How far do you consider the issues of identification and segregation or selection as in need of clear distinction? Is identification vital whether we intend to segregate or not? Why?

3   On what exceptional talents ought public money to be spent? A 'star' footballer? Olympic swimmer? or what? Can you suggest where a line should be drawn?

4   How far do you feel that the interests of an apparently talented child will be best served by concentrating on a particular talent—

(*a*) in a special school which purports to give a general education as well;

(*b*) in the ordinary school with a special programme of tuition?

Are your views in any way dependent on whether the 'talented' youngster maintains his performance later in life?

5 Some people, perhaps a great many, believe that gifted children are already sufficiently advantaged not to need any special attention either in the ordinary school or elsewhere. How far do you agree with this general position? What major qualifications would you wish to make, if any?

GUIDELINES SECTION C

Future development
The staff are requested either individually, or as a group, to formulate under the headings suggested an outline of the organization for a school and its supportive agencies such that it might be said to be able to provide optimally for all, or most, of its gifted children. Since the arrangements proposed are hypothetical, consideration of costs need not enter the discussion particularly. It would nevertheless be helpful if staff would indicate those arrangements and facilities which they consider to be viable possibilities now, as distinct from those that seem inevitably to be rather remote.

Areas of possibility

1 Grouping systems
(i) The ideal organization—size of school, pupil/teacher ratio etc.
   (ii) Methods of facilitating activities which would occur in the ideal situation but which cannot occur now. E.g. combining schools and groups.

2 Staffing
(i) Balance in terms of age, sex, specialisms covered etc.
   (ii) Qualifications and team characteristics needed.
   (iii) The part played by supportive agencies, including parents and television authorities.
   (iv) The need for staff actively to counsel parents.
   (v) Arrangements for cooperation and consultation.

3 Timetables and curriculum content
(i) Methods and materials needed for individualized challenges to be given to gifted children. New equipment—Audio-visual aids etc., likely to be useful.
   (ii) Minimum facilities, e.g. swimming pool.
   (iii) Areas of activity not now available that ought to be.

GENERAL HEADINGS FOR CASE STUDIES

1 Agencies involved in recognition
   2 Age at which recognition occurred
   3 Type of giftedness involved
   4 Educational difficulties experienced, if any
   5 Aspects of environment, apart from school, thought to have been facilitative of the child's development

6 Features of school provision thought to have facilitated the child's growth

7 Details of home background

8 Implications of the case study for improving provisions in future

9 Any other information likely to be significant in the general context of this document.

Appendix 5

A voucher scheme for extra-mural activities

1   Teachers involved would be paid volunteers offering an activity.

2   They would be recognized experts in the field to be studied.

3   Classes would be limited in size.

4   All children, including those in private schools, would possess vouchers expendable in no other way than by that child in a recognized class.

5   Attendance would be voluntary and no child would attend more than one type of activity in a given period.

6   The teachers involved would include as much as possible those known to children in 'day' school, and classes could occur during lunchtime breaks as is customary now. Other experts approved by the LEA would, however, be involved, e.g. swimming coaches, ballet teachers etc.

7   Schools and school equipment, e.g. pottery kiln, would be made available and schools would be the normal venue apart from the extended activity centres themselves.

8   Parental opinion on the kinds of activities to be included would be the starting point for determining the nature of the extra-mural programmes to be attempted.

A scheme such as the above, if proved feasible, would have a number of very substantial advantages over the present haphazard chaos, and result in both an extension in the use of educational facilities, and a real increase in the recognition and development of talent. At a single stroke it would greatly increase parental interest where it is most lacking. It would enable primary teachers to make extended use of their professional expertise, if they so wished, and at some little profit to themselves. Talented children would surely be better served in this way than by having professional teachers waste their time and talent in activities such as school meal supervision. Finally it might provide one long-term solution to the intractable problem as to which extra-mural activities should receive public support within any given locality and which should not.

Appendix 6

Tables referred to in the main text: a.1–a.28

Table a.1 Learning rates and teachers' expectations: item B.2 (xii) analysed by type of school, teaching experience and level of responsibility

		No reply	Emphatically agree/approve	agree/approve	disagree/disapprove	disagree/disapprove	Emphatically disagree/disapprove	Qualified reply	Totals
		n %	n %	n %	n %	n %	n %	n %	n %
Teaching experience	No information	3 10	15 48	10 32	2 6	1 3	0 0	0 0	31 8·4
	0–4 years	7 13	22 39	18 32	4 7	4 7	1 2	0 0	56 15·1
	5–9 years	2 2	37 42	36 41	9 10	2 2	2 2	0 0	88 23·8
	10+	8 5	95 55	43 25	14 8	7 4	4 2	1 1	172 46·5
Level of responsibility	No information	0 0	6 55	2 18	2 18	1 5	0 0	0 0	11 3
	Headteachers	2 3	42 54	21 27	5 6	5 6	3 4	0 0	78 21·1
	Deputy heads	1 3	24 62	10 26	4 10	0 0	0 0	0 0	39 10·5
	Assistants	18 8	97 44	74 34	18 8	8 4	4 2	4 2	220 59·5
Type of school	Infants	6 11	31 55	13 23	2 4	3 5	1 2	1 2	56 15·1
	Juniors	4 3	54 42	46 35	17 13	5 4	3 2	1 1	130 35·1
	Middle	2 9	10 43	6 26	3 13	1 4	1 4	0 0	23 6·2
	Infant/junior	7 6	66 56	34 29	5 4	4 3	2 2	0 0	118 31·9
	Preparatory	2 10	7 35	8 40	2 10	1 5	0 0	0 0	20 5·4

Table a.2 Item B.3 (i) (age-range 5–8): day release to special classes

		No reply		Emphatically agree/approve		approve		uncertain		disagree/disapprove		Emphatically disagree/disapprove		Qualified reply	
		n	%	n	%	n	%	n	%	n	%	n	%	n	%
Teaching experience	No information	6	19	1	3	6	19	5	16	5	16	8	26	0	0
	0–4 years	4	7	9	16	6	11	7	13	14	25	16	29	0	0
	5–9 years	14	16	5	6	7	8	11	13	25	28	26	30	0	0
	10+	22	13	13	8	13	8	22	13	39	23	63	37	0	0
Level of responsibility	No information	2	18	0	0	2	18	1	9	1	9	5	45	0	0
	Headteachers	5	6	5	6	5	6	10	13	16	21	37	47	0	0
	Deputy heads	6	15	4	10	3	8	3	8	15	38	8	21	0	0
	Assistants	34	15	19	9	22	10	31	14	51	23	63	29	0	0
Type of school	Infants	5	9	9	16	6	11	5	9	12	21	19	34	0	0
	Juniors	20	15	8	6	10	8	12	9	37	28	43	33	0	0
	Middle	5	22	1	4	1	4	4	17	8	35	4	17	0	0
	Infant/junior	13	11	9	8	11	9	18	15	24	20	43	36	0	0
	Preparatory	4	20	1	5	4	20	5	25	2	10	4	20	0	0
Totals		47	13	34	9	35	9	48	13	90	24	116	31	0	0

Note: For this and the following tables of this format, the horizontal totals are given by the right-hand column of table a.1. A group of students is included in the lower line of totals.

Table a.3 Item B.3 (i) (age-range 9–13): day release to special classes

		No reply		Emphatically agree/approve		agree/approve		disagree/disapprove		disagree/disapprove		Emphatically disagree/disapprove		Qualified reply	
		n	%	n	%	n	%	n	%	n	%	n	%	n	%
Teaching experience	No information	4	13	7	23	16	52	1	3	1	3	2	6	0	0
	0–4 years	9	16	13	23	19	34	4	7	5	11	5	9	0	0
	5–9 years	15	17	15	17	34	39	9	10	3	9	7	8	0	0
	10+	27	16	32	19	57	33	21	12	17	10	18	10	0	0
Level of responsibility	No information	3	27	3	27	3	27	0	0	1	9	1	9	0	0
	Headteachers	10	13	14	18	30	38	9	12	4	5	11	14	0	0
	Deputy heads	7	18	9	23	8	21	5	13	7	18	3	8	0	0
	Assistants	36	16	41	19	85	39	21	10	20	9	17	8	0	0
Type of school	Infants	23	41	12	21	14	25	1	2	3	5	3	5	0	0
	Juniors	10	8	24	18	46	35	17	13	18	14	15	12	0	0
	Middle	4	17	1	4	6	26	5	22	5	22	2	9	0	0
	Infant/junior	19	16	26	22	46	39	11	9	6	5	10	8	0	0
	Preparatory	0	0	3	15	14	70	1	5	0	0	2	10	0	0
Totals		56	15	77	21	138	37	35	9	32	9	32	9	0	0

Table a.4 Item B.3 (ii) (age-range 5–8): full-time super-selective classes

	No reply n	%	Emphatically agree/approve n	%	agree/approve n	%	disagree/disapprove n	%	disagree/disapprove n	%	Emphatically disagree/disapprove n	%	Qualified reply n	%
Teaching experience														
No information	5	16	1	3	1	3	4	13	10	32	10	32	0	0
0–4 years	6	11	0	0	2	4	5	9	12	21	31	55	0	0
5–9 years	9	10	1	1	5	6	8	9	24	27	41	47	0	0
10+	21	12	4	2	8	5	8	5	34	20	96	56	1	1
Level of responsibility														
No information	3	27	0	0	0	0	0	0	3	27	5	45	0	0
Headteachers	5	6	2	3	2	3	7	9	14	18	48	62	0	0
Deputy heads	5	13	2	5	2	5	0	0	10	26	20	51	0	0
Assistants	29	13	2	1	12	5	18	8	53	24	105	48	1	0
Type of school														
Infants	7	13	1	2	3	5	2	4	13	23	30	54	0	0
Juniors	17	13	3	2	8	6	6	5	28	22	67	52	1	1
Middle	4	17	0	0	0	0	2	9	10	43	7	30	0	0
Infant/junior	12	10	1	1	4	3	11	9	24	20	66	56	0	0
Preparatory	2	10	1	5	1	5	4	20	5	25	7	35	0	0
Totals	42	11	8	2	22	6	28	8	85	23	184	50	1	0

Table a.5 Item B.3 (ii) (age-range 9–13): full-time super-selective classes

		No reply	Emphatically agree/approve	———	———	disagree/disapprove	Emphatically	Qualified reply
Teaching experience	No information	4 13	3 10	8 26	1 3	10 32	5 16	0 0
	0–4 years	10 18	5 9	7 13	10 18	10 18	14 25	0 0
	5–9 years	13 15	6 7	20 23	10 11	21 24	18 20	0 0
	10+	22 13	21 12	26 15	11 6	28 16	64 37	0 0
Level of responsibility	No information	2 18	0 0	3 27	0 0	3 27	3 27	0 0
	Headteachers	9 12	9 12	8 10	5 6	13 17	34 44	0 0
	Deputy heads	5 13	5 13	4 10	1 3	10 26	14 36	0 0
	Assistants	34 15	21 10	46 21	26 12	43 20	50 23	0 0
Type of school	Infants	21 38	8 14	7 13	1 2	9 16	10 18	0 0
	Juniors	10 8	12 9	24 18	15 12	26 20	43 33	0 0
	Middle	3 13	1 4	4 17	3 13	7 30	5 22	0 0
	Infant/junior	15 13	11 9	20 17	12 10	22 19	38 32	0 0
	Preparatory	1 5	3 15	6 30	1 5	4 20	5 25	0 0
Totals		50 14	38 10	73 20	35 9	70 19	104 28	0 0

Table a.6 Item B.3 (xii) (age-range 5–8): streaming

| | | No reply | | Emphatically agree/approve | | agree/approve | | | | | | Emphatically disagree/disapprove | | Qualified reply | |
| | | | | | | | | | | disagree/disapprove | | | | | |
		n	%	n	%	n	%	n	%	n	%	n	%	n	%
Teaching experience	No information	3	10	0	0	14	45	2	6	4	13	8	26	0	0
	0–4 years	4	7	3	5	8	14	7	13	9	16	25	45	0	0
	5–9 tears	8	9	4	5	8	9	8	9	22	25	38	43	0	0
	10+	23	13	17	10	17	10	20	12	20	12	74	43	1	1
Level of responsibility	No information	2	18	0	0	2	18	0	0	2	18	5	45	0	0
	Headteachers	5	6	5	6	6	8	10	13	10	13	41	53	1	1
	Deputy heads	6	15	2	5	4	10	9	23	6	15	12	31	0	0
	Assistants	25	11	17	8	35	16	19	9	37	17	87	40	0	0
Type of school	Infants	6	11	0	0	10	18	2	4	9	16	29	52	0	0
	Juniors	16	12	12	9	11	8	16	12	19	15	56	43	0	0
	Middle	3	13	0	0	5	22	5	22	3	13	7	30	0	0
	Infant/junior	10	8	12	10	10	8	12	10	22	19	51	43	1	1
	Preparatory	3	15	0	0	11	55	3	15	2	10	1	5	0	0
Totals		38	10	25	7	51	14	41	11	62	17	152	41	1	0

Table a.7 Item B.3 (xii) (age-range 9–13): streaming

		No reply (n %)	Emphatically agree/approve (n %)	agree/approve (n %)	disagree/disapprove (n %)	Emphatically disagree/disapprove (n %)	Emphatically disapprove (n %)	Qualified reply (n %)
Teaching experience	No information	3 10	9 29	13 42	1 3	1 3	4 13	0 0
	0–4 years	10 18	13 23	7 13	5 9	10 18	11 20	0 0
	5–9 years	13 15	15 17	16 18	11 13	14 16	18 20	1 1
	10+	25 15	45 26	32 19	20 12	11 6	36 21	3 2
Level of responsibility	No information	1 9	1 9	3 27	1 9	1 9	4 36	0 0
	Headteachers	9 12	17 22	13 17	12 15	6 8	19 24	2 3
	Deputy heads	7 18	7 18	12 31	3 8	2 5	8 21	0 0
	Assistants	35 16	57 26	40 18	21 10	27 12	38 17	2 1
Type of school	Infants	22 39	10 18	7 13	5 9	4 7	8 14	0 0
	Juniors	10 8	29 22	20 15	16 12	17 13	36 28	2 2
	Middle	2 9	4 17	8 35	2 9	1 4	5 22	1 4
	Infant/junior	17 14	33 28	21 18	13 11	14 12	19 16	1 1
	Preparatory	1 5	6 30	12 60	1 5	0 0	0 0	0 0
Totals		52 14	84 23	79 21	41 11	39 11	71 19	4 1

Table a.8 Size of school and teachers' views on streaming in the first school and middle school: a further analysis of item B.3 (xii)

Roll	No reply		Emphatically agree/approve		agree/approve		disagree/disapprove		disagree/disapprove		Emphatically disagree/disapprove		Qualified reply	
	n	%	n	%	n	%	n	%	n	%	n	%	n	%
First school														
0–99	2	7	2	7	4	14	4	14	4	14	12	43	0	0
100–199	1	4	2	8	4	15	6	23	1	4	12	46	0	0
200–299	11	12	8	9	20	22	6	7	16	18	30	33	0	0
300–399	6	12	2	4	5	10	3	6	11	21	24	46	1	2
400+	8	9	5	5	12	13	14	15	16	17	37	40	0	0
Middle school														
0–99	3	11	6	21	9	32	4	14	3	11	3	11	0	0
100–199	2	8	11	42	4	15	6	23	0	0	3	12	0	0
200–299	20	22	19	21	22	24	4	4	12	13	14	15	0	0
300–399	14	27	10	19	8	15	6	12	5	10	8	15	1	2
400–499	10	11	22	24	15	16	10	11	10	11	22	24	3	3
500+	3	5	14	24	10	17	7	12	6	10	18	31	0	0

Table a.9 Item B.3 (iii) (age-range 5–8): periodic specialization

		No reply	Emphatically agree/approve	agree/approve	disagree/disapprove	Emphatically disagree/disapprove		Qualified reply
		n %	n %	n %	n %	n %	n %	n %
Teaching experience	No information	5 16	5 16	15 48	1 3	4 13	1 3	0 0
	0–4 years	4 7	19 34	15 27	6 11	7 13	5 9	0 0
	5–9 years	9 10	27 31	27 31	6 7	11 13	8 9	0 0
	10+	17 10	51 30	50 29	22 13	17 10	14 8	1 1
Level of responsibility	No information	2 18	2 18	5 45	0 0	1 9	1 9	0 0
	Headteachers	3 4	26 33	24 31	12 15	7 9	6 8	0 0
	Deputy heads	6 15	11 28	14 36	4 10	3 8	1 3	0 0
	Assistants	25 11	63 29	64 29	19 9	28 13	20 9	1 0
Type of school	Infants	4 7	30 54	16 29	1 2	2 4	3 5	0 0
	Juniors	15 12	30 23	39 30	17 13	15 12	13 10	1 1
	Middle	4 17	4 17	6 26	3 13	2 9	4 17	0 0
	Infant/junior	9 8	35 30	38 32	13 11	15 13	8 7	0 0
	Preparatory	4 20	3 15	8 40	1 5	4 20	0 0	0 0
Totals		37 10	106 29	118 32	36 10	43 12	29 8	1 0

Table a.10 Item B.3 (iii) (age-range 9–13): periodic specialization

		No reply		Emphatically agree/approve		agree/approve		disagree/disapprove		Emphatically disagree/disapprove				Qualified reply	
		n	%	n	%	n	%	n	%	n	%	n	%	n	%
Teaching experience	No information	4	13	13	42	13	42	0	0	1	3	0	0	0	0
	0–4 years	9	16	27	48	15	22	2	4	1	2	2	4	0	0
	5–9 years	15	17	45	51	20	23	2	2	3	3	3	3	0	0
	10+	24	14	86	50	46	27	5	3	6	3	4	2	1	1
Level of responsibility	No information	2	18	7	64	2	18	0	0	0	0	0	0	0	0
	Headteachers	7	9	43	55	20	26	4	5	2	3	2	3	0	0
	Deputy heads	5	13	22	56	9	23	1	3	2	5	0	0	0	0
	Assistants	39	18	99	45	63	29	4	2	7	3	7	3	1	0
Type of school	Infants	23	41	25	45	7	13	1	2	0	0	0	0	0	0
	Juniors	11	8	56	43	45	35	3	2	8	6	6	5	1	1
	Middle	3	13	10	43	7	30	2	9	0	0	1	4	0	0
	Infant/junior	15	13	72	61	24	20	3	3	2	2	2	2	0	0
	Preparatory	1	5	7	35	11	55	0	0	1	5	0	0	0	0
Totals		53	14	180	49	105	28	9	2	13	4	9	2	1	0

Table a.11 Degrees of correspondence among teachers' views related to selection and segregation

	(Ages 5–8)			(Ages 9–13)			
	Super selection	Periodic specializa-tion	Streaming	Day release	Super selection	Periodic specializa-tion	Streaming
(Ages 5–8)							
Day release	41·16 / 0·230	154·77 / 0·416	48·94 / 0·249	156·05 / 0·417	18·88 / 0·158	311·81 / 0·544	29·70 / 0·386
Super selection		277·97 / 0·523	134·90 / 0·393		73·09 / 0·300	434·21 / 0·608	249·79 / 0·502
Periodic specialization			47·68 / 0·246			65·55 / 0·285	5·62 / 0·087
Streaming							38·26 / 0·222
(Ages 9–13)							
Day release	274·86 / 0·520	12·81 / 0·130	47·53 / 0·246		85·86 / 0·322	83·33 / 0·318	14·10 / 0·137
Super selection		94·41 / 0·336	16·90 / 0·149			233·71 / 0·490	77·31 / 0·308
Periodic specialization			88·45 / 0·451				72·99 / 0·300

Note: The upper figure gives χ^2, the lower C.

Table a.12 Summary of views on items B.3 (i), (ii), (iii), (xii)

	Item	No reply		Emphatically agree/approve		agree/approve ——————— disagree/disapprove						Emphatically disagree/disapprove		Qualified reply		
		n	%	n	%	n	%	n	%	n	%	n	%	n	%	
Day release	B.3 (i) (5–8)	47	13	34	9	35	9	48	13	90	24	116	31	0	0	Day release
	B.3 (ii) (9–13)	56	15	77	21	138	37	35	9	32	9	32	9	0	0	
Super selection	B.3 (ii) (5–8)	42	11	8	2	22	6	28	8	85	23	184	50	1	0	Super selection
	B.3 (ii) (9–13)	50	14	38	10	73	20	35	9	70	19	104	28	0	0	
Periodic specialization	B.3 (iii) (5–8)	37	10	106	29	118	32	36	10	43	12	29	8	1	0	Periodic specialization
	B.3 (iii) (9–13)	53	14	180	49	105	28	9	2	13	4	9	2	1	0	
Streaming	B.3 (xii)(5–8)	38	10	25	7	57	14	41	11	62	17	152	41	1	0	Streaming
	B.3 (xii)(9–13)	52	14	84	23	79	21	41	11	39	11	71	19	4	1	

Table a.13 Item B.3 (vi) (age-range 5–8): enrichment with the normal unstreamed class

		No reply		Emphatically agree/approve		approve		disagree/disapprove				Emphatically disapprove		Qualified reply	
		n	%	n	%	n	%	n	%	n	%	n	%	n	%
Teaching experience	No information	6	19	15	48	7	23	2	6	1	3	0	0	0	0
	0–4 years	8	14	37	66	6	11	3	5	1	2	1	2	0	0
	5–9 years	14	16	40	45	24	27	5	6	2	2	3	3	0	0
	10+	25	15	104	60	24	14	14	18	1	1	3	2	1	1
Level of responsibility	No information	3	27	7	64	0	0	1	9	0	0	0	0	0	0
	Headteachers	4	5	54	69	10	13	8	10	0	0	1	1	1	1
	Deputy heads	7	18	19	49	9	23	4	10	0	0	0	0	0	0
	Assistants	40	18	116	53	42	19	11	5	5	2	6	3	0	0
Type of school	Infants	9	16	39	70	6	11	2	4	0	0	0	0	0	0
	Juniors	20	15	64	49	28	22	10	8	2	2	6	5	0	0
	Middle	7	30	12	52	2	9	1	4	1	4	0	0	0	0
	Infant/junior	15	13	73	62	18	15	9	8	1	1	1	1	1	1
	Preparatory	3	15	7	35	7	35	2	10	1	5	0	0	0	0
Totals		54	15	211	57	67	18	24	6	6	2	7	2	1	0

Table a.14 Item B.3 (vi) (age-range 9–13): enrichment within the normal unstreamed class

		No reply		Emphatically agree/approve		agree/approve		disagree/disapprove		Emphatically disagree/disapprove				Qualified reply	
		n	%	n	%	n	%	n	%	n	%	n	%	n	%
Teaching experience	No information	8	26	15	48	6	19	2	6	0	0	0	0	0	0
	0–4 years	17	30	29	42	4	7	4	7	1	2	1	2	0	0
	5–9 years	18	20	40	45	20	23	5	6	1	1	4	5	0	0
	10+	31	18	95	55	26	15	15	9	2	1	2	1	1	1
Level of responsibility	No information	2	18	8	73	0	0	1	9	0	0	0	0	0	0
	Headteachers	9	12	49	63	11	14	8	10	0	0	0	0	1	1
	Deputy heads	7	18	20	51	6	15	4	10	2	5	0	0	0	0
	Assistants	57	26	102	46	39	18	13	6	2	1	7	3	0	0
Type of school	Infants	29	52	21	38	3	5	3	5	0	0	0	0	0	0
	Juniors	16	12	65	50	29	22	12	9	1	1	7	5	0	0
	Middle	5	22	15	65	2	9	1	4	0	0	0	0	0	0
	Infant/junior	22	19	69	58	15	13	8	7	3	3	0	0	1	1
	Preparatory	3	15	8	40	7	35	2	10	0	0	0	0	0	0
Totals		76	21	193	52	62	17	26	7	5	1	7	2	1	0

Table a.15 Item B.3 (xiii) (age-range 5–8): a widening of the school curriculum

		No reply		Emphatically agree/approve				disagree/disapprove		Emphatically disapprove				Qualified reply	
		n	%	n	%	n	%	n	%	n	%	n	%	n	%
Teaching experience	No information	5	16	11	35	8	26	4	13	3	10	0	0	0	0
	0–4 years	5	9	21	38	15	27	8	14	5	9	1	2	1	2
	5–9 years	13	15	23	26	20	23	13	15	9	10	8	9	2	2
	10+	25	15	41	24	30	17	38	22	14	8	22	13	2	1
Level of responsibility	No information	3	27	5	45	1	9	2	18	0	0	0	0	0	0
	Headteachers	4	5	25	32	12	15	21	27	7	9	8	10	1	1
	Deputy heads	7	18	7	18	9	23	9	23	3	8	4	10	0	0
	Assistants	35	16	59	27	51	23	31	14	21	10	19	9	4	2
Type of school	Infants	7	13	17	30	11	20	9	16	7	13	4	7	1	2
	Juniors	23	18	27	21	25	19	25	19	12	9	18	14	0	0
	Middle	3	13	10	43	4	17	2	9	2	9	1	4	1	4
	Infants/juniors	14	12	36	31	26	22	24	20	7	6	8	7	3	3
	Preparatory	2	10	6	30	7	35	2	10	3	15	0	0	0	0
Totals		49	13	101	27	88	24	64	17	31	8	32	9	5	1

Table a.16 Item B.3 (xiii) (age-range 9–13): a widening of the school curriculum

		No reply		Emphatically agree/approve		agree/approve		disagree/disapprove				Emphatically disagree/disapprove		Qualified reply	
		n	%	n	%	n	%	n	%	n	%	n	%	n	%
Teaching experience	No information	4	13	17	55	7	23	2	6	1	3	0	0	0	0
	0–4 years	11	20	26	46	12	21	5	9	1	2	1	2	0	0
	5–9 years	17	19	30	34	18	20	14	16	4	5	3	3	2	2
	10+	29	17	61	35	28	16	29	17	12	7	12	7	1	1
Level of responsibility	No information	2	18	7	64	1	9	0	0	1	9	0	0	0	0
	Headteachers	11	14	32	41	13	17	13	17	3	4	6	8	0	0
	Deputy heads	6	15	15	38	5	13	8	21	1	3	4	10	0	0
	Assistants	42	19	81	37	46	21	29	13	13	6	6	3	3	1
Type of school	Infants	24	43	20	36	6	11	3	5	2	4	1	2	0	0
	Juniors	16	12	41	32	31	24	22	17	11	8	9	7	0	0
	Middle	2	9	11	48	3	13	4	17	1	4	1	4	1	4
	Infant/junior	18	15	52	44	17	14	21	18	3	3	5	4	2	2
	Preparatory	1	5	10	50	8	40	0	0	1	5	0	0	0	0
Totals		61	16	143	39	79	21	50	14	18	5	16	4	3	1

Table a.17 Item B.3 (xi) (age-range 5–8): more peripatetic specialist teachers

		No reply		Emphatically agree/approve				disagree/disapprove				Emphatically disagree/disapprove		Qualified reply	
		n	%	n	%	n	%	n	%	n	%	n	%	n	%
Teaching experience	No information	4	13	7	23	11	35	2	6	3	10	4	13	0	0
	0–4 years	2	4	27	48	15	27	7	13	3	5	2	4	0	0
	5–9 years	11	13	23	26	25	28	13	15	9	10	7	8	0	0
	10+	17	10	52	30	43	25	30	17	14	8	15	9	1	1
Level of responsibility	No information	2	18	4	36	2	18	1	9	0	0	2	18	0	0
	Headteachers	3	4	28	36	20	26	15	19	7	9	5	6	0	0
	Deputy heads	5	13	12	31	10	26	5	13	3	8	3	8	1	3
	Assistants	24	11	65	30	62	28	32	15	19	9	18	8	0	0
Type of school	Infants	4	7	30	54	15	27	3	5	1	2	3	5	0	0
	Juniors	15	12	29	22	33	25	26	20	14	11	12	9	1	1
	Middle	4	17	9	39	6	26	2	9	1	4	1	4	0	0
	Infant/junior	8	7	39	33	31	26	21	18	9	8	10	8	0	0
	Preparatory	3	15	2	10	8	40	1	5	4	20	2	10	0	0
Totals		34	9	115	31	101	27	57	15	33	9	29	8	1	0

Table a.18   Item B.3 (xi) (age-range 9–13): more peripatetic specialist teachers

		No reply		Emphatically agree/approve		agree/approve		disagree/disapprove		disapprove		Emphatically disapprove		Qualified reply	
		n	%	n	%	n	%	n	%	n	%	n	%	n	%
Teaching experience	No information	4	13	10	32	10	32	4	13	1	3	2	6	0	0
	0–4 years	10	18	38	68	6	11	1	2	0	0	1	2	0	0
	5–9 years	15	17	40	45	19	22	8	9	4	5	2	2	0	0
	10+	19	11	91	53	42	24	11	6	6	3	2	1	1	1
Level of responsibility	No information	2	18	5	45	2	18	1	9	0	0	1	9	0	0
	Headteachers	6	8	45	58	19	24	7	9	1	1	0	0	0	0
	Deputy heads	4	10	21	54	9	23	3	8	1	3	0	0	1	3
	Assistants	36	16	108	49	47	21	14	6	9	4	6	3	0	0
Type of school	Infants	22	39	30	54	2	4	1	2	0	0	1	2	0	0
	Juniors	7	5	59	45	39	30	11	8	8	6	5	4	1	1
	Middle	2	9	16	70	3	13	2	9	0	0	0	0	0	0
	Infant/junior	16	14	70	59	22	19	9	8	1	1	0	0	0	0
	Preparatory	1	5	3	15	11	55	2	10	2	10	1	5	0	0
Totals		49	13	186	50	89	24	26	7	12	3	7	2	1	0

Table a.19 Item B.3 (xiv) (age-range 5–8): greater involvement of outside agencies

		No reply		Emphatically agree/approve		agree/approve		disagree/disapprove				Emphatically disagree/disapprove		Qualified reply	
		n	%	n	%	n	%	n	%	n	%	n	%	n	%
Teaching experience	No information	5	16	12	39	10	32	0	0	2	6	2	6	0	0
	0–4 years	7	13	24	43	13	23	7	13	3	5	2	4	0	0
	5–9 years	12	14	26	30	30	34	11	13	4	5	5	6	0	0
	10+	21	12	63	37	48	28	25	15	8	5	7	4	0	0
Level of responsibility	No information	3	27	5	45	2	18	0	0	0	0	1	9	0	0
	Headteachers	1	1	35	45	21	27	13	17	4	5	4	5	0	0
	Deputy heads	5	13	13	33	12	31	7	18	2	5	0	0	0	0
	Assistants	37	17	72	33	66	30	23	10	11	5	11	5	0	0
Type of school	Infants	6	11	24	43	20	36	2	4	2	4	2	4	0	0
	Juniors	16	12	46	35	38	29	17	13	8	6	5	4	0	0
	Middle	5	22	9	39	4	17	4	17	0	0	1	4	0	0
	Infant/junior	16	14	42	36	30	25	18	15	5	4	7	6	0	0
	Preparatory	3	15	4	20	8	40	2	10	2	10	1	5	0	0
Totals		46	12	130	35	114	31	45	12	18	5	17	5	0	0

Table a.20   Item B.3 (xiv) (age-range 9–13): greater involvement of outside agencies

	No reply		Emphatically agree/approve		approve		disagree/disapprove		Emphatically disagree/disapprove		Emphatically disapprove		Qualified reply	
	n	%	n	%	n	%	n	%	n	%	n	%	n	%
Teaching experience														
No information	4	13	14	45	12	39	0	0	1	3	0	0	0	0
0–4 years	10	18	32	57	9	16	3	5	2	4	0	0	0	0
5–9 years	13	15	46	52	20	23	7	8	0	0	1	1	1	1
10+	21	12	91	53	40	23	16	9	0	0	4	2	0	0
Level of responsibility														
No information	2	18	7	64	2	18	0	0	0	0	0	0	0	0
Headteachers	6	8	47	60	20	26	4	5	0	0	1	1	0	0
Deputy heads	4	10	19	49	10	26	5	13	0	0	1	3	0	0
Assistants	36	16	111	50	49	22	17	8	3	1	3	1	1	0
Type of school														
Infants	21	38	24	43	8	14	2	4	1	2	0	0	0	0
Juniors	7	5	71	55	35	27	13	10	1	1	3	2	0	0
Middle	2	9	11	48	5	22	4	17	0	0	0	0	1	4
Infant/junior	17	14	72	61	20	17	7	6	0	0	2	2	0	0
Preparatory	1	5	5	25	13	65	0	0	1	5	0	0	0	0
Totals	48	13	197	53	88	24	28	8	3	1	5	1	1	0

Table a.21   Chi squares and contingency coefficients for B.3 (xi), (xiv)

	More peripatetics (9–13)	More outside agencies (5–8)	(9–13)
B.3 (xi) (5–8) (more peripatetics)	55·04 0·263	13·46 0·134	76·67 0·306
B.3 (xi) (9–13) (more peripatetics)		24·55 0·179	6·14 0·091
B.3 (xiv) (5–8) (more outside agencies)			39·34 0·225

Table a.22 Item B.3 (iv) (age-range 5–8): early promotion to more advanced groups

		No reply		Emphatically agree/approve		agree/approve		disagree/disapprove		disagree/disapprove		Emphatically disagree/disapprove		Qualified reply	
		n	%	n	%	n	%	n	%	n	%	n	%	n	%
Teaching experience	No information	5	16	3	10	14	45	3	10	3	10	3	10	0	0
	0–4 years	5	9	9	16	10	18	10	18	12	21	13	17	0	0
	5–9 years	7	8	8	9	30	34	10	11	16	18	17	19	0	0
	10+	20	12	27	16	41	24	24	14	25	15	33	19	2	1
Level of responsibility	No information	2	18	1	9	3	27	2	18	0	0	3	27	0	0
	Headteachers	4	5	15	19	22	28	11	14	12	15	13	17	1	1
	Deputy heads	5	13	4	10	14	36	8	21	2	5	5	13	1	3
	Assistants	27	12	27	12	56	25	26	12	42	19	42	19	0	0
Type of school	Infants	3	5	11	20	19	34	6	11	7	13	10	18	0	0
	Juniors	15	12	11	8	25	19	24	18	20	15	34	26	1	1
	Middle	4	17	4	17	5	22	4	17	3	13	3	13	0	0
	Infant/junior	12	10	20	17	35	30	12	10	22	19	16	14	1	1
	Preparatory	4	20	1	5	10	50	1	5	4	20	0	0	0	0
Totals		38	10	49	13	96	26	49	13	65	18	71	19	2	1

Table a.23 Item B.3 (iv) (age-range 9–13): early promotion to more advanced groups

		No reply		Emphatically agree/approve				disagree/disapprove				Emphatically disagree/disapprove		Qualified reply	
		n	%	n	%	n	%	n	%	n	%	n	%	?	%
Teaching experience	No information	4	13	9	29	13	42	1	3	2	6	2	6	0	0
	0–4 years	9	16	17	30	10	18	7	13	7	13	6	11	0	0
	5–9 years	13	15	24	27	27	31	9	10	6	7	8	9	1	1
	10+	23	13	48	28	46	27	21	12	15	9	17	10	2	1
Level of responsibility	No information	1	9	3	27	2	18	1	9	2	18	2	18	0	0
	Headteachers	8	10	21	27	23	29	10	13	8	10	7	9	1	1
	Deputy heads	5	13	11	28	10	26	7	18	0	0	5	13	1	3
	Assistants	36	16	63	29	61	28	20	9	20	9	19	9	1	0
Type of school	Infants	21	38	16	29	6	11	2	4	6	11	5	9	0	0
	Juniors	9	7	31	24	39	30	19	15	12	9	18	14	2	2
	Middle	2	9	8	35	6	26	5	22	1	4	1	4	0	0
	Infant/junior	16	14	38	32	31	26	12	10	11	9	9	8	1	1
	Preparatory	2	10	4	20	14	70	0	0	0	0	0	0	0	0
Totals		50	14	101	27	100	27	40	11	40	11	36	10	3	1

Table a.24 Item B.3 (v) (age-range 5–8): admittance to nursery or infant school before normal age

		No reply		Emphatically agree/approve				disagree/disapprove		Emphatically disapprove				Qualified reply	
		n	%	n	%	n	%	n	%	n	%	n	%	n	%
Teaching experience	No information	3	10	9	29	11	35	3	10	3	10	1	3	1	3
	0–4 years	3	5	15	27	14	25	9	16	8	14	7	13	0	0
	5–9 years	8	9	25	28	19	22	10	11	9	10	17	19	0	0
	10+	17	10	54	31	42	24	16	9	13	8	29	17	1	1
Level of responsibility	No information	2	18	5	45	1	9	2	18	0	0	0	0	1	9
	Headteachers	2	3	29	37	19	24	7	9	4	5	17	22	0	0
	Deputy heads	5	13	10	26	13	33	4	10	3	8	3	8	1	3
	Assistants	23	10	59	27	53	24	25	11	26	12	34	15	0	0
Type of school	Infants	3	5	21	38	14	25	6	11	7	13	4	7	1	2
	Juniors	16	12	31	24	25	19	18	14	13	10	27	21	0	0
	Middle	3	13	5	22	9	39	1	4	2	9	3	13	0	0
	Infant/junior	8	7	42	36	28	24	11	9	9	8	19	16	1	1
	Preparatory	2	10	3	15	10	50	2	10	2	10	1	5	0	0
Totals		32	9	107	29	95	26	41	11	38	10	55	15	2	1

Table a.25 Item B.3 (vii) (age-range 5–8): vertical grouping

		No reply		Emphatically agree/approve		agree/approve		disagree/disapprove		Emphatically disagree/disapprove				Qualified reply	
		n	%	n	%	n	%	n	%	n	%	n	%	n	%
Teaching experience	No information	11	35	1	3	5	16	4	13	7	23	3	10	0	0
	0–4 years	10	18	12	21	11	20	10	18	8	14	5	9	0	0
	5–9 years	19	22	6	7	15	17	25	28	12	14	10	11	0	0
	10+	33	19	23	13	37	22	30	17	19	11	26	15	4	2
Level of responsibility	No information	4	36	1	9	2	18	1	9	3	27	0	0	0	0
	Headteachers	9	12	9	12	19	24	21	27	9	12	8	10	3	4
	Deputy heads	8	21	5	13	10	26	4	10	5	13	6	15	1	3
	Assistants	53	24	27	12	37	17	43	20	29	13	30	14	1	0
Type of school	Infants	8	14	12	21	12	21	7	13	13	23	3	5	1	2
	Juniors	30	23	12	9	21	16	31	24	11	8	23	18	2	2
	Middle	4	17	5	22	6	26	4	17	3	13	1	4	0	0
	Infant/junior	22	19	13	11	26	22	24	20	16	14	15	13	2	2
	Preparatory	10	50	0	0	2	10	3	15	3	15	2	10	0	0
Size of school	0–99	7	25	3	11	6	21	4	14	4	14	4	14	0	0
	100+	2	8	2	8	10	38	3	12	4	15	2	8	3	12
	200+	21	23	13	14	16	18	18	20	15	16	7	8	1	1
	300+	8	15	5	10	11	21	14	27	8	15	6	12	0	0
	400+	24	26	16	17	12	13	16	17	7	8	16	17	1	1
	500+	12	21	3	5	13	22	13	22	8	14	9	16	0	0

Table a.26   Item B.3 (vii) (age-range 9–13): vertical grouping

		No reply		Emphatically agree/approve		agree/approve		disagree/disapprove		Emphatically disagree/disapprove		Qualified reply	
		n	%	n	%	n	%	n	%	n	%	n	%
Teaching experience	No information	11	35	2	6	7	23	1	3	5	16	5	16	0	0
	0–4 years	20	36	6	11	2	4	11	20	9	16	8	14	0	0
	5–9 years	26	30	8	9	14	16	17	19	12	14	10	11	1	1
	10+	41	24	19	11	22	13	33	19	22	13	30	17	5	3
Level of responsibility	No information	3	27	2	18	2	18	1	9	2	18	1	9	0	0
	Headteachers	17	22	4	5	12	15	22	28	8	10	12	15	3	4
	Deputy heads	7	18	6	15	5	13	7	18	4	10	8	21	2	5
	Assistants	72	33	23	10	26	12	32	15	34	15	32	15	1	1
Type of school	Infants	25	45	6	11	2	4	6	11	10	18	6	11	1	2
	Juniors	28	22	14	11	13	10	34	26	12	9	26	20	3	2
	Middle	3	13	2	9	7	30	5	22	3	13	3	13	0	0
	Infant/junior	35	30	13	11	16	14	17	14	21	18	14	12	2	2
	Preparatory	8	40	0	0	6	30	0	0	2	10	4	20	0	0
Size of school	0–99	8	29	4	14	4	14	4	14	3	11	5	18	0	0
	100+	2	8	2	8	4	15	3	12	7	27	5	19	3	12
	200+	32	35	9	10	11	12	16	18	9	10	13	14	1	1
	300+	18	35	4	8	6	12	11	21	8	15	5	10	0	0
	400+	26	28	12	13	11	12	14	15	10	11	18	20	1	1
	500+	13	22	4	7	9	16	13	22	11	19	7	12	1	2

Table a.27   Item B.3 (viii) (age-range 5–8): teaching machines

		No reply		Emphatically agree/approve		approve		disagree/disapprove				Emphatically disagree/disapprove		Qualified reply	
		n	%	n	%	n	%	n	%	n	%	n	%	n	%
Teaching experience	No information	8	26	2	6	8	26	2	6	5	19	5	16	0	0
	0–4 years	9	16	5	9	6	11	12	21	11	20	13	23	0	0
	5–9 years	12	14	10	11	20	23	15	17	15	17	15	17	1	1
	10+	27	16	21	12	30	17	42	24	22	13	30	17	0	0
Level of responsibility	No information	3	27	0	0	5	45	2	18	0	0	1	9	0	0
	Headteachers	4	5	12	15	15	19	27	35	13	17	7	9	0	0
	Deputy heads	5	13	6	15	8	21	9	23	2	5	9	23	0	0
	Assistants	45	20	20	9	36	16	33	15	39	18	46	21	1	0
Type of school	Infants	9	16	5	9	10	18	9	16	13	23	10	18	0	0
	Juniors	18	14	17	13	25	19	31	24	17	13	21	16	1	1
	Middle	4	17	5	22	3	13	1	4	5	22	5	22	0	0
	Infant/junior	19	16	11	9	23	19	28	24	14	12	23	19	0	0
	Preparatory	7	35	0	0	3	15	1	5	5	25	4	20	0	0
Totals		57	15	40	11	67	18	72	19	64	17	69	19	1	0

Table a.28 Item B.3 (viii) (age-range 9–13): teaching machines

		No reply		Emphatically agree/approve		agree/approve		disagree/disapprove				Emphatically disagree/disapprove		Qualified reply	
		n	%	n	%	n	%	n	%	n	%	n	%	n	%
Teaching experience	No information	6	19	6	19	15	48	1	3	2	6	1	3	0	0
	0–4 years	12	21	13	23	15	27	8	14	2	4	6	11	0	0
	5–9 years	17	19	18	20	22	25	19	22	7	8	4	5	1	1
	10+	26	15	45	26	41	24	38	22	10	6	12	7	0	0
Level of responsibility	No information	2	18	2	18	7	64	0	0	0	0	0	0	0	0
	Headteachers	9	12	26	33	15	19	19	24	4	5	5	6	0	0
	Deputy heads	5	13	8	21	12	31	9	23	2	5	3	8	0	0
	Assistants	46	21	46	21	59	27	38	17	15	7	15	7	1	0
Type of school	Infants	24	43	12	21	14	25	2	4	2	4	2	4	0	0
	Juniors	11	8	35	27	35	27	32	25	9	7	7	5	1	1
	Middle	2	9	8	35	7	30	2	9	3	13	1	4	0	0
	Infant/junior	21	18	25	21	27	23	28	24	5	4	12	10	0	0
	Preparatory	4	20	2	10	9	45	2	10	2	10	1	5	0	0
Totals		62	17	86	23	103	28	67	18	26	7	25	7	1	0

Appendix 7

Additional school case studies

Three case studies are given here to supplement those recorded in Chapter 7.

SCHOOL G:

Location: small borough	*SES* Wide range.
Roll 530	*Staff* 17 (6 male)
Age range 7–11 years.	*Peripatetics* 3
School time 9–12, 1.30–3.50	

Grouping systems

(i) Children are grouped into 16 classes (4 × 4) according to age and ability, i.e. they are streamed into ABCD and each class has a one year range chronologically. The AB and C classes are considerably larger than the D streams; the former are 38, the latter are 21 only.

(ii, iii, iv) Within class groupings are idiosyncratic in that they depend upon the individual class teacher. Some make extensive use of groupings, whereas others tend towards class activities mainly. The D streams stress 'group' activities most, but it is impossible to generalize in actual fact, and nobody knows just how much time any individual child spends on 'individual' learning—whatever this means to teachers who refer to it. In the 'basic skills' group activities are common and based on ability. Social groups are frequent in other activities—projects etc.

Small groups occur in connexion with visits by 3 peripatetic teachers:

(*a*) Remedial (5 mornings per week) selected by IQ and reading ability. (All children are tested in the first year by county psychologist.)

(*b*) Violin—children selected by ability and enthusiasm of parents. (Music tests as such are not used to identify potential musicians.)

(*c*) French—usually half a class, but sometimes whole class if the class teacher has no French at all.

(v) The purpose of streaming is to enable the teacher to meet a more homogeneous ability group and to put the slow learners in classes only two thirds the size of the others. The headteacher believes that general intellectual ability is a reality but that artistic abilities are found not infrequently in children of lower intelligence.

Staffing patterns
(i) Graded posts are awarded for French, English, music, PE and there is a deputy head (woman) plus senior man. No PSR is available for mathematics etc.

(ii, iii) Class teachers operate almost entirely independently. There is no specialization outside music, PE and French, and the latter is frequently a highly cooperative affair between class teacher and visitor, extra-mural music involves several teachers in recorder playing. The English PSR co-ordinates the school magazine entries.

The construction of schemes of work has sometimes been a cooperative undertaking amongst 3 or 4 members of staff especially interested in one particular field, e.g. maths.

There has been some cooperation with other teachers in the town in connexion with environmental studies and an institute course, but this has not been of a type which might properly be called 'cooperative' teaching.

The main area of 'team' and 'cooperative' work thus comes perhaps in connexion with extra-mural activities (see below).

Staff meetings are not regular formal affairs. These occur only in connexion with special events. A very great deal of informal discussion occurs in break and lunch times, and this suffices for ordinary requirements and contacts. The head spends a great deal of his time discussing problems with individual teachers.

(iv, v) Advisers and inspectors play very general roles and are of no help in terms of gifted children except in special, almost accidental circumstances. The local PE adviser, for example, is keen on 'trampolinists'. They have emerged in the high school though, not in the primary school.

The music adviser organizes annual concerts which give opportunities for outstanding children to perform in the town orchestra, and the high school master is now starting a boys' choir for outstanding singers.

Timetable and curriculum content
i) The school timetable merely lays down the restraint required by use of rooms, specialist teacher activities, swimming bath visits (4th year) etc. Otherwise classes operate individual timetables.

Class programmes are flexible and it is not possible to state accurately how much time is devoted to any particular activity. In general the mornings are devoted to 'basic work' and the more 'creative' activities and project work occurs in the afternoon.

The curriculum is not stated in any detail, but recognizes the following activities: mathematics, French, English, art and craft (including pottery).

PE and games, projects (environmental studies), RE and music, movement and drama. Reading can be considered a separate activity and remedial groups and D streams.

Most of the detailed programmes in classes derive from:

1 Textbooks—mathematics, language skills and French.

2 Teachers' handbooks—music, PE etc.

3 Reading schemes—lower school and D streams. Other children read library books: there is no SRA scheme for able pupils.

It has not been necessary to approach the secondary schools for suggestions as to what might be useful for very able 4th year pupils. 'Width' studies are offered at this stage, and not 'depth' studies as such.

(ii) Homework is not given unless children ask—and they frequently do this.

There is an extraordinarily comprehensive extra-mural programme which permits and encourages very able children to widen their interest and increase their skills considerably. The details are given in full below:

Table a.29 An extra-mural programme

Day and time	Activity	Year and No. of children		Venue
Mondays				
12.45–1.15	Pinball	4th year	14	Playground
1–1.25	Recorders	3rd year	20	Class 3
	Craft	4th year	10	Class 3
1–1.25	Preparation for games	3rd year (alternate weeks)	78	Class 5 and 7
			63	Class 6 and 8
1–1.25	Craft and chess club	4th year	21	Class 4
1–1.25	Recorders	4th year	17	East Hall
2.50–4.20	Violins	2nd and 4th years	3×6	Library
3.50–4.20	Recorders	4th year	17	East Hall
3.50–4.20	Swimming	4th year	24	Pool
Tuesdays				
1–1.25	Recorders	2nd year Cl. 9 and 10	14	Class 2
1–1.25	Recorders	2nd year	6	Class 3
	Craft	4th year	20	Class 3
1–1.25	Upper school choir	3rd/4th years	100	West Hall
1–1.25	Craft/chess club	4th year	21	Class 4
1–1.25	Craft	3rd year	24	Class 8

Day and time	Activity	Year and No. of children		Venue
3.50–4.20	West Leigh Singers		60	East Hall
3.50–4.20	Swimming	4th year Class 3	20	Pool
Wednesdays				
12.45–1.15	Pinball	4th year	14	Playground
1–1.25	Lower school choir	1st/2nd years (Cl 9–16)	60	East Hall
1–1.25	Games preparation	Class 1 and 4	62	Field
1–1.25	Stamp club	2nd/3rd/4th years	36	Class 8
3.50–4.20	Folk dancing	3rd/4th years	30	Assembly/ Dining Hall
3.50–4.20	Swimming	4th year	24	Pool
Thursdays				
9–10.30	Violins	2nd/4th years	3 × 6	Library
12.45–1.15	Pinball	4th year	14	Playground
1–1.25	Recorders	Class 9 and 10	14	Class 2
1–1.25	Recorders	3rd year 2nd year	20 20 } 40	East and West Halls
1–1.25	Games preparation	Class 2 and 3	77	Field
1–1.25	Craft	3rd year	24	Class 8
3.50–4.20	Drama	4th year	30+	Assembly/ Dining Hall
3.50–4.20	French club	3rd year	20	Class 11
3.50–4.20	French club	4th year	30	East Hall
3.50–4.20	Swimming	4th year (Class 3)	20	Pool
3.50–4.50	Football	3rd/4th years (1st and 2nd school team)	24	Field
Fridays				
12.45–1.15	Pinball	4th year	14	Playground
1–1.25	Gym club	4th year	24	West Hall
1–1.25	Chess club	4th year	21	Class 4
1–1.25	Stamp club	2nd/3rd/4th years	36	Class 8
3.50–4.20	Swimming	4th year	20	Pool

The range of interests represented on the staff is shown by this extra programme. Some expertise can be claimed in the following fields as well: mathematics, science (astronomy), art, music, French. But the influence of the attitude towards 'broadening' rather than 'deepening' is clearly seen in the areas of extra-curricular activities as represented here. French is possibly an exceptional case.

4 (iv) *AVT*

Equipment includes: 8 tape recorders, 3 filmstrip projectors, 3 record players, TV and radio. No use is made of these materials for the individualization of instruction and children are not permitted to use expensive equipment on their own.

Linking structures

The PTA is not formalized, but parents are encouraged to come to school and each is sent a formal invitation to an appointment with the teacher every year. 99 per cent of parents take advantage of this arrangement.

No parents are involved as teachers' 'aides' although they help with school events in a variety of ways.

Reports are issued each year and record cards for each child are kept in school.

The school psychological service will help with any problem but is concentrated on work with slow learners. No advice on treatment of very able pupils has been required or offered.

The school takes part in local team leagues—hockey and football and even pinball. There is an annual inter-schools athletic meeting which also stimulates able children appreciably. There are no links however with local soccer clubs, athletic associations, swimming clubs and the like. Apart from the school leagues noted, 'extra-links' are in connexion with musical activities, e.g. musical festival for choirs and recorders: the junior choir of the music school. There are no Saturday morning activities in, say, art, science, mathematics or music organized by the LEA.

Recognition and treatment of gifted children

As far as intellectually gifted children are concerned the school clearly has all the advantages and disadvantages of the streaming situation. The most outstanding point is that the very able children are always in very large groups, and hence tend to have a greater degree of 'class' teaching than do slow learners. The able are not of course alone in this, but they could easily suffer most.

Recognition of specific intellectual gifts is probably less effective, if only because individualization of learning in, say, mathematics, language skills and French cannot be carried far enough. Occasionally small groups of extremely able children are formed, even within the A streams, but such outstanding children do not appear every year it seems.

Recognition in other fields is probably effective but little use can be made of teachers' capabilities unless special programmes of work are also available. In games, for example, the school effectively coaches up to the level of the school team. There is no avenue beyond this however, and this state of affairs applies in most fields. Even in music, the possibilities open to the young instrumentalist appear to be very limited outside the school itself; and in swimming the possibility of developing really outstanding talent is small since children do not go to the baths until the 4th year.

Special note of the extensive range of extra-mural activities has already been made. This system must evoke a considerable number of very skilful children in the fields concerned, and the only problem arising would seem to be in connexion with 'continuity'. How far can children who demonstrate high ability in these activities carry them forward into the secondary level? Or to somebody outside the school itself?

Staff views and comments

1   Gifted children need:

(i) special care if they are not to be under-achievers. Some are certainly idle and do not 'stretch' themselves.

(ii) to avoid frustration and boredom due to 'class' teaching. Probably happens to a greater extent in an unstreamed class.

(iii) countervailing care against emotional and social imbalance.

(iv) competition in 'fields' where they are able; otherwise risk of complacency and 'big headedness'.

(v) some gifted children do not become aware of their own potential.

(vi) to be detected—staff not sure how good at recognition they really are. Certainly better at academic types than musicians and artists, and possibly we miss the 'creative' more unconventional types.

(vii) to meet teachers gifted in similar ways.

2   Specialization: not keen on specialization except under careful control. Class teacher should be with own class $\frac{2}{3}$ of the time. Clubs out of school time are the only answer really since we already specialize enough.

3   Use of extra staff: towards making smaller groups within the classes as they now are since there is no hope of reducing the actual class sizes to, say, twenty.

4   Staff co-operation would be facilitated by setting aside actual school time for meetings—perhaps once per week. There is little concerted discussion of individual children since staff meetings are so difficult to organize so that everybody can be there.

5   Reading is sufficiently organized without the use of SRA schemes.

6   BBC *Springboard* programme has provided good opportunities for children to pursue school work at home as well, and the 'gifted' child benefits greatly here. This type of 'homework' is thought to be of greater value than 'progress' papers because children enjoy the former.

7   Projects are better done when children are provided with some kind of study guide.

SCHOOL H:

Location : large town centre.	*SES* Middle/high
Roll 540+	*Staff* 15 (3 male)
Age range 5–11 years	*Peripatetics* 8
School time 9–12, 1.30–4.00	

Grouping system

(i) (*a*) Children grouped into 14 classes each unstreamed and stretching across one year in terms of age. There is no vertical grouping and no streaming anywhere.

(*b*) Special grouping systems for certain activities cut across the main classes as follows: 1 athletics; 2 swimming; 3 art; 4 needlework; 5 pottery; 6 music; 7 academic work. (See section below on curriculum content.)

For each of these groupings children are selected by ability and each activity is tested at given regular intervals with a view to recognizing the more able. Athletics testing is an annual affair: academic work is examined more frequently, say, spelling tests every fortnight.

(ii, iii) Systems of within class groupings depend heavily upon the individual teacher and hence it is impossible to examine the true degree of individualization which occurs even in sequential subjects like mathematics. A rough estimate would be $\frac{1}{3}$ time is wholly class activity with $\frac{2}{3}$ smaller groups. Individual work is achieved to some extent in mathematics and language by the use of graded work cards, reading schemes and graded textbooks. Each class has textbooks which cover two or three age ranges. Once children attain a reading age of 9.0 they are encouraged to read library books and leave the reading schemes.

(iii, iv) Class activities dominate games, PE, music (singing), TV and radio broadcasts. The small group activities are dominant in extra-mural sessions.

(v) Class activities ought to be confined to those requiring social contacts and wide ranges of abilities and interests. One other function relates to maintenance of a corporate spirit and class enthusiasm, pride in belonging etc. In fact of course class activities occur too frequently and even in mathematics and language work simply because of pressure of numbers.

Small group activities serve a variety of functions and permit able children to go forward at a faster rate than others—if formed by ability. Most groups are friendship or social groups however and enable gifted children to help less able pupils, gain experience of leadership and so on. Teachers find such tasks useful in freeing them to help the less able more frequently.

Staffing patterns

(i, ii) *Areas of co-operation:* There is no 'team' teaching but considerable specialization occurs. No one teacher takes the whole school for a single activity but the following subjects tend to be taught by someone other than the class teacher: athletics and games; swimming, art and needlework, pottery, music, remedial groups, French.

Peripatetic teachers are responsible for instrumental lessons for violin, cello, clarinet, flute, piano, guitar, and advanced recorders. Voice training and recorders are extended by music teachers who are also class teachers.

Staff discussions are informal and no regular formal staff meetings are held. No teacher has special responsibility for mathematics or language development, and no one is specifically required to identify able pupils.

(iii, iv) *Advisers and other agencies :* Advisers and inspectors do not normally provide a source of further expertise for use with gifted pupils. General advice on general matters is seen to be their function. No regular help is required or received from other external agencies.

Timetables and curriculum content

(i) School programme: merely a convenient exercise in organization of specialization areas, use of hall, TV etc. There are no syllabuses provided but certain textbooks are distributed and used by teachers as sources of work. There is a rigid testing programme.

Class programme: largely determined by individual teachers. Mornings are largely devoted to 'basic skills', and the more 'creative' activities occur in the afternoons.

There is no timetable of extra-mural activities and these depend upon haphazard arrangements by staff individually.

Curriculum Activities comprise the following:

1 Music with instruments as under Staffing patterns (ii)
2 Mathematics
3 PE (including swimming, if parents pay, from 6+)
4 Games (excluding soccer)
5 Art and craft, including pottery
6 Languages—English and French
7 Reading as a skill for language
{ 8 Centres of interest (environmental studies) }
{ 9 Religious education   }

It is important to notice that anybody who shows promise in any area will get one or two hours per week of special tuition in that area from the age of 7+ on either from the headteacher or from a peripatetic helper or as part of extra-mural sessions. No mention is made of movement (ballet) work or drama as such but horse riding may be a possibility.

(ii, iii) As noted, detailed content of work is not suggested, and detailed records of children's achievements are not kept although there is a 'system of recognition'. Able children are seen to 'emerge' and the aim of the school is not so much a 'balanced' education for every child, but to find and develop 'every child's forte'. In the end, it is contented, a more 'balanced' individual results.

(iv) *Individualization and AVT:* There is relatively little use of AVT and the stock of equipment is limited to items commonly found in all schools. No 'programmed' learning of any kind occurs and there is a shortage of tape recorders and 'quiet' rooms for language work. Scientific apparatus is non-existent. There are no calculators, laboratory equipment, trampolines etc., electronic materials, cameras.

Links with other elements
Parent/school relationships are close and the PTA meets regularly. It provides money in relative abundance but no use is made of parents themselves to help teachers in their work.

The psychological service provides no special help or advice with regard to able children; nor are there links with any other local agencies—other than the town and country orchestras which provide advanced instrumental tuition. The usual museum and library services are available but there are no links with the secondary schools. There are no Saturday morning classes available in any areas but music.

Recognition and treatment of gifted children
Since almost every activity in the school was looked upon as a dimension of individual differences wherein a gifted pupil could 'emerge', a very large number of children can be said to be receiving special attention on account of their outstanding potential. The individual talents of members of staff are geared to extending certain groups by means of 'specialist' timetabling and extensive extra-mural work.

Attitudes of staff
Question 5 (p. 222): The statement is quite false. Gifted children are sometimes hypersensitive to their own occasional failures and need more encouragement than they sometimes receive. They are not always accepted and need the support of adults just as slow learners do if they are to be acceptable to themselves as well as to others. Frequently they combine the emotions of a child with the outlook of an adult.

Question 1: Main need is for a lot of attention from adults; for meeting other children who are equally outstanding; for extension through very small group and individual activities.

Programmed learning has its place, but there are no suitable 'kits' about at present.

Question 2: All should be identified. Intelligence tests are not the best way, even for intellectually gifted children. Experienced teachers can do it effectively.

Question 3: Any talent beneficial to the public should be supported. There are dangers in tying teachers to, say, local clubs of, say, soccer and swimming since these may be 'coloured' by too much 'professionalism' perhaps. Teachers should organize a greater number and variety of club activities for young children, e.g. cycling associations, rambling, and so on. The LEA give no encouragement whatsoever to such activities yet spend large sums on 'activity centres' for 'teenagers'.

Staff generally favour keeping able children in the ordinary school, yet (paradoxically?) encourage children to try for choir school scholarships etc. Consensus seems to be that early recognition is often misleading and precocious children often 'fizzle out'.

Additional points

1   Some children are talented in several spheres and are frustrated by their inability to attend fully to all areas of interest, e.g. the boy who has ballet lessons and sees them as good training for soccer but not cricket.

There is no solution beyond keeping all the options open throughout the primary school years at least.

2   Book supplies are restricted despite the availability of a library loan service.

3   The organization of small special groups is crucial to the provision for able children.

4   More teachers or teaching time must somehow be made available.

5   There is a wide range of talent on the staff itself. Only science seems to be the glaring 'hole'.

6   The attempt to give children an opportunity to explore a wide field of activities is not always matched in teachers' minds with the concomitant duty to provide conditions whereby 'exploration' can become real study.

7   The standards of attainment now reached depend to no small extent upon the early recognition of potential talent and the continuous efforts of teachers to nourish it unencumbered by notions of 'equality' and 'fairness' which prevent some schools from giving anybody any special attention in anything.

SCHOOL J:

Location Rural village	*SES* Low
Roll 60 mixed	*Staff* 2 + 1 (3/5)
Age range 5–11 years	*Peripatetics* 2
School time 9–12, 1.30–3.30	

Grouping systems

(i) There are three classes grouped by age into infant, middle and upper juniors during mornings. In the afternoons, the school divides into two equal halves again by age. Thus groupings are 'vertical' and work programmes are difficult to arrange. Individualization is achieved to some extent by the use of textbooks, workbooks, and 'teacher made' workcards. Some activities, however, have to be taken in larger groups, e.g. BBC Maths where only two groups operate.

Class activities dominate games, PE and music. Usually everybody joins in story time and religious instruction.

(ii) The aims of the groupings are not made explicit since practical considerations force the various groupings on teachers anyhow and there is no point in stressing difficulties. If staffing were more liberal the great age ranges within classes would be reduced as a first essential step to more efficient teaching. The advantages of vertical grouping include:

(*a*) Social development—the older help the younger.

(*b*) Teacher organization—the older can assist as teacher 'aides' on occasion.

(*c*) Teacher keeps children longer and gets to know them very well. May be more effective for recognizing a child's gifts.

The major difficulty is in providing the able child with a challenge from his peers.

Staffing patterns

(i, ii) No staff meetings of a formal kind are necessary since the group comprises only three and they meet over lunch daily. There is no specialization of any kind and the teacher has to be all things to all children all the time as well as he can.

(iii, iv) No peripatetic teachers are in use for, say, violin teaching, but a remedial teacher takes small groups of six children for $1\frac{1}{2}$ hours per week, and all the junior girls are taught needlework one afternoon per week by a visiting teacher.

Other agencies include the county library service and museum lending service, but the most able children do not have access to a wide enough range of books.

The vicar helps occasionally with religious instruction.

There are no links with the secondary school staff, nor are parents used in the school in any way.

Advisers and inspectors have in some cases been of special help and have joined in the teaching, especially with regard to music and science.

Timetable and curriculum content

There is no timetable, the classes operate entirely independently. The mornings are devoted to 'basic skills' however in the main and the more creative activities take place in the afternoons. Generally the whole class will be doing mathematics before play and English afterwards. Centres of interest occupy much of the remaining time.

The activities recognized in the school include:

Music (mainly singing and playing 'home-made' instruments—instrumental opportunities additionally are recorder and violin for those who purchase instruments)

Games and PE—includes swimming and cross-country running
Art and craft (including pottery)
Mathematics
Science
Environmental studies (centres of interest)
Religious instruction
Language (English but not French).

There is no extra-mural timetable but children play recorders during lunch hours or work at topics if they wish.

Homework is not set, nor is it given even if asked for owing to unfortunate complaints from some parents that individual children are receiving special treatment. To some extent it has even been difficult to put very able children to work on different books from the rest of the class for similar reasons.

(iii) No syllabuses are laid down. The infants work from a reading scheme and make use of Cuisinaire Rods and Dienes Blocks but no sequence of work is printed in a document, and the infant teacher operates on the basis of her experience. No detailed records are kept since teachers know the children well, and are aware of their individual progress. No use is made of standardized tests of any kind except in connexion with the remedial groups and the 11+ selection examination.

Some sequential work derives from the usual textbooks in mathematics and language skills and the topics covered year by year generally run in four yearly cycles to avoid repetition with the same children. Generally Book IV texts are the most advanced in use but one or two children have worked from Cundy & Rollett. (This led to parental objections and will not happen again presumably.) BBC *Maths Workshop* also provides a sequential strategy which is developmental. It does not apparently lend itself to individual progress at all well, and is basically a class/group activity.

Language work is less organized in terms of development sequences outside actual reading skills. Children do most of their writing and reading in connexion with their science and topic work.

In music, art and craft etc., children work on spontaneous projects (in groups) without having a particular developmental pattern to follow. The headteacher feels that, despite some excellent work in these fields, the need for outside expertise to guide the work along developmental lines is urgently necessary if we are to approach nearer to the ideal. He is here comparing what he achieves in some fields with those he achieves in science which is his own particular interest. There is no doubt that the latter area of work is easily amongst the most advanced to be found, and it is important to note that the art and craft of which he is so self-critical is better than is found in many places where complete satisfaction with the standards achieved is expressed with confidence.

(iv) *Use of AVT* No use is made of tape recorders, slide projectors, teaching machines etc., for the individualization of learning as such. The usual equipment is available of course for use by the teacher including radio and TV. In addition the school possesses less common aids in having:

(i) Single lens reflex camera
(ii) A 6″ telescope
(iii) A 40 gallon aquarium
(iv) A microscope

The school also possesses extra items bought in connexion with Nuffield Science scheme.

Links with outside agencies
The school is isolated really and has no links with local clubs and associations. There is no schools games league and no schools orchestra. The headteacher would very much like to start an astronomical society but the population is too small. There are no links with other schools either.

The PTA is non-existent as aforementioned.

The psychological service is not used except for cases of ineducability of which there are very few indeed. An IQ test is given to all children at 8 years but an exceptionally able child would not receive any special attention as a result of recognition in this testing programme. Only the teachers would be interested in the upper end of the scale.

Recognition and treatment of gifted children
Intellectually gifted children are recognized only through the 11+ procedure in any formal sense. Outstanding children do appear from time to time but the staff do not feel that they have suffered particularly by not having the competition of other very able children. At the same time the present situation is seen as inadequate since it is difficult to individualize learning to a sufficient degree and in any event it is impossible fully to stretch the most outstanding child in the group if he never meets other children equally good.

The treatment of children who are able in the less academic fields is very inadequate indeed in some sense. This is largely due to the fact that the school provides a very wide range of opportunities so that a number of children discover their potential in, say, games or pottery. The development of these interests beyond the capabilities of the teacher (who cannot of course be gifted in every sphere that he opens up to children) is where a major problem presents itself. A small staff of two or three, however talented, cannot cope properly with ten or twelve curriculum activities equally well. In music, for example, there can be no school choir or orchestra as these appear in the larger school.

On the other hand one cannot help but feel that boys with a propensity for scientific studies are likely to be held back when they move from School J to the secondary school, unless there is a good deal of individualization arranged in that stage.

Staff views and general comments

All gifts of social value should be developed as far as they can go in primary school. There should be no 'brake' put on progress merely in order to avoid secondary work. Since classes are smaller in the rural school the child has a better chance of having this potential recognized than he would in a class of 40. At the same time the teacher finds it very difficult to know what treatment to afford such children and the advisory services are inadequate from this point of view. A larger team of visiting specialists would undoubtedly be of great value and it ought to be possible to make stronger and more frequent contact with other schools in the area.

One disadvantage of the small village community would seem to be the fact that parents also know all the children well and hence when teachers want to try to individualize progress by giving one child more advanced work than another they are likely to be faced with complaints about unfair treatment etc.

Sport tends to be difficult. School J cannot compete even in 7-a-side soccer so the headteacher has tended to move away from competitive team games to cross-country running. The need for some measure of competition to stimulate the most able pupils in any field is well recognized.

The main difficulty is the maintenance of a wide range of activities and at the same time have staff capable enough to carry every gifted child along his chosen path. There is a minimum size of staff below which this cannot be done without some external aid system and School J is below this minimum size in the view of the staff themselves.

Appendix 8

Research proposals

In education it is impossible clearly to distinguish between 'pure' research and those activities more frequently termed 'curriculum development'. Nevertheless in a Schools Council context it is useful to consider those investigations which are directly orientated towards the work of the teacher in school separately from others which, however interesting in themselves, will not produce knowledge or materials which can readily help teachers to improve their provisions and practices. The proposals briefly described below are thus subsumed under two separate headings according as it is judged appropriate in terms of these considerations.

Curriculum development projects

One major difficulty facing teachers of gifted children is their ignorance of the developmental patterns which characterize various physical and mental activities. They are thus unable to describe clearly:

(*a*) where they intend the individual child shall go next;

(*b*) the precise standing any individual has achieved at any particular point in time;

(*c*) how this level of achievement relates to normal patterns of growth and to what would appear to be, in all the circumstances of his life, the child's true potential within the activity area being considered.

Teachers are moreover presented with the further difficulty of having no knowledge of the effects of different approaches to the teaching of some particular skill in terms of how the normal pattern of development can be altered, expedited, or retarded.

Clearly these are generalizations. Our knowledge is greater in some areas than others and the following merely suggest what appear to be major gaps affecting the development of real talent:

PHYSICAL SKILLS

There appears to be a severe shortage of films which show the developmental patterns associated with the teaching of e.g. trampolining, movement and dance, modern gymnastics. There appears to be an almost complete absence of films which compare and contrast developmental patterns and rates as these occur under the two distinct conditions of (i) expert tuition and (ii) encouragement by a general practitioner.

It is thus recommended that an investigation of these shortages be initiated through the various Schools Council Subject Committees with a view to producing such films as soon as possible. A start should be made first with regard to those activities which are relatively new in the primary school curriculum since it is here that such key guides to teaching procedures and standards are most needed.

MENTAL SKILLS

Attention has been drawn in our paper to the grave dangers in an unrestricted spread of programmes so vague and unstructured as to warrant the term 'enrichment': programmes which are never evaluated in any but the most useless general terms. The Schools Council has a responsibility for enabling teachers properly to evaluate their children's work, their own expectations in relation to children's abilities, and their own methods of approach. There is, in some areas anyhow, a plethora of advice on method, rather than methods, but little is available by way of collections of exemplars of children's work in a very wide variety of topics or project areas which would enable teachers to make useful comparisons. There are of course collections of children's poems, and in the best of these children's ages are given. But this is mere scrabbling: what is needed is an organization which continuously monitors the schools and systematically publishes collections of work together with the related backgrounds of the children concerned. Space will not permit a detailing of what would be most valuable here but a statement of the goal is sufficient. The aim should be to achieve vicariously and in a most economical manner what a good teacher could achieve for himself by visiting a very large number of schools over a very long period of time and examining children's products for himself.

Individualized learning units

Closely connected with curriculum development is the dearth of equipment and material which will enable gifted children to pursue individually a structured study in depth.[1] Some well-known 'packages' are available, but there are few deliberately aimed at the very advanced primary child. Production of such materials would have a most immediate impact on the schools and ought to be put in train at once. In this context it should be noted that we have in mind not merely the 'paper' unit; a very widespread use of cassette tapes is essential and the present failure to use videotapes for the purposes outlined can only be ascribed to a massive failure by authorities to appreciate their possibilities in terms of the individualization of study and learning.

One rapid method for producing the required materials would be to work through the Open University. The author has discussed this with Professor Williams and his colleagues, and it is recommended that support for their project be considered. One project would be insufficient however, and would not necessarily stress the essential relationship between the contents and structure of the learning package and the abilities and backgrounds of children of different ages. A further difficulty would be the direct and close supervision of the teaching which accompanied learning unit construction, and for this, location of a production unit in a local college of education would be very advantageous. Finally it would be necessary in some places to provide actual teaching machines. If this were to be overlooked every learning unit would closely resemble in terms of methodology every other one, and that could be disastrous.

At least three projects might thus usefully be considered: one located in the Open University, making specific use if possible of TV components in source units; a second located in a local college or university, and a third organized directly by an LEA, perhaps in conjunction with its local college and making use of local radio in some of its units.

Support teams in rural areas

No LEA at the present time has a team of specialists with good primary school experience which could provide direct teaching help to smaller schools in rural areas. Without Schools Council support it is unlikely that anybody will investigate the possibilities although the Nuffield Foundation has done a little along the lines proposed. A joint LEA Schools Council experiment would have very great and immediate benefits both for the schools involved and the system generally. *Inter alia* it would provide indicators as to the best use of teachers as and when pupil/teacher ratios in primary schools are reduced. Without such investigation it is likely that an increasing pupil/teacher ratio may be accompanied by a decreasing teacher-effectiveness index.

Instrumental music

The development of musical talent is perhaps catered for rather better in present circumstances than are other forms of ability. There would however appear to be a concentration only upon musical education which is linked to cheaper instruments, and brass for example is almost entirely absent in primary schools. The reasons for this particular ommission are obscure and need investigation but meantime there would appear to be a strong case for a mini-project in one or two schools with the goal of ascertaining just how far the introduction of other than the usual instruments evokes talent in children previously unsuspected of possessing it. The Schools Council Music Committee could easily organize and oversee such a project with quite small resources relative to the pay-off in terms of extending our knowledge of latent musical talent.

Individualization—the present position

It has been shown that individualization as here defined has not progressed far in schools. It is however necessary that research on a considerable scale should be mounted in order to discover just how far progress is being achieved. It is suggested therefore that what is necessary in general terms is a programme of research complementary to that already mounted by the NFER into the daily activities of teachers. In the present case the focus would be wholly on the moment by moment activity of the child, with the findings being analysed in relation to already specified dimensions of individualization. The proposal by the NFER to pursue this investigation clearly should receive careful and sympathetic consideration.

Research possibilities to support curriculum projects

Since the Schools Council is unlikely to find itself able to do more than draw attention to certain research possibilities these are merely listed below to complete the preceding sections:

1   Examination of the effect of linking PSRs to school size especially as regards effect on movement of experienced staff to large schools.

2   Work studies of the degree of individualization actually achieved in schools of different size, pupil-teacher ratio, age group systems etc.

3   Examination of the factors involved in creating differences between schools in terms of length of school day, extra-mural programmes and levels of interaction with other schools.

4   Investigation of the influence of parental instruction by teachers in (say) mathematics on the learning of their children in school, i.e. an experimental application of Suzuki method to other fields than music, without of course excluding the latter.

5   A trial on local radio or TV of an 'Open University' for primary children. Schoolteachers might volunteer as remunerated tutors for an experimental period.

6   A survey and comparison of teachers' judgements of children with regard to interests, aptitudes, abilities etc. with those of their parents independently obtained.

7   Investigation of the incidence of rules which restrict use by children of electronic equipment, free movement and so on, in the interests of safety.

8   Investigation of the ability structures of children who score very highly on IQ tests, mathematics tests and other more specific academic fields.

9   Research into the efficiency of recognition of giftedness in relation to the maladjusted: is it true that a maladjusted child stands a much greater chance of being thought gifted than a well integrated person?

Notes

1   In March 1973 the Programme Committee of the Schools Council approved a grant of £35,000 to Northampton College of Education to develop learning units for gifted children within the age-range 7–10. Further information about this project, which will be directed by Dr Ogilvie, will be available from the Project Information Centre, Schools Council, 160 Great Portland Street, London W1N 6LL.

Bibliography and References

Anderson, J. E. 'The Nature of Abilities' in *Talent and Education*, ed. E. P. Torrance (Modern School Practices Series), Minnesota University Press/Oxford University Press, 1960, p. 20

Bridges, S. A. *Gifted Children and the Brentwood Experiment*. Pitman, 1969.

Butcher, H. J. *Human Intelligence*. Methuen, 1968.

Central Advisory Council for Education (England), *Children and their Primary Schools* (The Plowden Report), HMSO, 1967.

Central Advisory Council for Education (Wales), *Primary Education in Wales* (The Gittins Report), HMSO, 1967.

De Haan, R. F. and Havighurst, R. J. *Educating Gifted Children*. University of Chicago Press, 1961.

Entwistle, N. J. and Welsh, J. 'Correlates of School Attainment at Different Ability Levels', *British Journal of Educational Psychology*, February 1969.

Eysenck, H. J. and White, P. O. 'Personality – the Measure of Intelligence', *British Journal of Educational Psychology*, XXXIV, 1964, 197–202.

Gallagher, J. J. *Teaching the Gifted Child*. Allyn and Bacon, Boston Mass., 1964.

Gallagher, J. J. and Crowder, T. 'The Adjustment of Gifted Children in the Regular Classroom', *Exceptional Children*, 23, 1957, 306–12.

Getzels, J. W. and Jackson, P. W. *Creativity and Intelligence*. Wiley, New York, 1962.

Gold, M. J. *Education of the Intellectually Gifted*. Merrill Books, Columbus Ohio, 1965.

Haddon, F. A. and Lytton, H. 'Teaching Approach and the Development of Divergent Thinking Abilities in Primary Schools', *British Journal of Educational Psychology*, Vol. 38, No. 2, 1968.

Hayes, K. G. 'Genes, Drive and Intellect', *Psychological Reports*, 10, University of California, 1962, 299–342.

Heim, A. W. and Watts, K. P. 'An Experiment on Practice, Coaching and Discussion of Errors in Mental Testing', *British Journal of Education*, XXVII pt III, Nov. 1957. 199–211.

Hildreth, G. H. *Introduction to the Gifted*. McGraw-Hill, New York, 1966.

Hoyle, E. *Gifted Children and their Education*. Unpublished, 1969, p. 12. Obtainable from Professor Hoyle, School of Education, University of Bristol.

Hudson, L. *Contrary Imaginations*. Methuen, 1966.

Hudson, L. *Frames of Mind*. Methuen, 1968.

Inlow, G. M. *Emergent in Curriculum*. Wiley, New York, 1966.

Kallen, H. M. 'The Meaning of Unity among the Sciences' in *Structure, Method and Meaning*, ed. P. Henle, H. M. Kallen and S. K. Langer, Liberal Arts Press (USA), 1951.

Kough, J. *Practical Programmes for the Gifted*. Science Research Associates, Chicago, 1960.

Lunn, J. C. B. *Streaming in the Primary School*. NFER, 1970.

McNemar, Q. Address to 72nd Annual Convention of American Psychological Association, 1964.

Miles, T. R. 'On Defining Intelligence', *British Journal of Educational Psychology*, XXVII pt III, Nov. 1957, 153–65.

Morris, J. M. *Standards and Progress in Reading*. NFER, 1958, pp. 320–1.

Ogilvie, E. 'Creativity, Intelligence and Concept Development', unpublished Ph.D. thesis, Southampton University, 1970.

Pidgeon, D. A. 'School Type Difference in Ability and Attainment', *Educational Research*, Birmingham University, June 1959.

Pidgeon, D. A. 'Intelligence: a Changed View', *Educational Research News*, NFER, May 1969.

Pringle, M. L. Kellmer. *Able Misfits*. Longman, 1970.

Proctor, M. *The Education of Gifted Children* (Occasional Papers no. 11), ILEA, 1966.

Shouksmith, G. *Intelligence, Creativity and Cognitive Style*. Batsford, 1970.

Terman, L. M. 'The Discovery and Encouragement of Exceptional Talent'. *American Psychologist*, Vol. 9 No. 6, June 1954, 221–30.

Torrance, E. P. *Guiding Creative Talent*. Prentice-Hall, 1962.

Various 'Symposium on the Effects of Coaching and Practice in Intelligence Tests: V: Conclusions'. *British Journal of Educational Psychology*, XXIV pt II, 1954, 1–5.

Vernon, P. E. 'The Development of Current Ideas about Intelligence', in *Genetic and Environmental Factors in Human Ability*, ed. J. Meade and A. S. Parkes, Oliver and Boyd, 1966.

Wallach, M. A. and Kogan, N. *Modes of Thinking in Young Children: A Study of the Creativity Intelligence Distinction*. Holt Rinehart and Winston, New York, 1965.

Wallach, M. A. and Wing, C. W. *The Talented Student*. Holt Rinehart and Winston, New York, 1969.

Yamamoto, K. 'Thresholds of Intelligence in Academic Achievement of Highly Creative Students', *Journal of Experimental Education*, Vol. 32 No. 4, 1964, 401–5.

Index

011499

This book is to be returned on or before
the last date stamped below.